Dictionary of language testing

STUDIES IN LANGUAGE TESTING...7

Series editor: Michael Milanovic

Also in this series:

Dictionary of language testing

Alan Davies, Annie Brown, Cathie Elder, Kathryn Hill, Tom Lumley, Tim McNamara

University of Melbourne

Desktop publishing work by Paulo Pinto da Cunha

Published by the Press Syndicate of the University of Cambridge
The Pitt Building, Trumpington Street, Cambridge CB2 1RP, UK
40 West 20th Street, New York, NY 10011–4211, USA
10 Stamford Road, Oakleigh, Melbourne 3166, Australia

First published 1999

Printed in Great Britain at the University Press, Cambridge, UK

British Library cataloguing in publication data

University of Cambridge, Local Examinations Syndicate
Dictionary of language testing

Alan Davies, Annie Brown, Cathie Elder, Kathryn Hill, Tom Lumley,
Tim McNamara

1. Education. Assessment 2. Education. Tests. Setting

ISBN   0 521–651018   hard cover
        0 521–658764   paperback

Contents

Series Editor's Note

The Language Testing Dictionary represents a substantial contribution to the field of language testing and credit needs to be given to the Melbourne team for undertaking the work. The dictionary has taken six years to write and has been rigorously reviewed on an on-going basis throughout this period. Its 600 or so entries are clearly written and aim to communicate to a wide range of readers with varied background experience. The team, led by Alan Davies, approached the project in a systematic and organised manner and their approach is documented in both the preface and appendix to this volume.

Many of those involved in Applied Linguistics and EFL/ESL have found language testing a daunting area. This is partly because of the emphasis on numbers and 'difficult' statistical techniques and partly because there is a large amount of terminology and jargon to contend with. I hope that the dictionary will contribute to making language testing more transparent, and help to demystify some aspects of it. In this way, it will strengthen the field and help it to mature. It should be useful to students at all levels as a source of reference and guidance. The entries are not unduly long, but are often accompanied by references to further reading thus making it valuable to most professionals in the field of applied linguistics as a reference document.

The dictionary will complement the multilingual glossary, published as volume 6 in this series. Both volumes will help to make language testing more accessible, which is consistent with the overall aims of this series.

Preface

Work on this Dictionary of language testing began in 1991, soon after the inception of the Language Testing Research Centre (LTRC) in the University of Melbourne. During the last six years, a number of colleagues[1] have participated in the preparation of the volume, but the final writing has been done by the listed authors (Davies, Brown, Elder, Lumley, McNamara from the beginning, Hill joining later). Progress has been irregular and always dependent on other commitments. But the slow pace can in part be explained by our insistence on making the Dictionary a team effort: draft entries have been prepared by one author and then panelled by the team, revised and often repanelled.

As the article contained in Appendix 1 (Davies 1996) explains, the process of writing was always as important to the team as the eventual product. When we started writing there was a clear felt need: we found ourselves establishing a Centre in which most members of staff were new to the field of language testing. Both to cater for learning about the field and at the same time to facilitate communication with one another, we realised our need for a common terminology, a dictionary. And, of course, if we needed one, then it was very likely that others new to language testing would have the same need. So we saw a role for our dictionary both as process and as product. And so it has turned out, at least as far as process is concerned. We have all learned through the need to be specific in our definitions and then to justify our decisions to colleagues who can be the severest of critics.

For the most part the division of first drafts was allocated randomly: we did not permit choices to be made on the basis of individual knowledge. Our thinking was that if language testing has a coherence as a profession then it should have a broad basis of common knowledge shared by all practitioners. Hence our early agreement that we would all attempt whatever entries came our way. To some extent as we have neared completion (and in order to ensure completion) that random principle has been retired; but until recently it has been an important principle to which we have adhered.

The Dictionary contains some 600 entries, each listed under a headword. Cross-referencing takes two forms: within entries, references to other entries are bolded; where there is no substantive entry, the cross-referencing follows

---

[1] Chris Corbel, Lis Grove, Kieran O'Loughlin, Joy McQueen, Yap Soon Hock

the stand-alone headword. Our selection of headwords is based on advice from colleagues, scanning of current textbooks in the field and of dictionaries and encyclopedias in adjacent fields (eg psychometrics, applied linguistics, statistics). Inevitably our choice is subjective and not final. But that is true of course of any selective dictionary. We have tried to keep in mind a potential colleague who may or may not have experience in the field but who has a need for information. Our dictionary is intended as a first stage in meeting that need, but it is not intended to do more than provide an orientation and where appropriate indicate where next to look. Hence the references which follow many of the entries and which are collected together at the end of the book. For the most part, the area of language testing sufficiently delimited itself for our selection purposes; this was not so with statistics where we found ourselves constantly tempted to add to its representation. That temptation we have tried to resist on the grounds that we were not in the business of offering a dictionary or indeed a mini-text on how to do statistics. There are, after all, many excellent such books available.

Our hope now is that the Dictionary as product will prove as valuable to others as the Dictionary as process has to us. We welcome suggestions for additions, emendations, etc., which we will be happy to incorporate in any subsequent edition.

Our thanks to Natalie Stephens who has maintained our data base over these last years and to Fiona Watson who has produced from our varied fonts a professionally formatted text.

Alan Davies,
November 1997

Reference

Davies, A. (1996) The role of the segmental dictionary in professional validation: constructing a dictionary of language testing. In Cumming, A. & Berwick, R. (Eds.) *Validation in Language Testing*. Clevedon Multilingual Matters: 222–35.

Dictionary of language testing

a

ability

Current capacity to perform an act. Language testing is concerned with a sub-set of cognitive or mental abilities, and therefore with **skills** underlying behaviour (for example, reading ability, speaking ability) as well as with potential ability to learn a language (**aptitude**).

Ability has a more general meaning than terms such as: **achievement**, **aptitude**, **proficiency**, **attainment**, while **competence** and **knowledge** are sometimes used as loose synonyms.

Ability is difficult both to define and to investigate, no doubt because, like all **constructs**, it cannot be observed directly. Much of language testing is concerned with establishing the **validity** of such constructs.

See also: **factor analysis, performance, true score**
Further reading: Bachman 1990; Carroll 1987

ability estimates

See **estimates**

accuracy

An assessment category commonly used in subjectively assessed speaking and writing tasks, particularly in relation to grammatical accuracy. Raters are required to give an estimate of each candidate's ability to produce well-formed grammatical structures; these estimates generally relate to a **proficiency scale** which may or may not include descriptions of typical performance at each level.

Accuracy may also refer to word choice, or to surface features such as spelling and punctuation (in the assessment of writing) and pronunciation (in the assessment of speaking).

See also: **assessment criteria**

achievement

See **achievement test**

achievement test

Also **attainment test** (UK)

Achievement refers to the **mastery** of what has been learnt, what has been taught or what is in the syllabus, textbook, materials, etc.

An **achievement test** therefore is an instrument designed to measure what a person has learned within or up to a given time. It is based on a clear and public indication of the instruction that has been given. The content of achievement tests is a sample of what has been in the syllabus during the time under scrutiny and as such they have been called parasitic on the syllabus.

An achievement test may be distinguished both from a **proficiency test** and from an **aptitude test** by their uses. A set of grammar test items may be used as an achievement test if all the items have been part of the learners' syllabus; as a proficiency test if adequate performance on these items is required for some real world performance; and as an aptitude test if they provide the means of puzzling out the grammar of an unknown language so as to indicate language learning ability.

The view that an achievement test should measure success on ultimate course objectives rather than on course content is not widely held, largely because such an approach removes the achievement-proficiency distinction.

Because achievement tests are typically used at the end of a period of learning, a school year or a whole school or college career, their results are often used for decision making purposes, notably selection.

See also: **sampling**, **predictive validity**

Further reading: Anastasi 1988; Davies 1990

ACTFL

The **American Council on the Teaching of Foreign Languages** (ACTFL). Well known in language testing for the 'ACTFL Proficiency Guidelines' (1986), and the earlier provisional 'Proficiency Guidelines'

(1982). These provide **rating scales** with **descriptors** at six levels for the four **skills**, and are intended for assessing language students in schools and colleges. A descriptor is a representative sample of a particular range of ability, each one incorporating all lower level descriptors. The authors claim that the Guidelines are atheoretical (and therefore widely useable), proficiency-based and intended for global assessment. The ACTFL Guidelines were based on the **Interagency Language Roundtable (ILR)** Language Skill Level Descriptions. The best known ACTFL test is probably the **Oral Proficiency Interview** (OPI) test.

The ACTFL Guidelines have been much discussed in terms of their underlying holistic-universal view of proficiency, which takes account neither of separate **abilities** nor of differential progress across the skills. Their contribution has been mainly to the development of **direct** or real-life language **performance testing**. The oral proficiency tests using interview (OPI) and tape (**SOPI**) illustrate a real-life test and a semi-real-life one.

See also: **ILR, ASLPR, FSI**

Further reading: Bachman 1990; American Council on the Teaching of Foreign Languages (ACTFL) (1986)

adaptive testing

Also **tailored test**

A form of individually tailored testing, also known as sequential, branched, tailored, individualised, programmed, dynamic, response-contingent, deriving from the paper-and-pencil exercises of the programmed instruction movement of the 1950s and 1960s. These exercises were of two main kinds: linear and branching. They both provided a teaching unit in which successful progress through a series of frames indicated that satisfactory learning had taken place. In the linear programme success was judged by a prompt at the end of each frame; in the branching programme alternative routes were available for faster learners.

Adaptive tests have become fashionable through the use of variable-branching strategies based on **IRT** and administered by computer. Using a strategy which relates difficulty of **item** to **ability**, the student is repeatedly presented with the next most difficult item until there is no further **score** gain on the **trait** under test. This strategy is known as the maximum information adaptive testing strategy.

The principle underlying all types of adaptive testing is that items are chosen to reflect the level at which the candidate is estimated to be performing, thus generating a more efficient test. The entry level may be determined by a previously determined **proficiency** level, by performance on an initial item, **task** or pre-test, or by age (for example in deciding which of a battery of L1 reading tests to administer). The accuracy of the final assessment may, therefore, be influenced by the accuracy of the initial judgement.

Adaptive tests may be administered in a variety of formats including individual interview (for example certain types of **oral proficiency interview**), pencil-and-paper format or computerised format. The most successful use of adaptive testing is in **computer adaptive testing**.

Further reading: Anastasi 1990; Bachman 1990

administration

Test administration involves the delivery of a set of test tasks to a group of **candidates** under specified conditions. Depending on the type of test, it may be administered by a language expert (a teacher or a trained **interlocutor**) or by a non-expert (often called an invigilator). Where the work is not specialised, training is rarely undertaken; however, for public tests administrators are frequently given detailed instructions regarding their duties and the resolution of problems. This information may cover the venue, lay-out of tables and chairs, registration of candidates, equipment needed (eg tape-recorders), aids allowed to candidates (eg dictionaries), sequencing of test components (including distribution and collection of papers and timing of tests), and instructions to be given to candidates. Expert test administrators, most commonly used in subjective assessment, are generally trained to ensure that the administration, including selection and delivery of **tasks**, is carried out correctly, thereby ensuring fairness to all candidates.

advantage

See **impact (2)**

affective reaction

The emotional reaction or engagement of a **test taker** to a test. Affective reactions are recognised as influencing the quality of the test **performance**, and as such will contribute to **measurement error**. While individual and group affective reactions to tests and test types have been recorded, the relationship between particular reactions and performance appears not to be stable (anxiety producing better performance in some cases and poorer performance in others, for example), and hence cannot be adjusted for.

See also: **motivation, test anxiety**
Further reading: Porter 1991

agreement (in CRM)
See **dependability**

alpha coefficient
See **Cronbach's alpha**

ALTE
See **Association of Language Testers in Europe**

alternate forms, alternative forms
Also **equivalent forms**

Although the terms alternate and **parallel forms** (versions) are used inter-changeably, alternate form is a more general term.

Ideally, alternate forms of a test are two or more tests designed to the same specifications. Each form should correspond in terms of: number of test **items**, type of item, content of items, difficulty level of item, as well as in instructions, time allowed, etc. It is sometimes the case that actual alternate forms do not correspond to these demands and are simply two tests which have been designed to be parallel but lack the empirical evidence.

Alternate forms are useful in experimental and follow-up studies and in guarding against loss of test security because they avoid the need to administer the same test twice. They are also traditionally used in establishing test **reliability** based on the same principle as **test-retest** reliability. The argument is of course the same. If the test-retest reliability of Grammar test A can be measured by the size of the correlation between two administrations (as close in time as possible) of the same test to the same group of students, then it will also be measured by the correlation between the administration of Grammar test A1 and of Grammar test A2 to the same students. However, since equivalence is very hard to be sure about, it is usual now to assess reliability by the **split-half** procedure (in practice yet another permutation of the test-retest method) or by **internal consistency** reliability. An advantage of **IRT** methods of test analysis is that test equivalence can be guaranteed through the **anchoring** method.

Item banks from which items can be drawn to desired specifications (in eg **computer adaptive testing**) provide for the continuous construction of alternate forms.

See also: **validity, generalisability theory**
Further reading: Anastasi 1990; Cronbach 1964

analysis of covariance (ANCOVA)
See **ANCOVA**

American Council on the Teaching of Foreign Languages (ACTFL)
See **ACTFL**

analysis of variance
Also **ANOVA**

A statistical procedure which allows the comparison of the **means** and **standard deviations** of three or more groups in order to examine whether significant differences exist anywhere in the data. The procedure tests whether the observed values of the groups might all belong to the same **population**, regardless of group, or whether at least one set of observations seems to come from a different population. What the procedure does is to compare the variability of values within groups with the variability of values between groups. A significant result in ANOVA is achieved if the within-group variance is smaller than the between-group variance, the argument being that groups which are distinct are likely to represent different populations.

ANOVA is used in language testing in experimental situations, such as when tests are used to compare the effect of different treatments on language learning. For example the same test might be given to three groups, the first of which has been given intensive oral practice, the second a set of taped listening materials and the third reading-only practice. If the **variance** of 'between the groups' test scores is larger then the variance of 'within the groups' test scores, we would conclude that in our experiment there is an effect on language learning. To determine which treatment is producing the effect we need to perform a priori or post-hoc comparison of means using tests such as Tukey's or Sheffé's.

The research question asked in the above example is straightforward in that it asks only about the effect of different treatments on the language learning outcome. This use of ANOVA is known as a one-way ANOVA. More complex designs can be used. In a two-way ANOVA the **interaction** effect between treatment and the variable 'sex' of testees might be examined and in a three-way ANOVA the further variable 'first language' of testees might be added to the analysis. One possible result of the analysis could then be that the reading-only treatment group members do better but only when they are (a) female and (b) have a Romance language as their first language. On the other hand, the taped-materials group members might do better when they have Japanese as their first language, but there is no interaction in this case with sex of testee. In other words, we might discover that the effect of the different treatments on test score depends on sex of testee or first language of testee, or both.

ANOVA is also fundamental to procedures used in **generalisability theory**.

See also: **multiple regression, sampling, hypothesis**

analytic scoring

A method of **subjective** scoring often used in the assessment of speaking and writing **skills**, where a separate score is awarded for each of a number of features of a **task**, as opposed to one global score. In the assessment of writing the functional trisection of content, organisation and structure is commonly represented in the assessment categories. In **speaking tests**, commonly used categories are **pronunciation** or **intelligibility**, **fluency**, **accuracy** and **appropriateness**.

Advantages claimed for the analytic method of scoring are that:

- raters are required to focus on each of the nominated aspects of performance individually, thus ensuring that they are all addressing the same features of the performance;
- it allows for more exact diagnostic reporting of literacy or oracy development, especially where skills may be developing at different rates (reflected in a marked profile);
- it leads to greater reliability as each candidate is awarded a number of scores.

A criticism commonly made of analytic scoring is that the focus on specified aspects of the performance may divert **raters'** attention from its overall effect. This problem may be at least partially overcome by requiring raters to give an overall impression score in addition to the analytic scores. A further problem with analytic scoring lies in the possibility of a **halo effect** distorting the score due to the number of judgements required. The main practical disadvantage of this method of scoring is that it is time consuming compared with **holistic scoring**.

An issue which has to be dealt with where analytic scoring is used is whether to, or how to, weight the different scores.

See also: **weighting, criteria, holistic scoring, multiple-trait scoring**
Further reading: Hamp-Lyons 1991b

anchoring

A technique used to **equate** two **test forms** but which avoids the need for a group of candidates to take both tests by simulating this statistically. Anchoring may be of two kinds: anchoring of **test items** and anchoring of **test takers**. In the first type, a subset of items (the anchor test) is administered to two groups of candidates in addition to one full form of the test (typically either an old form or a new form). Scores on the anchor test are then used to estimate the performance of the combined group on both forms of the test, and hence to compare the two tests. This procedure is used in normal administrations of operational tests as part of the process of development of new versions, obviating the need for special administrations where candidates are required to take two full tests. In the second type of anchoring, a small subset of candidates takes both forms of the test and their performance across the two is used to estimate the performance of the other candidates on both forms, and hence to compare the tests.

Anchoring is also used in the extension of an **item bank**: existing items with known properties are used as the anchors for the analysis of new items, again avoiding the necessity of **trialling** all the items on the same candidates.

Further reading: Petersen *et al.* 1993

ANCOVA

Analysis of covariance. A variant of **ANOVA** which allows for pre-existing differences in a variable which is not the focus of the research, but which might otherwise affect the results and lead to faulty conclusions to be controlled. For example, we may want to investigate the efficacy of three different test preparation methodologies by comparing the performance of three groups of students on a particular language test at the end of a course. Using ANCOVA, pre-existing **ability** differences amongst the groups can be controlled by taking into account a **pre-test** score on some common measure. In other words, there is no need to eliminate particularly high ability or low ability students in order to control the variable ability across these two groups: rather the effect of ability is controlled statistically.

ANOVA

See **analysis of variance**

answer key

See **key**

anxiety

See **test anxiety**

a posteriori test validation

Latin for 'from what comes after': procedures used to establish what a test actually measures after it has been developed. This process may include the use of statistical procedures, such as **multi-trait multi-method**, or the soliciting of expert opinion.

> *See also:* **validation, a priori test validation**
> *Further reading:* Weir 1988

applied linguistics

Two opposing views of applied linguistics as a discipline are prevalent: the first may be labelled the weak view, the second the strong view.

The view of applied linguistics as a weak discipline suggests that linguistic theories and procedures may be applied to other disciplines, eg the study of literary texts or writing a syntax for a computer program. An alternative weak view is that linguistics may be an important reference point in a number of (not necessarily connected) areas of language work. For example, speech pathology, communication engineering, speech technology, cognitive science, language in education, discourse analysis, interpreting and translating. This version of applied linguistics has been called 'linguistics applied' to distinguish it from the strong version, 'applied linguistics'.

The view of applied linguistics as a strong discipline normally refers to the institutionalised discipline of applied linguistics which concerns itself largely with language learning and teaching (and sometimes remediation, as in speech pathology). This version of applied linguistics attempts to be both problem based (or focused) and theoretically oriented. The theories (and methodologies) drawn on come not only from linguistics but also from other disciplines such as education, sociology, psychology, etc. To what extent this strong applied linguistics can achieve its own all-embracing theory has yet to be seen, although it is not clear that it need do so any more than other problem or professionally-oriented disciplines (eg engineering, medicine, social work, law).

Since language testing is focused on major 'problems' in language work, and is firmly committed to the measurement of language learning in context, it occupies a central position within a strong applied linguistics.

> *Further reading:* Davies 1990; Bachman 1990

appropriacy

See **appropriateness**

appropriateness

Also **appropriacy**

An assessment **category** or **criterion** reflecting sociolinguistic competence: the relationship between language, the language users and the context of use. Such conventions of language use determine the extent to which the performance of a language **task**, or function, is viewed as appropriate. Assessments of appropriateness in relation to spoken or written language usually require **raters** to focus on the register or style of language used and the extent to which it is appropriate to the task.

a priori test validation

Latin for 'from what comes before': procedures to ensure that a test will actually measure what it is intended to measure before the test is developed. The process normally involves a **needs analysis** to provide a description of the test **domain** and may also involve review of **test content** during the course of test development.

See also: **a posteriori test validation**

Further reading: Weir 1988

aptitude

The extent to which an individual possesses specific language learning ability. Research is somewhat unclear on the existence of a general language aptitude **variable**; various aptitude tests have attempted to define and operationalise the **construct** in various ways.

See also: **aptitude test**, **Modern Language Aptitude Test**, **Language Aptitude Battery**

Further reading: Carroll 1981; Skehan 1989

aptitude test

An instrument to measure the extent to which an individual possesses specific language learning **ability**. Such tests are usually used for selection and diagnosis and for prediction of language learning success. Research is somewhat unclear on the existence of a general **aptitude variable** and the tests that exist normally claim to predict success only in terms of defined learning outcomes or distinct methodologies.

Data from major aptitude tests suggests that phonetic coding ability (sound discrimination and memory), grammatical sensitivity (recognising the grammatical function of words), rote learning ability for new sound and meaning associations and inductive learning ability for language patterns are components of language aptitude. Experimental results indicate that also important to language aptitude are: language processing ability, ability to make sense of and learn from decontextualised data, and experience of early language learning in the mother tongue. Other **variables** which are said to influence language aptitude are grammatical knowledge, listening ability, range of (mother tongue) **vocabulary** and **motivation**.

See also: **aptitude**, **Modern Language Aptitude Test**, **Language Aptitude Battery**

Further reading: Carroll 1981; Skehan 1989

ASLPR (Australian Second Language Proficiency Ratings)

See **ISLPR (International Second Language Proficiency Ratings)**

assess

See **rate**

assessment

A term often used interchangeably with testing; but also used more broadly to encompass the gathering of language data, including test data, for the purpose of **evaluation** and making use of such instruments as **interview**, case study, questionnaire, **observation** techniques. More narrowly the term is used to indicate assessment procedures which do not involve tests.

Assessment may be of the language **ability** of one learner or of a group of learners; or of the effectiveness of a language teaching operation. Most broadly, assessment contributes to an evaluation through assessment of the learner(s), and assessment of the whole teaching operation including curriculum, methods, materials, resources, plans and staffing.

See also: **diagnosis**, **measurement**

Further reading: Anastasi 1990; Cohen *et al.* 1992

assessment criteria

See **criterion**

Association of Language Testers in Europe (ALTE)

Set up in 1990 to bring together providers of language examinations in the various European Union states. ALTE's main objectives are:

- to establish common levels of proficiency;
- to establish common standards for all stages of the language testing process;
- to collaborate on joint projects.

Members in 1998 included providers working in Catalan, Danish, Dutch, English, Finnish, French, German, Greek, Irish, Italian, Luxembourgish, Norwegian, Portuguese, Spanish and Swedish, as well as an Associate member working in Russian.

The Waystage and Threshold specifications have had a significant influence on the examinations produced by ALTE and were used in the creation of Levels 1 and 2 in the ALTE Framework of Levels. ALTE members are currently taking part in the evaluation of Vantage Level, which was produced in collaboration between them and the **Council of Europe**.

Further reading: ALTE Handbook, ALTE Newsletters

attainment

See **achievement test**

attainment test

See **achievement test**

attitude scale

A technique for measuring attitude, that characteristic tendency to react consistently favourably or unfavourably to a **stimulus** (persons, objects or concepts). In the case of language testing the stimulus is a language or speakers of a language. Attitudes tend to be quite stable and less subject to factual input than are beliefs or opinions. There are two reasons for caution with regard to attitude studies: the first is that measured attitude does not necessarily predict behaviour; the second, that much of the data comes from self-reports.

In all attitude scales respondents indicate their agreement or disagreement with a series of statements about the object of the attitude. Different approaches have been devised to achieve **unidimensionality** (or homogeneity) of items on a scale, the best known being those associated with **Thurstone**, **Guttman** and **Likert**.

Attitude scales have been widely used in **applied linguistics** to study

motivation in second and foreign language learning. In many such studies the matched-guise technique has been used, itself based in part on Osgood's **semantic differential**.

Further reading: Anastasi 1990; Anderson 1981

authentic

A **language test** is said to be authentic when it mirrors as exactly as possible the content and **skills** under test, eg a conversation test to test for conversation skills or an essay test to test for writing essay skills or a test of medical English for non-English speaking doctors wishing to work in English medium. The qualification 'as exactly as possible' is important since complete authenticity is unachievable in a test which by its nature is a special occasion. A measure of authenticity may be added in tests by simulating reality through the use of spoken and written texts which have been collected and not specially written.

In any case, the 'real life' view of authenticity is surely partial in its assumption that authenticity can be achieved only through completely **direct tests**. But there is a compelling argument that authenticity can in fact be achieved through a parallelism in the test of the skills, processes, **abilities**, etc. which underlie **criterion** behaviour.

See also: **communicative competence**

Further reading: Bachman & Palmer 1996

authenticity

See **authentic**

b

background knowledge

Prior knowledge of content in tests. Relevant to tests of all four skills, but of particular relevance to tests of **reading comprehension** in which the reading **stimuli** or **texts** may be more familiar to some candidates than others, leading to test **bias**. Tests of **languages for specific purposes** (LSP) are the source of both concern and research in this area given that the purpose of **LSP testing** is usually not to test for content but to use content to provide a familiar discourse. In so doing LSP tests avoid being either over specific or over general. Non-specific (or general) tests also draw on candidates' knowledge of the world: however, the assumption is made by test constructors that the background knowledge such tests call on is indeed general, that is, available to every member of the **population** under test, and therefore cannot be a cause of bias. Arguments about bias with regard to both general and specific tests may therefore arise out of a disagreement as to whether the background knowledge being demanded is too specific.

See also: **variance**, **domain**
Further reading: Bachman 1990; Weir 1988

backwash

See **washback**

band

See **level, proficiency scale**

band descriptor

See **descriptor**

base group

See **reference group**

battery

See **test battery**

BEC

See **Business English Certificates**

bell-shaped curve

See **normal distribution**

benchmark

The establishing of a standard (in experiments and **evaluation** projects) against which to measure subsequent progress.

bias

A factor or factors inherent within a test that systematically prevents access to valid estimates of **candidates' ability**. One consequence, which is increasingly the subject of litigation, is that the scores of a particular subgroup of candidates (the **focal group**) will be systematically different from those of the majority group (the **reference group**). Bias may be claimed on the grounds that the difference derives from factors irrelevant to performance on the **criterion** measure.

In language testing the most frequently cited sources of group bias tend to be:

- **rater** error prompted for example by greater **severity** of judgements in relation to a particular group of candidates;
- **background knowledge**, including cultural background and content knowledge which may limit the capacity of a particular group to deal with the linguistic demands of a **task**;
- **test method** or **format** (eg **multiple-choice**) which may be more manageable for one group than for another.

Investigations of test bias are central to the construct **validation** process. When found, bias is considered to represent a violation of the **unidimensionality** assumption, that is, that test **scores** have a common meaning for all **test takers**.

Among techniques commonly used for investigating test bias are **factor analysis** and other multivariate techniques such as **structural equation modelling**, which explore the structure of intercorrelations among test components. To detect potential bias at the item level (commonly termed **differential item functioning**), the **Mantel-Haenszel** procedure or analogous **IRT** standardisation techniques are the most commonly applied.

It is useful to distinguish between construct bias (described above) and predictive bias, A test which is construct valid for candidates of different language background (ie it measures the same **skill** or configuration of skills in the same way for each group) may nevertheless be a biased predictor of performance in some other domain. An English language test for example may be equally valid as a measure of proficiency for both long-term immigrants and overseas students with temporary residence visas but as a predictor of future academic performance it may be less powerful for the latter group, because of the range of other social factors, such as ability to acculturate to the academic culture and access to support systems, which may contribute to study outcomes. Predictive bias is generally determined on the basis of **regression** equations.

See also: **test fairness**, **sampling error**, **validity**
Further reading: Cole & Moss 1993; Jensen 1980

bilingual

A person who knows two languages is said to be bilingual. Because it is difficult to determine the level of **proficiency** required in both languages to be classed as bilingual it is convenient to regard bilingualism as a continuum ranging from those equally fluent in both languages to those with very partial proficiency in a foreign language. Bilingual tests such as the **Bilingual Syntax Measure** have been devised to determine the extent of balanced bilingualism in an individual.

Further reading: Harley *et al.* 1987

Bilingual Syntax Measure (BSM)

A published language test which was widely used in the 1970s at a time when the notion of language 'balance' in an individual was thought to be important. Its purpose was to determine among young children in a migrant community the degree of 'balance' between the home and the school language in order to devise appropriate support for both. Such a view is still of interest in **bilingual** education and in some areas of second language acquisition research, but in language testing the methodology in the Bilingual Syntax Measure (pictures used to stimulate grammatical responses to an **interviewer**) is now less current.

Further reading: Burt, Dulay and Hernandez-Chavez 1975; Pienemann 1985

bimodal distribution

A single **distribution** with two separate **modes**, unlike the classical normal curve which has only one. Since abilities are assumed to be distributed uniformly in a **population**, a bimodal distribution indicates that the **sample** under test represents not one but two populations.

See also: **normal distribution**
Further reading: Hatch & Lazaraton 1991

binary choice item

See **objective item**

biserial correlation

Now rarely used. The statistic normally used where one variable is dichotomous is the **point–biserial correlation**.

BSM

See **Bilingual Syntax Measure**

Business English Certificates (BEC)

BEC (Business English Certificates) were introduced by **UCLES** between 1993 and 1996. They are tests in English as a Foreign Language for business purposes. The **examinations** test reading, writing, listening and speaking in work-related situations. There are three levels: BEC 1 (lower-intermediate), BEC 2 (upper-intermediate) and BEC 3 (advanced). Stage One of the examinations comprises Reading, Writing and Listening. Candidates who achieve Grades 1 or 2 in the Speaking have this recorded on their certificates. Initially the BEC examinations were only available in Asia, but they are now offered all over the world.

C

CAE
See **Certificate in Advanced English**

calibration
The calibration of a test involves the determination of the value of **test items** against a particular measurement scale, in other words it reflects **item difficulty**. While calibrated values of items could be based on expert opinions, the term is more commonly used where the measures of item difficulty are based on empirical data, as is the case with the use of either classical measurement theory or **item response theory** in **test analysis**. The process of calibrating items gives meaning to the scale values in terms of the knowledge or skills required to succeed at **tasks** within a particular range of values.

CALT
See **computer-assisted language testing**

Cambridge (examinations)
See **University of Cambridge Local Examinations Syndicate**

Cambridge Young Learners English Tests (YLE)
The Cambridge Young Learners English Tests were introduced in 1996 on a pilot basis and have been available since mid-1997. They are tests to assess the English of 7- to 12-year-old primary learners and are available at three **levels**: *Starters*, *Movers* and *Flyers*. The *Flyers* test (the highest level test) is roughly equivalent to the **Key English Test**. At each level there are three components: Listening, Reading and Writing, and Speaking. There are no Pass or Fail grades; instead candidates receive an Award showing a number of badges out of a total of five for each component, the minimum being one

badge for each component attempted.

candidate

A term used to refer to any person undertaking a test or **examination.** Other terms commonly used in language testing are **examinee, test taker** or **testee.**
  See also: **test-taker feedback**

case reliability estimate

In **item response theory** analysis, the term 'case' is used to refer to **candidates**, thus case reliability is an estimate of the accuracy or **reliability** with which the test as a whole measures the group of candidates. Unlike in **classical measurement theory** where one global estimate of reliability is obtained, IRT takes into account that measurements of ability will be more accurate closer to the **mean** of the score distribution. Hence in order to calculate the case reliability, the **standard error of measurement** for every point along the scoring continuum is taken into account.

CAT

  See **computer-adaptive test**

categorical data

  See **nominal scale**

category

  See **nominal scale, structural equation modelling**

CBT

  See **computer-assisted language testing**

ceiling effect

Also known as 'lack of headroom', the effect of most **candidates** scoring near the top of the **scale** on a particular test, with the result that the test does not discriminate adequately amongst higher **ability** learners. This effect occurs particularly with subjective ratings where **raters** score most candidates highly. In such cases, it can be counteracted through the use of more detailed **descriptors**, by **rater training**, or by limiting the percentage of high scores allowed. However, it may also occur through a test being too easy for the test **population** or where an **interviewer** provides such easy tasks that a candidate is not given the opportunity to demonstrate his/her full ability.

The ceiling effect may not be a problem for **achievement tests** or **mastery** tests (where it may be acceptable for most candidates to achieve a high score) or if the test is a **selection test** used to identify the high ability candidates.

central tendency

A term used to summarise the central point in the **distribution** of values in a data set. There are three common measures of central tendency, the **mode**, the **median** and the **mean**. The choice of which measure to use will depend on the type of data (and hence the meaningfulness of any one of these measures) and the purpose of the analysis. Different statistical procedures may require the use of one or other measure of central tendency.

See also: **normal distribution**

Certificate in Advanced English (CAE)

CAE was introduced by **UCLES** in 1991 and meets the needs of people requiring English for study or professional purposes. The tasks in the **examination** emphasise real-world situations and activities. CAE is part of a coherent suite of UCLES examinations in English as a Foreign Language, which, in addition to the CAE, include the **Key English Test**, the **Preliminary English Test**, the **First Certificate in English**, the **Certificate of Proficiency in English**, the Cambridge Examination in English for Language Teachers and several examinations in English for business.

The present components of CAE are: Reading, Writing, English in Use, and Listening papers, and a Speaking test. Each paper is equally weighted in order to determine the **score**, carrying 20% of the total marks. CAE is recognised by many British universities as fulfilling English language entry requirements.

Certificate of Proficiency in English (CPE)

One of the first public tests of English as a Foreign Language, CPE was introduced by **UCLES** in 1913 to meet the special needs of foreign teachers of English. Over time CPE has become part of a coherent suite of UCLES examinations in English as a Foreign Language which, in addition to the CPE, include the **Key English Test**, the **Preliminary English Test**, the **First Certificate in English**, the **Certificate in Advanced English**, the Cambridge Examination in English for Language Teachers and several examinations in English for business.

The present components of CPE are: Reading Comprehension, Listening Comprehension, Composition, Interview, Use of English. The CPE **score** is determined by a weighted over-all grading over the five papers. In certain countries (eg Greece) CPE is accepted as a qualification for teaching English in the state system. It is also recognised by British universities as fulfilling language entry requirements.

Certificates in Communicative Skills in English (CCSE)

The Certificates in Communicative Skills in English were introduced by **UCLES** in 1990 as the replacement for **CUEFLT (Communicative Use of English as a Foreign Language Test)**. They test the **ability** of **candidates** to use English communicatively. Reading, writing, listening and speaking are assessed separately and four different **levels** are available. Candidates may enter for one, two, three or four **skills** at the levels suited to their ability, though only at one level per skill in each sitting. Level 1 corresponds approximately to **Preliminary English Test**, Level 2 to a grade C/D in **FCE**, Level 3 approximately to **Certificate in Advanced English** and Level 4 to a grade B/C in **CPE**.

certification

The public recognition of a test performance. In language testing certification may be linked to the **ability** to carry out particular language-based tasks (eg to present an oral report, or to fill out forms adequately), or to the candidate's ability to fulfil the requirements of a particular job (eg tour guiding or teaching). It may also be used to reflect students' progress through, or completion of, a course of instruction.

While certification is often associated with **competency-based assessment** (or, in the US, **minimum competence testing**), language tests used for certification can take many forms and reflect different views of language **proficiency**.

Chi-square

A non-parametric statistical test which tells us about the relationship between two nominal **variables**. Specifically, it describes the extent to which the pattern of frequencies observed departs from that which would be expected were the variables to be totally unconnected.

The Chi-square statistic will indicate the extent to which the observed frequencies depart from the expected frequencies, and hence the significance of the relationship between the variables.

In language testing, Chi-square may be used to investigate test **bias** by examining differences in the proportion of each **candidate** type responding correctly to an item. This is known as the **Mantel-Haenszel** procedure.

classical analysis

See **classical test theory** and **item analysis**

classical reliability

See **reliability**

classical reliability theory

See **reliability**

classical test theory

Also known as classical **true score** measurement theory, according to which an **observed score** (on a test) is made up of a true score and an error score. The **standard error of measurement** of a test is an index of the extent to which the observed score is influenced by the error score. Since the purpose of a test is to achieve reliable observed scores, ie as close as possible to true scores, much of the effort put into test construction concerns ways of promoting and estimating test **reliability**. Although classical theory is still much in vogue, its inability to handle different types of error and its total reliance on the sample under test have been criticised.

Classical test theory has since the 1950s been challenged by an alternative model known now as **generalisability theory**. Generalisability theory reminds us that reliability is not static since it is a function of the circumstances under which the test is developed, administered and interpreted. A further challenge is found in the **IRT** models which go beyond generalisability theory in order to allow the expression of the relationship of item difficulty and individual ability within a single framework.

Further reading: Bachman 1990; Henning 1987

.

cloze (test)

A language testing technique first used by Wilson Taylor in the 1950s as a means of assessing the **readability** of newspapers. In the last 40 years the cloze technique has been very widely used in the language testing field to test reading comprehension as well as general language **proficiency**.

Here is an example of the technique.

Fill in the gaps in the following passage:

The room seemed empty when I first went in. But it wasn't.
I (1) _____around and saw near (2) _____ window a kitten
playing (3) _____ the curtain. Then as (4) _____ turned I
saw, on (5) _____ sofa, a blue cot. (6) _____ I looked closer,
I (7) _____ it contained a baby.

In order to provide help to the reader it is customary to begin deletions after the first sentence. The deletions in the above passage are: (1) looked; (2) the; (3) with; (4) I; (5) the; (6) When; (7) saw.

The name cloze is a deliberate phonic reminder of the psychological Gestalt theory whereby recall of incomplete visual shapes tends towards closure. At the same time, on the linguistic side, the cloze test legitimately appeals to language redundancy, which allows for loss of information as messages are exchanged by repetition at various levels. For example, the sentence: 'those three books are expensive' provides the information of a plural subject four times (those + three + books + are), allowing therefore for mishearing or misreading of one or more items of information.

While **gap-filling** tests (of which cloze is one version) have always implicitly appealed to such theories, the claim of cloze is stronger by virtue of its deliberate use of random text deletion. The argument is that redundancy is best accessed if its limitation is random. Traditional cloze tests (known as random cloze) typically use a deletion rate of every 5th, 7th, 9th, ie *n*th word. An alternative method also in use is known as rational cloze. Here the deletions are chosen on rational grounds, for example every adjective, noun, modal, preposition, article, etc. While random cloze does not differ greatly in terms of difficulty from one deletion rate to another, rational cloze deletion types vary considerably: for example nouns are very difficult indeed to replace.

There are two main types of cloze scoring:

* verbatim word scoring, whereby the deleted word is the only correct

choice;
- acceptable word scoring, whereby any acceptable replacement is correct.

There are critics of both methods. Verbatim scoring is criticised because it places too heavy a reliance on the original text which, it may be said, could easily have used other words. It is also very difficult to achieve high scores on, even for educated native speakers.

Acceptable scoring raises problems because the list of possible replacements is not finite, with the effect that different markers may produce different results. An agreed list may be drawn up but to some extent this defeats the purpose of allowing acceptable scoring.

Other presentations of cloze are in use, notably the display of possible replacements in multiple-choice format (often at the side or bottom of the text). Such a presentation is of course a disguised verbatim method which permits higher scores.

Because **native speakers** find difficulty with cloze tests and therefore cannot easily be appealed to as the standard to reach, radical changes in cloze method have been researched, notably the **c-test**.

While cloze tests may be justified in terms of **construct validity** through their tapping into language redundancy, they are hard to justify in terms of **content validity**. Quite what they test remains unclear except from the evidence of correlational studies. Nevertheless, in spite of this lack of content validity (and it may be said of **face validity**), they remain hugely popular, in part, no doubt, because they are among the easiest of tests to construct.

See also: **pragmatic expectancy grammar**
Further reading: Oller 1979; Alderson 1979; Alderson *et al.* 1995

clozentropy

A technique based on **cloze** which provides a measure of the **test taker**'s ability to draw on the linguistic context to predict meaning. Clozentropy employs an entropy measure (derived from information theory) which indexes the compatibility of a test taker's responses with those of a **criterion** group of native speakers. After **weighting**, a **score** is assigned to each answer an individual gives for an item according to the proportion of the criterion group who gave that same answer. The candidates' total score, the sum of all the weighted **responses** they gave to the test, shows by how much they differ from the **norm** established by the criterion group. Thus, a testee whose responses coincide with a large number of the criterion group will get a high score, while one whose responses are unusual compared with those of the criterion group will get a low score.

An advantage claimed for clozentropy is that it avoids the disadvantages of both 'exact word' and 'acceptable word' cloze scoring. A problem, however, is that a response may be unusual and not a good choice, or unusual and a clever choice, and the test is not able to distinguish between these. Clozentropy also raises the basic question associated with all cloze tests, that of what they measure.

See also: **pragmatic expectancy grammar**, **integrative test**
Further reading: Darnell 1970; Reilly 1971

coefficient

See **correlation coefficient**, **regression**

coherence

An aspect of **discourse competence** which involves the sequencing of ideas in a spoken or written text. Coherence is often included as an aspect of the **assessment** of writing, frequently linked with **cohesion** in the same assessment category, or otherwise being included explicitly or implicitly in assessment categories addressing the organisation of the content (the argument and ideas put forward), or the overall communicative quality of the text.

cohesion

An aspect of discourse competence which consists of the explicit marking of semantic relationships through reference, substitution, ellipsis and conjunction. Cohesion is commonly included within **assessment** categories for the assessment of writing in particular, but may also feature in the assessment of oral skills. Cohesion is frequently in the same assessment category as **coherence**.

Further reading: Halliday & Hasan 1976

communicative competence

An attempt to make **linguistic competence** situationally appropriate. Linguistic competence is concerned only with the native speaker's awareness of the formal patterning of his/her language, thus ignoring the equally important awareness of how to use those patterns appropriately.

Hymes proposes that **appropriateness** of language use requires four kinds of awareness:

- whether something is possible;

- whether something is feasible;
- whether something is appropriate in context;
- whether something is ever actually performed.

Examples often quoted of communicative incompetence include expressions lacking politeness and being informal when formality is required, as in a job interview.

Whether the 'awareness' communicative competence provides is **knowledge**, **ability** or control remains disputed. What is generally agreed is that communicative competence is not just performing linguistic competence because it involves control over the rules of language use. In other words, communicative competence, like linguistic competence, is rule-governed.

For language testing the Canale and Swain formulation has been influential, incorporating as it does linguistic competence, **sociolinguistic competence**, **discourse competence** and **strategic competence**. While some progress has been made in recent years in making language tests more communicative through the use of **authentic** stimulus materials and emphasising the productive **skills** of speaking and writing, the number of published tests of **communicative language tests** remains small. Those currently in use give evidence by what they omit that testing constraints make it difficult to accommodate crucial features of natural language use, such as interaction and unpredictability, which are important components of communicative competence.

Further reading: Hymes 1972; Bachman 1990; Canale & Swain 1980

communicative language tests

Tests of communicative skills, typically used in contradistinction to tests of grammatical knowledge. Such tests often claim to operationalise theories of **communicative competence**, although the form they take will depend on which dimensions they choose to emphasise, be it specificity of context (**LSP tests**), **authenticity** of materials or the simulation of real-life performance. An early communicative language test was the **RSA Communicative Use of English as a Foreign Language Test**, designed to test the use of English in what are typically seen as non-linguistic or real-world tasks.

Communicative Use of English as a Foreign Language Test (CUEFLT)

An early communicative language test, designed for the **Royal Society of Arts** on the basis of a feasibility study. The test, originally known as the

Communicative Competence Test (and therefore 'Co-Co'), has in recent years been taken over by **UCLES** and is now known as the RSA/UCLES Certificates in Communicative Skills in English (CSE). The original format remains: four **skills** labelled Reading, Writing, Listening and Oral Interaction, each at four **levels**. The skills are independent of one another which allows for candidacy on the same occasion in skills at different levels. One of the major communicative aspects of the test has been its use of **'authentic'** materials.

See also: **communicative competence**
Further reading: Morrow 1977

comparability

See **test equivalence**

competence

See **linguistic competence, discourse competence, pragmatic competence, strategic competence**

competency-based assessment

An approach to assessment which places primary emphasis on the competencies needed by the learner to perform a particular job adequately. In the teaching and assessment of language, the focus is on the intended outcomes of language training, that is, the sorts of **tasks** a person may be expected to deal with in the target situation, for example as an engineer, a teacher or a university student. Such assessment is necessarily **criterion-referenced**.

There is some controversy surrounding competency-based assessment of language, with its opponents accusing it of being both behaviourist and atomistic. The main difficulty in assessing language within such a framework is in defining what the necessary **skills** or competencies are and in establishing **mastery levels**, particularly where language skills are only one contributing factor in success (occupational knowledge and personal qualities being other relevant skills).

See also: **minimum competence testing, performance test**

composition test

A test of writing ability in which candidates are required to write one (or more) composition or essay. Composition tests are common in tests of English for academic purposes, where the purpose of the test is to predict which candidates will best be able to cope with the demands of academic essay writing. In the USA in particular composition tests are widely used in universities, where both native speaker and non-native speaker entrants to university are required to demonstrate their essay writing skills. However, composition tests may also be used in tests of general writing **proficiency**, especially in the school context, although in such cases the **assessment criteria** may focus less on academic writing skills and more on the linguistic features of the writing. **Prompts** for composition tests may take many forms, and require varying amounts of pre-reading or subject knowledge.

See also: **LSP testing**, **writing test**, **essay test**
Further reading: Hamp-Lyons 1991a

comprehension

The act or ability of understanding spoken or written **text**. Comprehension, unlike production, can only be assessed indirectly.

Second-language comprehension skills are frequently assessed independently of production, through the use of a **listening comprehension test** or a **reading comprehension test**. They may, however, also be assessed in a more integrated manner, for example in an **oral interview** where 'comprehension' may be one of several **assessment** categories, or in conjunction with a **writing test** where the comprehension of input material is a prerequisite for the writing task.

computer adaptive test (CAT)

Computer adaptive tests are based upon the existence of a bank of **items**, all **calibrated** on a single ability-difficulty scale, against which the items are ranged and the candidates will be placed; **item response theory** provides the tool by which this can be done. The item difficulties are pre-programmed into the CAT, and are derived from large-scale administration of the items to a trial **sample**, typically at this stage in pen-and-paper **format**.

Computer adaptive tests aim to measure the **ability** of the **candidate** by matching as closely as possible the difficulty of the test item with the ability of the candidate (both of which are measured on the **scale** using units called **logits**). In the test, a candidate is presented with a selection of items from the bank. The particular items that any individual candidate encounters are chosen by the computer programme as a result of the responses of the candidate to successive questions. The first response of the candidate is used to form a provisional estimate of ability, and easier or more difficult items are successively selected on the basis of the revised estimates after each response. Thus, if item A is found to be too difficult for a candidate, an easier one will be selected. If this one, item B, proves to be too easy, then a third one, item C, will be selected of intermediate difficulty. By this means the programme arrives at closer and closer estimates of the candidate's ability with a corresponding narrowing of the range of difficulty of the items until the estimate is within an agreed level of precision.

Computer adaptive tests are claimed to facilitate greater accuracy of measurement as a result of presenting candidates with items which are at the maximum discrimination level, ie, are more or less at the candidate's level of ability, items of this type providing more information about the candidate than items which are too easy or too hard.

A practical advantage of computer adaptive tests is that test security is enhanced, as it is unlikely that two candidates would receive the same items in the same sequence. It is also extremely unlikely that a candidate will encounter the same items on successive administrations, thus allowing the test to be used over and over again on the same students. They are also said to be more efficient as fewer items are needed to determine a candidate's ability.

See also: **adaptive testing**
Further reading: Weiss 1990

computer-assisted language testing (CALT)

Also computer-managed language testing, computer-based (English) language testing, computer-enhanced language testing

Such terms are used to refer to the various uses of computers in the development and delivery of language tests, in addition to their more traditional use in test scoring, analysis and reporting. In fact, computers may be used at any point in the testing process, as follows:

Test items may be developed and stored on computer, accompanied by information on their properties (computer software to facilitate this process is readily available). The resulting collection of items, known as an **item pool** or **item bank**, can then be drawn upon in order to construct a test containing items with properties which match the **test specifications**. The test and its answer key are then stored in the computer, and may be either printed out as a pen-and-paper test or be administered by computer using appropriate test administration software.

The pen-and-paper test may then be scanned and scored by computer, and candidates' item responses and test **score** stored. Summary information on the test and the items may also be computed and stored. This information may then be formatted for reporting of the candidates individually or as a group. If the test is computer-administered, the information on candidates' performance will be computed and stored directly, without the need for score sheet scanning.

See also: **computer-adaptive testing**, **item bank**, **IRT**
Further reading: Baker 1993

computer-based language testing (CBT)
See **computer-assisted language testing (CALT)**

concurrent validity

A type of **validity** which is concerned with the relationship between what is measured by a test (usually a newly developed test) and another existing **criterion** measure, which may be a well-established **standardised test**, a set of judgements or some other quantifiable variable. If the two measures function similarly (ie they **rank** candidates in the same way), they are considered to have concurrent validity. Strictly speaking it is inappropriate to use an existing test as the criterion unless the new test represents an abbreviated or simplified version (eg a tape-based test as a replacement for a 'live' oral proficiency interview).

Concurrent validity is calculated by correlating the scores obtained by a single set of candidates on the two different measures and is commonly expressed in terms of the amount of **variance** (ie the square of the **correlation**) shared by the two.

The problem of concurrent validity is how much emphasis to put on the existing criterion measure. If the criterion is itself valid, then the need for the test under trial is questionable. On the other hand, if the test under trial represents a new departure, then there will be little point in validating it against the existing test, which is presumably regarded as an imperfect measure of the relevant **construct** of **ability**. If, for example, the new test aims to measure English for air traffic controllers, there will be little value in comparing performance on it with skills demonstrated on a test of general English. A high correlation between the two sets of scores would in fact invalidate the new test as a measure of specific-purpose **proficiency**.

See also: **construct validity**, **predictive validity**, **convergent validity**
Further reading: Anastasi 1990

confidence interval

A range of values of an estimate which is likely to contain the true value for the relevant **population** a certain percentage of the time. It is unlikely that a single value, or point estimate, such as the **mean** or **standard deviation** of a **sample**, will be exactly equal to the true value for the relevant population. Confidence intervals provide an indication of the accuracy of the estimate.

A 95% confidence interval indicates a 95% probability that the true value lies within the stated range of values. The wider the confidence interval, ie the greater the range of possible values, the higher the confidence level (ie the more confident we can be that the interval contains the true value for the population). The narrower the confidence interval, ie the more precise the estimate, the lower the confidence level. The confidence interval is usually given in standard deviation units around the mean.

consequential validity

An evaluation of the potential consequences of the use of test **scores** (including issues of **bias** and **fairness**). Consequential validity places the onus on the test developer to provide evidence not only that test interpretation and use are both in line with intended testing purposes, but that they are also in line with other social values, in other words, to ensure that the score-based interpretations and actions reflect accepted social values. For example, the developer of a basic **skills** test for schoolchildren should be aware of the likelihood of children of a non-native language background performing less well owing to linguistic problems, and this should be taken into account in the inferences that are drawn about performance by individuals, groups and schools, and the action that is taken as a result of the test scores should reflect this awareness.

Language test developers cannot, of course, be held responsible for uses of their tests which are beyond their control.

See also: **impact**, **validity**, **ethics**
Further reading: Messick 1992, 1993; Bachman & Palmer 1996

construct

The **trait** or traits that a test is intended to measure. A construct can be defined as an **ability** or set of abilities that will be reflected in test **performance**, and about which inferences can be made on the basis of test **scores**. A construct is generally defined in terms of a theory; in the case of language, a theory of language. A test, then, represents an operationalisation of the theory. Construct **validation** involves an investigation of what a test actually measures and attempts to explain the construct.

constructed-response item

Also **extended response**, **open-ended question**

A type of **test item** or **task** requiring **test takers** to formulate their own answers, rather than select from a range of alternatives provided. One main purpose for using constructed-response items is to allow an assessment of test takers' ability to produce language – **direct tests** of speaking or writing, therefore, always require constructed responses. Constructed-response items are to be distinguished from **forced-choice items**, where the correct answer is supplied amongst the **distractors**.

Constructed-response items take a variety of forms, for example:

- a **cloze** (or **summary cloze**) item, where the test taker has to supply a word or phrase;
- a **short-answer question** (often used in tests of **reading** or **listening comprehension**), where the test taker may have to supply as little as one word, or perhaps one sentence or more;
- an extended writing task, where the test taker has to write an extended answer, as in an **essay question**;
- an extended speaking task, such as a section of an **interview test**, or a **role play**. In an extended speaking task the response may be considered as a single turn, in response to a question, or a series of turns, which collectively constitute a complete response.

Because constructed responses are **subjectively scored**, some item types, for example cloze and short-answer questions, generally require a comprehensive **marking scheme** (including acceptable alternative answers), to ensure adequate **reliability**. It may also be necessary to include instructions to scorers about how to judge answers with grammatical or spelling errors.

In extended tasks (written or spoken), a **rating scale** is often used. This inevitably involves a high degree of subjectivity, and when the test also has important consequences, satisfactory **rater** reliability should be established. This is likely to require **rater training**, multiple rating of responses (written or spoken) and monitoring of rater characteristics.

See also: **writing test**, **speaking test**, **reading comprehension test**, **listening comprehension test**

Further reading: Weir 1993; Alderson *et al.* 1995; Hughes 1989

construct irrelevant variance

A type of systematic **measurement error** where there is some variance in the test **scores** that is due to factors other than the construct in question. In a reading test, for example, construct irrelevant variance may be introduced through a factor associated with **background** or cultural **knowledge**. Such variance contaminates the interpretations that are made on the basis of test scores, and hence negatively affects the **construct validity** of the test.

construct underrepresentation

One of two major threats to **construct validity**, the other being **construct irrelevant variance**. In construct underrepresentation the test does not include important aspects of the construct; it could be said to be too narrow.

construct validity

The construct **validity** of a language test is an indication of how representative it is of an underlying theory of language learning. Construct **validation** involves an investigation of the qualities that a test measures, thus providing a basis for the rationale of a test.

There could be said to be two aspects of construct validation: theoretical and empirical, both of which are concerned with the production of evidence or arguments to support the inferences that are made about **candidates** on the basis of their test performance. Construct validity is traditionally examined by determining the relationship between the empirical (patterns of scores on the test) and the theoretical (proposed explanatory concepts), so, for example a **factor analysis** may be undertaken to identify the number of factors (or constructs) in the test data and their relationship with one another. **Multi-trait multi-method analysis** is another classic form of construct validation which investigates the relationship between **scores** on tests, the construct being tested and the **test method**.

Recent views of construct validity consider a broader range of testing factors, including performance differences across different groups, times and settings, as well as investigating **candidate**, **rater** and **interlocutor** behaviour. Construct validity may also be said to subsume **content validity** as this pertains to the inferences made about candidates' **abilities** on the basis of their test performance.

See also: **convergent validity**, **discriminant validity**, **content underrepresentation**, **construct irrelevant variance**

Further reading: Messick 1993; Bachman 1990

content analysis

A stage of test development in which experts are called upon to examine the content of test **tasks** or **items** in order to judge what the test is measuring. **Content validity** is generally considered to include two aspects, relevance to and coverage of the **domain**, and therefore experts might be expected to comment on both of these in relation to the **test content**. Ideally, this is a systematic process, involving comparison of test items and tasks with the **test specifications**.

Experts are most commonly language teachers, although in **LSP tests**, they may be chosen for their subject knowledge (eg medical doctors might be consulted in a test of English for health professionals). This raises the questions of which representatives of the relevant field are consulted; whether or not they agree with each other; and what to do if there is disagreement.

See also: **validation**
Further reading: Alderson *et al.* 1995, Ch. 8; Bachman 1990

content validity

A conceptual or non-statistical **validity** based on a systematic analysis of the **test content** to determine whether it includes an adequate **sample** of the target **domain** to be measured. An adequate sample involves ensuring that all major aspects are covered and in suitable proportions. This target domain may be a particular teaching module or **knowledge** area (for an **achievement test**), a particular occupational or educational domain (for a specific purpose **proficiency test**), or indeed the whole of the language and its possible uses (for a general **proficiency** test).

In the development of a **performance test**, content validity is normally achieved by means of a thorough **needs analysis** of the target domain, upon which the test content is based. An achievement test seeks content validity by drawing a representative item **sample** from the syllabus on which it is based. For a general proficiency test, where the whole of the language is the target domain, content then becomes the **construct**.

Content validation may require making reference not only to the content of the test in terms of linguistic **skills**, but also in terms of conceptual content ('topic') and of the candidates' test responses.

See also: **construct validity**, **face validity**, **validity**
Further reading: Anastasi 1990; Bachman 1990; Messick 1993

convergent validity

A type of **validity** which is concerned with the similarity between two or more tests which are claimed to measure the same underlying **trait** or **ability** (eg two measures of **reading comprehension**). Convergent validity is established by comparing **scores** obtained by a single group of **candidates** on the different tests. A high **correlation** can be interpreted as evidence that the tests are similar to one another in what they are measuring. A weak correlation indicates that something else is being measured by one of the tests (eg

background knowledge, reasoning **skills, test wiseness**).

Convergent validity is a key component of **multi-trait multi-method analysis**.

See also: **validity, discriminant validity, alternate forms, parallel forms**
Further reading: Messick 1993

correction for guessing

A procedure whereby the measurement problem induced by **candidates'** guessing the answers to **test items** can be reduced. Where the correct answer is not known and guessing occurs, this can lead to an overestimation of the candidates' **ability**. The solution to this, correction for guessing, is nevertheless problematic in itself as it assumes that all candidates are affected by guessing to the same degree.

A correction for guessing is typically applied where large numbers of **forced-choice items** are used. The standard formula works on the assumption that if candidates do not know the answer they will choose randomly from amongst the alternatives, giving a one in x likelihood of guessing the right answer (where x is the number of alternatives per question).

However, this assumption has been criticised as being too simplistic, on the grounds that candidates would at least know enough to be able to eliminate those they know to be wrong, choosing randomly amongst those that then remain, and thus increasing their chances of guessing correctly to greater than $1/x$.

The **three-parameter latent trait model** provides a means for correcting for guessing by plotting rates of success on the item by **examinees** of different ability and by giving less credit than normal for correct responses to difficult questions. However, very large data sets are required for this analysis, as well as there being some concern about the validity of associating patterns of guessing with items rather than people. If there is concern about guessing, its effects can be avoided by the use of five or more **distractors** in forced-choice test items, or by extending the length of the test.

Further reading: Choppin 1990; Anstey 1966

correlation

A procedure which measures the strength of the relationship between two (or more) sets of measures which are thought to be related. For example, we may want to investigate the relationship between students' **scores** on one test and scores of the same group of students on a different test. This relationship is usually expressed as a numerical value known as the **correlation coefficient**.

Correlation is a measure of relatedness and does not in itself provide evidence of causality. Determining whether one of the **variables** has an effect on the other requires different methods of evaluation.

The most common **parametric** procedure is the **Pearson product–moment correlation**. Other, non-parametric, correlational procedures include **Spearman's rank–order correlation** (*Rho*) (used for **rank** order, or **interval data** which are not **normally distributed**), **point biserial correlation** (used where one variable is a dichotomous nominal variable and the other is an interval), **Kendall's coefficient of concordance** (for more than two variables) and phi (for two dichotomous variables).

A number of statistical procedures, such as **regression** and **factor analysis** are based on correlation.

See also: **reliability**

Further reading: Hatch & Lazaraton 1991

correlation coefficient

A value showing the degree to which two **variables** are related.

The coefficient for **Pearson's product–moment correlation** is denoted by '*r*' and for **Spearman's rank–order correlation** by '*ρ*' (rho). Possible values for correlation coefficients vary from –1 to +1. A coefficient of zero indicates that there is no relationship between the two **variables**, a coefficient of –1 indicates a perfect negative correlation, and a coefficient of +1 indicates a perfect positive correlation.

The most helpful way of interpreting particular values of the correlation coefficient is to calculate the explained **variance** (or degree of overlap). For Pearson's product moment correlation we can calculate the variance between two measures by squaring the '*r*' value. For example, if $r = 0.7$, the variance $= 0.7^2 = 49\%$. This means that the two measures have only 49% in common. This example demonstrates that, whilst a correlation may be statistically significant, it may not be important. This depends on what we are trying to establish. If we are calculating **inter-rater reliability** we would hope for a value as close to 1 (ie exact agreement) as possible. For other tests of relatedness, eg between a score on a test of academic English and first semester university grades, a much lower value may still be considered important.

Council of Europe

Founded in 1949, the Council of Europe is an intergovernmental organisation based in Strasbourg, France, whose main role is to strengthen democracy, human rights and the rule of law throughout its 40 member states. The Council of Europe is also active in promoting awareness of a European cultural identity and encouraging its development. Since 1989, the Council of Europe has become the main political focus for co-operation with the countries of central and eastern Europe.

To improve international understanding, co-operation and mobility, the Council of Europe has helped to develop a communicative approach to language learning and teaching which seeks to facilitate 'the freer movement of people and ideas'. Its work has been widely used in **curriculum** and examination reform, course and textbook design and teacher training. Models for defining learning objectives ('threshold levels') have been published for some twenty languages spoken in Europe. More threshold levels are in preparation, in addition to the lower 'Waystage' level and recently developed higher 'Vantage' level. These models provide the basis for testing and certification systems in many national and pan-European contexts, including the **Association of Language Testers in Europe** (ALTE).

Current priorities include the development of a Common European Framework of reference for describing objectives, methods and qualifications and informing others of decisions concerning these. The uses envisaged for a Common European Framework of reference include the planning of language learning programmes, language certification and self-directed learning. The proposed set of levels of proficiency illustrated in the Framework provides a basis for the comparison of qualifications. Work is also in progress on the development of a European Language Portfolio – a personal document in which learners can record their qualifications and other significant linguistic and cultural experiences in an internationally transparent manner, thus motivating learners and acknowledging their efforts to extend and diversify their language learning at all levels in a lifelong perspective.

Further reading: van Ek & Trim 1991; *Language Testing Update* 1996 (no. 20)

covariance

See ANCOVA

CPE

See **Certificate of Proficiency in English**

criterion

1. An external **variable** such as a syllabus, teacher's judgement, **performance** in the real world, or another test. A test aims to provide a means of representing the criterion as it is usually not possible to observe/measure

every element of the criterion. Performance on the test is used to predict a candidate's **performance** on the criterion.

2. An acceptable level of **knowledge** of, or performance on, a specific **domain** of language behaviour (eg English for air traffic controllers).

3. A quality on which test performance is judged. Successful performance of an assessment **task** may be characterised in terms of linguistic and non-linguistic criteria. For example, if the task is writing a letter, the linguistic criteria might include **fluency**, **coherence** and **cohesion**, and grammatical **accuracy**. Non-linguistic criteria might include task fulfilment and **appropriacy** of the layout. Different criteria may be given different **weighting** in calculating a candidate's final **score**. The choice and weighting of **assessment criteria** will depend on the testing purpose.

See also: **analytic scoring, criterion-referenced test, criterion-related validity, cut-score, mastery, multiple-trait scoring, subjective scoring, predictor**

Further reading: Cronbach 1964; Anastasi 1990; Davidson & Lynch 1993

criterion-referenced test(ing)

Also CRT, criterion-referenced measurement, **domain-referenced test**

A test that examines the level of **knowledge** of, or **performance** on, a specific **domain** of target behaviours (ie the **criterion**) which the **candidate** is required to have mastered. The test domain is typically, but not necessarily, a specific course of instruction (see **achievement test**). In this case criterion-referenced tests are useful for teachers both in clarifying teaching objectives and in determining the degree to which they have been met. Criterion-referenced tests are also often used for professional accreditation purposes, ie the test represents the types of behaviours considered critical for participation in the profession in question.

Test **scores** report a candidate's **ability** in relation to the criterion, ie what the candidate can and cannot do, rather than comparing his/her performance with that of other candidates in the relevant **population**, such as happens in **norm-referenced tests**. **Test results** are often reported using descriptive **scales** rather than a numerical score. In contrast to norm-referenced tests the **criterion**, or **cut-score**, is set in advance.

Strictly speaking, criterion-referenced tests are only concerned with whether candidates have reached a given point rather than with how far above or below the criterion they may be. Where used for **achievement testing**, a high pass rate is usually expected, ie we would hope that the objectives of the course of instruction had been met. Because of this expectation, teachers often react negatively to **proficiency tests** which, in order to fully test the capabilities of the more proficient candidates, typically contain items beyond the scope of the majority of the cohort.

Where they are tied to a specific syllabus, results on criterion-referenced tests have limited transferability across different settings. Furthermore, until test performance is compared with cohorts in comparable or subsequent courses, it may be difficult to decide on how to capture the criterion by means of a cut-score.

See also: **norm-referenced test**, **competency-based assessment**, **standard setting**

Further reading: Glaser 1963; Popham 1975; Hudson & Lynch 1984; Henning 1987

criterion-related validity

Also **external validity**

Criterion-related validity (which incorporates **concurrent** and **predictive validities**) of a new test is established statistically (using **correlation**) in terms of the closeness of a test to its **criterion**. The criterion may be an established (well-known) test or some other measure within the same **domain** (concurrent validity) or a future test (predictive validity). In both cases validity is judged in terms of how closely the new test correlates with the criterion measure. The relation of two **parallel forms** of a test with one another, which is a special case of the relation of a new test to a criterion test, is a matter of both **reliability** (ie **parallel forms reliability**) and **validity**, reminding us of the close link between the two.

Further reading: Messick 1993

Cronbach's alpha

A measure of **internal consistency** and **reliability**. Alpha indicates how well a group of **items** together measure the **trait** of interest by estimating the proportion of test **variance** due to common factors among the items. If all items on a test measure the same underlying dimension, then the items will be highly **correlated**, or covary, with all other items. The greater the **covariance** of the items, the higher the reliability estimate will be.

An extension of the **Kuder-Richardson formulae**, Cronbach's alpha is the mean of all possible **split-half reliability** coefficients. However, in contrast to the Kuder-Richardson formulae, alpha can describe the **variance** whether or not items are **dichotomously scored**. Values for alpha range from 0 to 1.0. Alpha provides a low estimate of reliability for a test which is designed to measure several traits or when the group of **test takers** is relatively homogeneous. When all items are measures of the same trait, increasing test length will improve reliability.

As with other measures of internal consistency, Cronbach's alpha is based on a single administration of the test and does not, therefore, take into account any variation which may occur from one **test administration** to another or from one assessor to another.

Further reading: Anastasi 1990

c-test

A variant of the **cloze test** in which the second half of every second word in a reading passage is deleted.

Further reading: Klein-Braley 1997; Jafarpur 1995; Weir 1993

CUEFLT

See Communicative Use of English as a Foreign Language Test

culture-fair test

Also culture-free, culture-reduced

A test which is designed in such a way that it does not favour members of one cultural group over another. The notion of cultural **fairness** arose in the context of IQ testing where it was claimed that the inferior performance of working class subjects on intelligence tests was due to cultural **bias** in the **test items**. Bias was thus linked to lack of familiarity with item content or with test-taking processes among particular groups of **candidate**s. These factors were considered irrelevant to the underlying capacities which IQ tests sought to measure.

Most attempts to produce 'culture free', 'culture-fair' or 'culture-reduced' tests are therefore directed towards eliminating topics or items which assume **background knowledge** or **skills** which are alien to a particular cultural group and may therefore mask their true **ability**. In language testing the task of producing culture-fair material may be particularly difficult because all language has some degree of cultural resonance and the process of neutralising a text or an item may reduce its **authenticity**.

Further reading: Ells 1951; Cattell 1940

curriculum

See **syllabus**

cut-score

Also **passmark**

A score that represents achievement of the **criterion**, the line between success and failure, **mastery** and non-mastery. Methods of establishing a cut-score always involve making some kind of subjective judgement regarding the acceptability of test **performance**. It is therefore essential firstly to ensure that those involved in making these judgements have the relevant expertise, and secondly to be specific about the type of evidence which will be used to support these judgements.

Cut-scores may be determined with reference to either an absolute or relative standard. Relative standards are commonly determined by administrative considerations. For example, if there are only 50 places on a course, only the first 50 candidates will be passed. Absolute standards, on the other hand, do not compare candidates with each other but with some type of external criterion, eg mastery of a specific range of skills.

There are three main types of method for determining a cut-score when using an absolute standard, all of which involve classifying **test takers** into higher and lower scoring groups.

- **Methods which focus on test items:**
  The cut-score may be determined by firstly classifying test items into groups according to difficulty (eg easy, medium, hard) and importance (eg essential, important, acceptable), and secondly making a judgement about the percentage of items in each group a borderline candidate is likely to get right.
- **Methods based on judgements about the adequacy of individual test takers:**
  The cut-score may be set at the point between scores associated with candidates judged to be 'qualified' (ie who meet the criterion) and those judged to be 'unqualified'. Alternatively, the cut-off may be set at the **median** score of a group of candidates judged to be minimally successful.
- **Methods involving judgement as to the percentage of candidates in a reference group who are 'qualified':**
  If, for example, 45% of the reference group (typically **trial** candidates) are considered 'qualified', a pass rate of 45% will be specified.

Regardless of the method adopted, the cut-score selected needs to ensure success on a critical number of test items on a specified range of language skills and at an appropriate level of difficulty. The cut-score also needs to be monitored against real-world evidence to ensure that qualified candidates are not unnecessarily excluded and/or unqualified candidates admitted. Whether the cut-score errs on the side of **leniency** or **severity** is influenced by a consideration of the harm caused by excluding qualified candidates as opposed to the harm caused by passing unqualified candidates. Contingency tables can be used to estimate the optimum cut-score.

See also: **standard setting**

Further reading: Cangelosi 1982; Angoff 1971; Livingston & Zieky 1982

d

dependability

Also **agreement**

1. In **criterion**-referenced measurement, refers to the internal dependability of the test as a sampling of the **domain** of interest. The **coefficient**, called the domain score dependability index, represents the proportion of **observed score variance**, and is the **criterion-referenced test** equivalent of the **reliability** coefficient derived for **norm-referenced tests**.

2. The extent to which decisions about **mastery**/non-mastery are accurately made on the basis of test **cut-scores**. Two classification errors can occur here: **false positive** (in which a candidate is deemed on the basis of his/her test **score** to be a master when in fact his/her domain score would indicate otherwise) and **false negative** (where a candidate is beneath the cut-off when in fact his/her domain score would indicate that he/she is indeed a master). Contingency tables indicate the false positive : false negative ratio.

Further reading: Berk 1984

dependent variable

See **variable**

descriptive assessment

The **reporting** in prose of subjects' abilities, rather than representing them as **scores**. In language testing such reporting is normally based on **criterion-referenced** assessment and may involve the use of **profiling** or **bandscales**. Descriptive **assessment** may also be based on informal **observation** in the classroom or on **portfolios**.

See also: **descriptor**

descriptive statistics

Statistics which provide summary data of the particular group measured. The range, **central tendency** and **standard deviation** of the group are frequently used descriptive statistics, as are **correlations** with data taken from the same or another group. For example, the performance of a group on a language test may be described in terms of the spread of **scores** and average scores. It may also be described in terms of how much better or worse the group performed than a parallel group, or how much the group has improved since the last time it was tested.

Descriptive statistics form the basis of **inferential statistics**; however such data cannot be used to infer the characteristics of the larger **population** unless the group described forms a representative **sample** of that population.

descriptor

A statement which describes the level of **performance** required of **candidates** at each point on a **proficiency scale**. Descriptors typically make reference to the level of linguistic **skill** required (for example level of grammatical **accuracy**, vocabulary range), to production skills (eg **fluency** and **intelligibility**), to the types of functions candidates can fulfil (eg asking questions, giving personal information, filling in forms), or to the content of the message (eg relevance of information, organisation of ideas).

See also: **analytic scoring**, **holistic scoring**

diagnosis, diagnostic test

Used to identify **test takers'** strengths and weaknesses, by testing what they know or do not know in a language, or what **skills** they have or do not have. Information obtained from such tests is useful at the beginning of a language course, for example, for **placement** purposes (assigning students to appropriate classes), for **selection** (deciding which students to admit to a particular course), for planning of courses of instruction or for identifying areas where remedial instruction is necessary. It is common for educational institutions (eg universities) to administer diagnostic language tests to incoming students, in order to establish whether or not they need or would benefit from support in the language of instruction used. Relatively few tests are designed specifically for diagnostic purposes. A frequent alternative is to use **achievement** or **proficiency tests** (which typically provide only very general information), because it is difficult and time-consuming to construct a test which provides detailed diagnostic information.

See also: **SLA**, **profile**
Further reading: Hughes 1989

dichotomous scoring, dichotomously scored

Describes **items** which are scored either right or wrong, ie **candidates** may score either zero or one for each item. Most commonly associated with **true/false** and **multiple-choice items**, this type of scoring is also possible for **short-answer questions** having several acceptable **responses**.

See also: **partial credit, test item**

dictation

An exercise where a passage is read aloud in fragments with sufficient pauses and at such a speed as to allow proficient **candidates** to write it down with complete **accuracy**. The passage may be read once or more than once.

Dictation is an **integrative test** in that it simultaneously assesses a range of **skills**, including listening, and involves processing in real time. The rationale for this testing technique comes from the **unitary competence hypothesis**, according to which there is no need for analysis or **sampling** from a particular **domain** of language nor for a **battery** of tests, each testing different language skills.

Whilst dictation tests tend to discriminate well among learners of different **ability** and are relatively easy to construct, it is generally considered that the lack of domain analysis and crude **sampling** reduce their **validity** as a testing technique. However, where **content validity** and **diagnosis** can be ignored, dictation may be used to provide an estimate of general language **proficiency**, for example, for the purpose of placing students in a general language instruction programme.

Devising an appropriate **marking scheme** for a dictation task is difficult. The most straightforward method of scoring dictation is to deduct one from the total number of words in the original text for each wrong or missing word. In this approach spelling mistakes, unless they are also structural errors, are ignored.

See also: **pragmatic expectancy grammar**
Further reading: Oller 1979; Baker 1993

DIF

See **differential item functioning**

differential item functioning (DIF)

Also **item bias**
A feature of a **test item** that shows up in a statistical analysis as a group

difference in the probability of answering that item correctly. The presence of differentially functioning items in a test has the effect of boosting or diminishing the total test **score** of one or other of the groups concerned.

DIF items may be regarded as biased only if group differences can be traced to factors which are irrelevant to the test **construct**. For example, on a test of Japanese **reading comprehension**, Chinese-background students may find it easier to read test questions which are formulated in characters than do their counterparts from English-speaking backgrounds, because of the script similarity between Chinese and Japanese. Any **performance** advantage for the Chinese students on this kind of test question cannot be treated as evidence of **bias**, since the **ability** to decipher characters is intrinsic to reading Japanese. On the other hand, if there is a negative DIF effect for questions which are formulated in English (ie Chinese-background students are less likely to get the right answer to these items than English-background students) this could be regarded as an instance of item bias, because the source of **difficulty** (ie reading skills in English) is unrelated to the ability under test.

To avoid confusion between real differences in ability and bias, most DIF detection techniques are performed on groups which are matched according to the **criterion** ability, usually the total test score.

Amongst the most robust DIF techniques are the **Mantel-Haenszel** method (basically an adaptation of the **Chi-square** test) and the analagous standardisation technique based on a **Rasch analysis**.

Further reading: Holland & Wainer 1993

difficulty

The extent to which a test or **test item** is within the **ability** range of a particular **candidate** or group of candidates. Most tests (except those with a very stringent selection or gate-keeping function) are designed in such a way that the majority of items are not too difficult (or too easy) for the relevant **sample** of test candidates. Preliminary **trialling** is often undertaken to ensure that this is the case. The notion of test difficulty is always relative to the underlying ability that is being measured and is therefore a key consideration in establishing a test's **validity** or **discriminability**.

See also: **item difficulty, item analysis, severity**

dimensionality

A measurement property of **scores** from a test: that responses from **candidates** on a set of **test items** display sufficiently consistent patterning as to allow candidates to be ranked or ordered in terms of whatever is being measured by the test. The most commonly used **item response theory** models require that test data display **unidimensionality** (that a single measurement **trait** or pattern is sufficient to account for candidates' test performance). If scores on a subset of the items display a different patterning from scores on the majority of items, we can say that the data display **multidimensionality**. This means that there will appear to be two (or more) types of patterning co-present in the data set such that candidates would be ranked differently on a subset of items from the way they would be ranked on other items. In such a case there will be unsatisfactory **model data fit** to a unidimensional measurement model. For example, on a writing task, **performance** in terms of handwriting or **mastery** of the conventions of spelling and punctuation may be unrelated to other, more cognitively demanding aspects of performance such as **text** organisation.

The assumption of unidimensionality should also be tested with different subgroups of candidates (eg girls and boys, or candidates from different language backgrounds) to ascertain that the structure of test scores is invariant across the groups. If not, the test may be regarded as biased, in that scores will have different meaning for each group.

It is necessary to distinguish psychometric from cognitive or psychological unidimensionality. The presence or otherwise of psychometric unidimensionality is an issue of score patterns, that is, it is a mathematical and statistical question which must be distinguished from the complexity and multidimensionality of the linguistic **skills** and **abilities** that underlie test performance, for example in reading or listening, considered from a cognitive or psychological perspective. In a test where two different kinds of abilities are being measured, statistical analysis of test data can establish whether a single consistent pattern can be observed in the overall set of responses; if performance on the two abilities is correlated, such a unidimensional pattern will be observed; if not, then no single pattern will be observed and the multidimensionality in the data will invalidate certain conventional procedures in test score interpretation. Explanations or interpretations of the multidimensionality may then be sought in theories of the substantial skills involved in performance. The appropriateness of the use of **IRT** procedures for the analysis of language test data has been debated in terms of their unidimensionality assumption.

See also: **bias**
Further reading: Henning 1987; McNamara 1996

directed-response

See **directed-response item**

directed-response item

A test **question** designed to elicit an answer whose content is tightly constrained. **Cloze** test, **gap-filling**, word-matching and substitution exercises as well as **multiple-choice** and **true/false** questions are all examples of items with directed responses. The major advantage of such items over **open-ended questions** is that they allow for ease and objectivity of scoring.

See also: **forced-choice item, constructed response item, key**

direct test

Also **face-to-face test**

A test which claims to measure **ability** directly by eliciting a **performance** approximating **authentic** language behaviour. This type of test is most commonly associated with the testing of speaking and writing. Examples of direct tests of speaking include simulated **interviews** and **role plays** whilst direct tests of writing include writing a letter or an essay. As the **receptive skills** are essentially unobservable, there is disagreement as to whether it is possible to have direct tests of reading or listening, even where authentic texts and **tasks** are included.

It has been argued that it is the underlying **language ability**, rather than performance of the task *per se*, which should be the object of interest. In this view a direct test is one which involves authentic processing on the part of the candidate and, as such, need not involve simulation of the **criterion** performance.

Because direct tests make it easier for **test users** to make the connection between test performance and future use, they tend to have higher **face validity** than **indirect tests**. However, direct tests should not be assumed to be intrinsically more valid than indirect tests.

See also: **communicative language test, performance test, validity**
Further reading: Davies 1978 (a/b); Bachman 1990; McNamara 1996

discourse competence

The component of **communicative competence** which is basically concerned with above-sentence-level **cohesion** and **coherence**. In the testing of speaking and listening **proficiency** these features are frequently included in the **assessment criteria** or **band scales**. In the testing of reading and writing they may form the basis of particular **test items**.

See also: **skills**
Further reading: Canale 1983; Bachman 1990.

discrete-point

A procedure in which each item is independent and focuses on a specific component of **language ability**, for example a syntactic point. This approach is based on the view that language consists of small elements which can be learnt and tested in isolation. In recent years the **validity** of this approach has been questioned.

See also: **integrative test, test item**

discriminability

See **item discrimination**

discriminant validity

A type of **validity** which is concerned with the dissimilarity between different measures rather than with similarity. It involves a comparison between tests or **sub-tests** which purport to measure different underlying **traits** or **abilities**. A low **correlation** can be interpreted as evidence that the tests are indeed different from one another in what they are measuring, provided that the **method** of **measurement** is the same for each test. In most cases, however, tests measuring different abilities (such as reading and writing) have different types of items (eg **forced-choice** for reading and **open-ended** for writing) so that differences in candidates' **scores** may be at least partly attributable to greater facility with one or other **item** type. For this reason discriminant validity also depends on evidence of **convergent validity**. In other words, the researcher must demonstrate that test A (reading ability) is more closely related to another measure of reading than to test B (writing ability).

The estimation of discriminant validity is a key component of **multi-trait, multi-method analysis**.

See also: **test method**

discrimination

A fundamental property of language tests (especially **norm-referenced**) in their attempt to capture the range of individual **abilities**. On that basis the more widely discriminating the test the better it is. In **classical test theory** item discrimination is an important indicator of a test's **reliability**.

See also: **item discrimination, item difficulty, item analysis**
Further reading: Henning 1987

discrimination index
See **item discrimination**

distractor
Any response in a **forced-choice item** which is not the **key**, ie it is not the correct choice but is offered as a means of ascertaining whether **candidates** are able enough to distinguish the right answer from a range of alternatives.

While distractors should not make greater demands on candidates' **ability** than the key, they should be sufficiently plausible to be selected as the correct option by a good number of candidates. Distractors which are chosen by very few candidates contribute little to the item because they effectively reduce the number of alternatives, thereby increasing the probability that candidates will arrive at the correct answer by **guessing** alone.

distribution
The spread and pattern of a set of data such as test **scores**.

Distributions are usually described in terms of their **central tendency** (**mean, median, mode**), variability or dispersion (range, **standard deviation, variance**), the relative position of scores (**percentiles, z-scores, stanine scores**), and relationship between scores (**correlation coefficient**).

Types of distribution include:
- normal, that is, represented by a curve which is **bell-shaped**, and symmetrically arranged about the **mean**;
- skewed – represented by a curve which is asymmetrical, with the majority of the scores occurring towards one end of the **scale**; and
- bimodal, with scores congregating at two distinct points on the scale.

See also: **normal distribution**
Further reading: Hatch & Lazaraton 1991

divergent validity
See **convergent validity**

domain
1. In **applied linguistics** this term is used to refer to the area of language use or the social correlate of a particular speech style or variety, normally marked by such features as topic of discourse, locale of discourse and relative status

of participants. The idea that language use varies according to social context is central to **LSP testing**.

2. In testing theory the term is used more broadly to denote that portion of the total universe of subject matter (linguistic or other) which is being tested or about which inferences are to be drawn. Domain is an important factor in needs/job analysis surveys and in test construction. Proper **sampling** from the domain is also central to **content validity**.

See also: **criterion, needs analysis**

domain-referenced test

An alternative (but less commonly used) term for **criterion-referenced test**. A domain-referenced test is constructed to take into account the major dimensions of the **criterion** behaviour or **domain** of language use which it is intended to represent so that its **items** elicit **performances** which are of relevance to that domain. Domain referenced tests are typically used for professional accreditation (eg tests of medical English for doctors, engineers, airline pilots who have been trained in a foreign language medium) and have the purpose of providing information about what **candidates** can or cannot do rather than determining their **scores** relative to those of other candidates. Many of these tests have a **minimum proficiency threshold** or **cut point** which indicates the level at which candidates can be deemed to have achieved adequate **mastery** of the target domain.

See also: **norm-referenced test**
Further reading: Popham 1975; Glaser 1963

e

EAP (English for Academic Purposes) test
See **LSP testing**

editing
An **item** type in which the **test taker** has to identify and/or correct the **errors** in a written **text**. Texts may include **authentic** learner errors or the errors may be deliberately introduced. Typically there is one error per line of text, but this may vary.

See also: **multiple-choice item**
Further reading: Alderson *et al.* 1995

Educational Testing Service (ETS)
See **ETS**

ELTS
1. The English Language Testing Service, which developed and delivered the ELTS test.

2. The test of the English Language Testing Service: a test of English for Academic Purposes, it was developed jointly by the British Council and **UCLES** between 1975 and 1979, and administered worldwide by them from 1980 to 1989. The ELTS replaced the **English Proficiency Test Battery**, and had as its purpose the assessment (for screening purposes) of the English **proficiency** of non-English-speaking students (typically overseas or international students) wishing to study in British universities.

The test consisted of five **sub-tests** in two sections: G1 (General Reading), G2 (General Listening), M1 (Study Skills), M2 (Writing) and M3 (Individual Interview). All candidates took the General Section (G1 and G2), while six versions of each Modular Section (M1, M2 and M3) were developed, according to the student's area of study. The six subject areas were: Life Sciences, Social Studies, Physical Sciences, Technology, Medicine and General Academic.

This test represented one of the boldest attempts to operationalise theories behind **LSP testing**. An evaluation of the test in the late 1980s led to its being replaced by the **IELTS**, which has now largely abandoned the subject-specific approach.

See also: **gatekeeping test**

Further reading: Criper & Davies 1988; Hughes *et al.* 1988; Alderson & Clapham 1992

English for Specific Purposes (ESP)

See **LSP testing**

English Language Battery (ELBA)

A test designed in the early 1960s to determine whether prospective overseas (international) tertiary students had adequate English to attend British universities. The English Language Battery (ELBA) was designed by Elisabeth Ingram on behalf of the University of Edinburgh on structuralist principles: test results (including students' outcomes) were collected over a period of about 15 years, providing at that time a unique data set for **predictive validity** studies.

See also: **English Proficiency Test Battery**

Further reading: Davies 1984

English Language Testing Service (ELTS)

See **ELTS**

English Placement Test (EPT)

A 100-**item multiple-choice test** of listening comprehension, grammar, vocabulary and reading comprehension for beginning and intermediate level speakers of English as a second language. Originating at the University of Michigan's English Language Institute, multiple forms are now commercially available to *bona fide* educational institutions for use in their ESL teaching programmes. The EPT is designed to group students into homogeneous **ability** levels. Further information available at www.lsa.umich.edu/eli/.

See also: **Listening Comprehension Test**, **MELAB**, **MTELP**

English Proficiency Test Battery (EPTB)

A test designed in the early 1960s to determine whether prospective overseas international tertiary students had adequate English to attend British universities. The English Proficiency Test Battery (EPTB) was designed by Alan Davies on behalf of the British Council and administered by them until 1980. Its design combined structuralist and sociocultural concerns and was eventually available in four parallel versions. Only **receptive skills** were tested. **Correlations** of between 0.4 – 0.5 with academic grades were reported. In 1980 the EPTB was replaced by the English Language Testing Service (**ELTS**), itself now replaced by the International English Language Testing System (**IELTS**).

Further reading: Hughes 1987; Davies 1984

entrance test

See **gatekeeping test**

EOP (English for Occupational Purposes) test
See **LSP testing**

EQS

A statistical software package for multivariate **structural modelling** analysis.
Further reading: Kunnan 1995

equate, equating

Also **equivalence**

The process of establishing the equivalence of individual **test items** or **tasks** or of entire tests.

When a comparison is to be made between **scores** provided by two or more tests or **test forms**, a procedure is normally used whereby either the tests are given to the same group of **test takers**, or a number of **samples** of test takers with similar characteristics each takes a different test. A common point of reference is thus established, and a common standardised **scale** may be constructed.

An alternative approach is to establish the characteristics (**difficulty**, **discriminability**, **reliability**) of individual test items or tasks, using, for example, **IRT analysis**, and thus to develop an **item bank**. Once a large enough pool, or bank, is developed, multiple forms of a test of known difficulty may then be constructed from these items. Items may be selected in order to produce tests of equal difficulty (**alternate forms** – horizontal equating); or of increasing difficulty (where test A is for beginners, for example, test B for intermediate learners, and test C for advanced learners – vertical equating).

See also: **test equivalence**, **concurrent validity**

equivalence

See **equate**, **test equivalence**

equivalent forms

See **alternate forms**

error

See **measurement error**, **standard error of measurement**, **Type 1 error**, **Type 2 error**, **sampling error**

error of measurement

See **measurement error**

error variance

The square of the **standard error of measurement**. Error variance is another way of expressing **test reliability**, in terms of the amount of **variance** in the **scores** that is due to **random error** – that is, the variation in the **observed scores** which cannot be explained by variation in the **true scores**; it is used as an alternative to the standard error of measurement and the **reliability** coefficient. In contrast to the reliability **coefficient** (where a high value indicates a reliable test), low error variance indicates a reliable test.

Further reading: Feldt & Brennan 1993; Anastasi 1990

ESP (English for Specific Purposes) test

See **LSP testing**

essay test

Essay examinations are widely used in school systems throughout the world at the end of courses and school levels to evaluate **achievement** and as **entrance tests**.

Essay examinations are usually more formal than **composition tests** and offered at higher levels of language instruction.

Further reading: Quellmalz 1990

estimates

The term used for measures of person **ability** and **item** parameters (**difficulty**, **discrimination** and **guessing**) produced in **latent trait models**. These estimates are given in **logits**, units of measurement on a logarithmic scale. The estimates for the specified number of item parameters and the ability parameter are calculated iteratively and simultaneously on the basis of the overall pattern of responses in the set of test data. The analysis may also provide an error estimate associated with each ability and item parameter estimate. The default setting for logit scales is typically for the **mean** item difficulty estimate to be set at zero logits and the **standard deviation** to be set at one logit.

See also: **one-parameter model**, **two-parameter model**, **three-parameter model**

Further reading: Wright & Masters 1982

ethicality

The quality of right doing according to a professional Code of Conduct or set of professional **standards**. **Language testers** are much exercised as to their own responsibility for the intervention of language tests and the **norms** they establish. One commonly proposed **benchmark** is to consider whether an alternative **assessment** procedure, or no procedure at all, would produce a more equitable outcome for test **candidates** or for society or both. For some, however, there is a fundamental conflict between a system which allocates educational and vocational opportunities according to merit, on the basis of results on **standardised tests**, and the assertion of constitutional rights of equality of opportunity in education and employment.

See also: **ethics**

Further reading: Cronbach 1964; Jensen 1980; Messick 1993; Joint Committee on Testing Practices (JCTP) 1988; Davies 1997(a/b)

ethics

The agreed rules of conduct of a group, profession or society. Among

language testers the increasing concern with the ethics of the activity appears to indicate a growing sense of professionalism. Among the issues currently being addressed are whether testing specialists should take any responsibility for decisions about non-intended use of tests following test construction; who decides what is valid; whether professionalism conflicts with individual morality; relationships with various **stakeholders**; **washback**; and the politics of the **gatekeeping** use of language tests (in, for example, immigration procedures). In recent years the **International Language Testing Association** (ILTA) and the **Association of Language Testers in Europe** (ALTE) have established **standards** or Codes of Practice, the aim being to make public to members and stakeholders the ethics of those professing language testing.

See also: **ethicality**

Further reading: Alderson *et al.* 1995, Ch. 11; American Education Research Association, American Psychological Association, and National Council on Measurement in Education 1985; Davies 1997b

ETS

Educational Testing Service, based in Princeton, New Jersey, was founded in 1947. Now the world's largest non-profit educational measurement institution, ETS develops achievement, occupational and admissions tests for clients in education, government and business. ETS annually administers tests to over nine million **candidates** world-wide. **TOEFL** is developed by ETS and **TOEIC** originated there.

evaluation

The systematic gathering of information in order to make a decision. Within a language education programme, evaluation may be carried out to provide information about the programme to **stakeholders**, such as sponsors, managers, teachers or parents, and to make decisions about the future of the programme. Where the effectiveness of the instruction is under investigation, **language tests** are frequently used as one component of the evaluation; typically **pre-** and **post-testing**, or **achievement testing** would be carried out, with or without a control group of subjects.

See also: **language programme evaluation**

examination

Also exam

A term generally used synonymously with 'test'. While there does not appear to be any clear distinction in meaning between the two terms, in certain contexts one may be preferred over the other, eg in certain institutional contexts or by particular examining bodies. The term examination is more likely to be used for **syllabus**-related **assessment**. A distinction may also be made on the basis of the assessment format: objective, **discrete-point** types of assessment being more likely to be termed 'tests', and subjective assessments being termed 'examinations'.

Further reading: Allen & Davies 1977

Examination for the Certificate of Competency in English (ECCE)

An intermediate-level ESL examination developed and administered by the English Language Institute of the University of Michigan (ELI-UM) at authorised sites world-wide. It is comparable to the **UCLES FCE**. The ECCE has four components: a Speaking section, a Listening section, a Grammar/Vocabulary/Reading Comprehension section and a Writing section. All test papers are scored at ELI-UM, which issues certificates to successful candidates for use in their home countries as evidence of intermediate-level English language **proficiency**. Further information available at www.lsa.umich.edu/eli/.

Examination for the Certificate of Proficiency in English (ECPE)

An advanced-level ESL examination developed and administered by the English Language Institute of the University of Michigan (ELI-UM) at authorised sites world-wide. It is comparable to the **UCLES CPE**. The ECPE has five components: a Speaking section, a Writing section, a Listening section, a Cloze section and a Grammar/Vocabulary/Reading Comprehension section. All test papers are scored at ELI-UM, which issues certificates to successful candidates for use in their home countries as evidence of advanced-level English language **proficiency**. Further information available at www.lsa.umich.edu/eli/.

examinee

A term used to refer to any person undertaking a test or **examination**. Other terms commonly used in language testing are **candidate**, **test taker**, **testee**.

See also: **test-taker feedback**

exit test

A form of **achievement test**, administered at the end of a course of study. **Scores** derived from exit tests may be used for various purposes. Scores on an exit test may be related to those obtained on an **entry test**, allowing a **pre-test post-test** comparison; scores may reflect the level of success obtained in mastering the course content; or they may act as a more general indication of the language **proficiency** of the **test takers**.

See also: **pre-test post-test design, proficiency test**

extended response

See **constructed-response item**

external validity

See **criterion-related validity**

f

face validity

The degree to which a test appears to measure the knowledge or **abilities** it claims to measure, as judged by an untrained observer (such as the **candidate** taking the test or the institution which plans to administer it).

For example, a **gate-keeping test** of oral **proficiency** administered prior to entry to a particular profession (such as engineering), which simulates actual workplace communication, can be said to have high face validity, even though the **skills** measured may not in fact be reliable **predictors** of future performance.

Conversely, if a **listening comprehension test** uses a speaker with a strong regional accent which is unfamiliar to the majority of candidates, the test may be judged as lacking face validity. Another example of poor face validity is the use of a **dictation** activity to measure an apparently unrelated ability, such as reading, even though there may be empirical evidence of a high **correlation** between the two skills.

Concerns for face validity are often dismissed as trivial because they have to do with appearances rather than with the underlying **construct** of ability being measured by the test. However, it has also been argued that failure to take issues of face validity into account may jeopardise the public credibility of a test (and indeed the curriculum on which the test may be based) and that the notion of test appeal is a practical consideration which test designers cannot afford to overlook.

Nor should it be taken for granted that **test takers** are inexpert judges. Candidates for a test of medical English, for example, may be better equipped than language experts to pass judgement about a text in their specialist area. Particularly in the development of **occupation-specific tests**, there may be a certain degree of overlap between face and **content validity**

face-to-face test

See **direct test**

facet

In the analysis of test data, a measurable aspect of a **performance** or its setting which is hypothesised to have an **impact** on **scores**; a technical term in generalisability theory and multi-faceted Rasch measurement. Facets modelled in such analyses typically include person **ability**, **item difficulty**, **rater** characteristics and **task** characteristics, though others (for example variability associated with **interlocutors**, **stimulus** mode, medium through which the performance is assessed) may also be considered.

See also: **generalisability theory**, **multi-faceted Rasch measurement**
Further reading: Bachman 1990

facet theory

Facet theory refers to approaches to investigating the **measurement** consequences of **variables** (termed '**facets**') in the **assessment** situation, particularly in **performance** assessment contexts, where there are likely to be many variables affecting the allocation of **scores**. For example, the characteristics of **raters**, **tasks** and **candidates** will have an effect on the judgement of **language ability**. Not all raters are equally harsh or consistent; where there is a choice of tasks, not all tasks present the same challenge; raters may react to irrelevant candidate characteristics such as gender, language background, etc. There may as well be interactions between the effects of these facets.

Two sets of techniques are available for the investigation of the effects of such facets: **generalisability theory** or G-theory and **multi-faceted Rasch measurement**.

facility

See **difficulty**

factor analysis

A procedure used to reduce the number of **variables** accounting for test performance by identifying the common underlying factor (or factors) shared by a series of **items** or tests. For example, you might want to know to what extent a general **proficiency** test, a **vocabulary knowledge test** and a **speaking test** measure the same **traits**, in order to justify the use of a single test (on the grounds that it measures much the same language traits as the others) or in order to validate a new test.

Factor analysis uses **correlation** to examine two components of score

variance: common variance (ie variance shared by the tests) and unique variance (comprising specific variance and **error** variance). A loading (ie the portion of the total variance contributed by a test to each factor) of 0.3 or above is, by convention, considered to indicate a substantial link between a factor and a test. However, having isolated the underlying factors, or components, it is often difficult to name them accurately.

Confirmatory factor analysis starts with some prior knowledge of the underlying factorial structure whereas for exploratory factor analysis the researcher has no preconceived ideas of what the factor structure should be.

See also: **correlation**

Further reading: Hatch & Lazaraton 1991

fairness

See **test fairness**

false negative

A person classified as failing on the basis of a test's **cut-score** but who would nevertheless have gone on to succeed in the area for which the test is used as a predictor. Critical scores, based on an acceptable level of risk, are determined by relating test scores to a **criterion**, typically **assessment** of **performance** in the target context; nevertheless any cut-score is likely to misclassify some **candidates** as false negatives or **false positives**. While lowering the cut-score would reduce the number of false negatives, it would also increase the number of false positives; **test users** need to consider the consequences of raising or lowering cut-scores. Contingency tables can be used to estimate the optimum cut-score.

See also: **mastery**

Further reading: Cronbach 1964

false positive

A person classified as passing on the basis of a test's **cut-score**, but who would nevertheless have gone on to fail in the area for which the test is a predictor. Critical scores, based on an acceptable level of risk, are determined by relating test scores to a **criterion**, typically **assessment** of **performance** in the target context; nevertheless any cut-score is likely to misclassify some **candidates** as false positives or **false negatives**. While raising the cut-score would reduce the number of false positives, it would also increase the number of false negatives; **test users** need to consider the consequences of raising or lowering cut-scores. Contingency tables can be used to estimate the optimum cut-score.

See also: **mastery**
Further reading: Cronbach 1964

FCE

See **First Certificate in English**

feedback

1. In communication theory the process whereby the sender of a message obtains a reaction from the receiver which enables him/her to check on the efficiency of the message.

2. In language testing the term generally refers to **test-taker feedback**, that is, comments by **test takers** on a test which may be used for post-**trialling** test revision or as a form of test evaluation.

field-specific test

See **LSP testing**

First Certificate in English (FCE)

Introduced by **UCLES** in 1939 as a preparatory examination to **CPE** it was originally known as the Lower Certificate in English. It quickly became popular, attracting many more candidates than CPE. It forms part of a coherent suite of UCLES examinations in English as a Foreign Language which, in addition to the FCE, include the **Key English Test**, the **Preliminary English Test**, the **Certificate in Advanced English**, the **Certificate of Proficiency in English**, the Cambridge Examination in English for Language Teachers and several examinations in English for business.

An extensively revised version of the examination was introduced in December 1996. The present components of the FCE are Reading, Writing, Use of English and Listening papers, and a Speaking test. Each paper is equally weighted in order to determine the **score**, carrying 20% of the total marks. FCE is recognised as proof of language ability at an intermediate level by educational institutions in Britain and abroad.

fit

See **model data fit**

fit statistics

Part of the output of Rasch-based analyses of test data. They provide very broadly similar information to the **discrimination indices** of traditional analysis.

Rasch analysis proceeds by estimating the underlying **ability** of **candidates** and the **difficulty** of **items**, and sometimes other relevant **facets** of the **assessment** context, eg judge **severity**, on the basis of the evidence of test data. In other words, it generalises on the basis of an observed data set. The generalisations are then in turn used to make specific predictions about **scores** for particular candidate, item and **rater** combinations. These predicted scores are then compared with the **observed scores** for each combination. Differences between observed and expected values are termed **residuals** and are aggregated for particular candidates, items or **judges**, and evaluated in terms of their statistical significance as indicating departures from the assumptions about the likely extent of normal variability in the data, as in most statistical tests.

Where more variability in the data for a candidate, item or judge is present than expected, the fit statistic will be relatively large. This indicates that the **measurement** model has been incapable of predicting or modelling the behaviour of the candidate, item or judge concerned, and thus no reliable picture of the underlying characteristic involved can be formed. Such a candidate, item or judge is said to be 'misfitting'. The practical consequences of this are that the candidate would need to be measured again, the item revised or the judge retrained.

When less variability than expected is found in the data, the fit statistic will be smaller than expected, and the candidate, item or judge concerned is said to be 'overfitting'. Explanations for this lack of variability, or predictability in the data, depend on the setting. For example, in the case of items, overfit may suggest a lack of independence between items; in the case of raters the use of too limited a part of the **rating scale** may be indicated.

Two fit statistics are commonly used: the *t*-statistic and the **mean** square statistic. Unweighted t or mean square fit values (**outfit**) include all the observations in the data set, and are thus sensitive to atypical outlying values. Weighted t or mean square values (**infit**) exclude such values, and are thus more sensitive to variability in the range of observations that are usually of most interest. For this reason, it may be more appropriate to be guided by infit values in the interpretation of test data.

See also: **model data fit**

fixed choice
See **forced-choice item**

fluency
An **assessment category** commonly used in the assessment of oral **skills**, less commonly in the assessment of writing skills. Fluency may include any or all of the following:
- the speed of utterance;
- a lack of hesitation, repetition, self-correction and other false starts;
- appropriate stress, rhythm and intonation; or
- a general ability to communicate ideas effectively.

Raters are typically required to give an estimate of each **candidate**'s fluency in relation to a **proficiency scale** which may or may not include descriptions of typical performance on this **criterion** at each **level**.

More generally, the term 'fluent' is used to describe a speaker who has a very good overall command of a foreign or second language; it may also be used to describe a good oral performance by a native speaker.

Further reading: Fulcher 1996

focal group
A term used in **DIF** or **bias** studies to describe the group of **test takers** which is the subject of investigation. **DIF** studies usually involve a comparison between the focal group (usually a minority) and the **reference group** (usually the majority).

forced-choice item
Any item which requires the test **candidate** to choose between **response** options which are provided to the candidate (usually on the test paper). **True/false** and **multiple-choice** responses are examples of forced-choice items. Forced-choice items have the advantage of being easy to score because, unlike **constructed-response items**, they do not require discretionary judgements on the part of **raters**.

Foreign Service Institute
See **FSI (scales)**

form

1. The formal features of **text**. In language testing, the focus of **assessment** may be on the formal features displayed in **test-taker** performance. These features generally include grammatical **accuracy** foremost, but also other aspects such as syntax, spelling and punctuation. Formal features may be contrasted with other characteristics concerned with the meaning, message or function of the text.

2. A version of a test.

See also: **alternate forms**, **test form**

formative assessment

A term based on the concept of formative **evaluation** used in evaluating programmes and projects. The formative part of **programme evaluation** attends to the process of a programme in order to provide immediate **feedback** which could lead to improvement. The summative part of programme evaluation, on the other hand, reports on the accountability of the product. Formative assessment procedures do not lend themselves as readily as formative evaluation of programmes to immediate feedback on teaching and run the risk of becoming a series of mini-summative assessments.

Further reading: Scriven 1991; Bachman 1990); Brindley 1995

FSI (scales)

A set of **language proficiency scales** developed in the early 1950s for the US Foreign Service Institute (FSI), the language teaching and accrediting agency of the US Government. The Australian Second Language Proficiency Ratings (**ASLPR**) and the **Interagency Language Roundtable (ILR)** scale for US government employees derive directly from the FSI scales, as do the American Council on the Teaching of Foreign Languages (**ACTFL**) Proficiency Guidelines.

See also: **scales**, **bands**

Further reading: Alderson 1991; Clark & Gifford 1988; Bachman 1990

g

gap-filling

An **item** type in which the **test taker** has to complete a **text** from which one or more words or phrases have been deleted. A list of possible choices is sometimes supplied, from which the candidate is required to select the correct option. This kind of item is used most commonly in tests of reading or listening comprehension, or of grammar. **Cloze** is a particular type of gap-filling item.

See also: **summary cloze, short-answer question**
Further reading: Alderson *et al.* 1995; Weir 1993

gatekeeping test

Also **entrance test, selection test**
A test used for purposes of selection. Typically, **test takers** are permitted to enter institutions or professions on the basis of their **performance** on one or more specified tests, sometimes in combination with other information.

In this sort of situation, **language testers** may be subject to conflicting demands from different **stakeholders** with regard to **test content, test methods** used or **standards**. For example, there may be strong pressure to develop a test which is quick and cheap to administer, but which may have poor **validity** and/or **reliability**.

One issue that always needs to be addressed in gatekeeping tests is what decision to make about those test takers close to the **cut-score**: in the most typical case, the aim is to exclude those who may not be competent, and test takers are not given the benefit of the **measurement error** associated with their test score; in other cases, the aim is to ensure that no test taker is wrongly excluded, and so **error** will generally operate to the advantage of the test taker. Language testers are sometimes responsible for the activity of setting standards and cut-scores; alternatively, information or advice may be provided by the test developers to assist **test users** (such as universities or professional accreditation bodies) in interpreting test **results** and thus setting their own cut-scores. **Criterion-related validity** is an important issue in deciding all these matters.

Because performance on a gatekeeping test generally involves major consequences for test takers, the claims to reliability and validity of the

assessment procedure need to be especially carefully evaluated. Effective procedures should be set up which will allow these to be continually monitored; this may require the continued involvement of the test developers in some aspects of **test administration** (eg selection and training of **raters**, or analysis of results).

See also: **test purpose, ethicality, consequential validity, validation, mastery, criterion**

generalisability theory

Also **G-theory**

An extension of **classical test theory**, differing mainly by its view of **measurement error**. Whereas classical theory considers **error** as a single entity (although derived from a variety of sources), generalisability theory aims to consider various sources of error separately, and estimate the contribution each makes to the overall error, employing **ANOVA** procedures. It is useful in such areas of test development and research as estimating the effect caused by varying the number of **items** or **tasks** in a test, or the number of **raters** involved in scoring each **performance**.

Further reading: Shavelson & Webb 1991

general language proficiency (GLP)

See **g factor, general proficiency test**

general proficiency test

A test where the behaviour under examination is language **proficiency** generalisable to a wide range of unspecified and unspecifiable contexts. There are large numbers of language tests which aim to make some general **assessment** of language **knowledge** or **ability**, although exactly what is included in this general proficiency is not always made very explicit. Such tests may assess ability to use one or more **macro-skills**, or may concentrate on knowledge of language systems; they may be **direct** or **indirect tests**. General proficiency tests may be contrasted with specific-purpose tests (**LSP tests**), where the **domain** of language use is more clearly specified.

See also: **g factor, proficiency test**

g factor

A general factor (of general **ability** or general intelligence), first claimed to have been identified by Spearman in 1904, using **factor analysis**. Spearman claimed that this general intelligence factor was first in any hierarchy of the factors making up intelligence, accounting for much of the **variance** in any of a wide variety of tests. On the basis of this theory, competence in or **aptitude** for language learning was considered to be closely correlated to this general intelligence factor. This notion of a general factor underlay the assumption that **language proficiency** was global and indivisible, as promoted in the late 1970s by Oller as General Language Proficiency (GLP). Oller's position was subsequently shown to be overstated.

See also: **unitary competence hypothesis**
Further reading: Spearman 1904; Oller 1979, 1983; Alderson 1981

global assessment

See **holistic assessment**

global rating/scoring

See **holistic scoring**

GLP

See **g factor; general proficiency test**

grade

1. A word (eg 'excellent') or phrase (eg 'above average') and/or a letter (eg 'B') or number (eg '3') that represents the **score** or **level** attained by a **test taker** during an **assessment** procedure. Grades may be allocated on the basis of **performance** on a single test or may summarise performance on a series of **sub-tests**. Grades are common for both **norm-referenced tests** and **criterion-referenced tests**; explanatory statements describing the level attained are sometimes provided for the latter.

2. To allocate a grade or **score** to a sample of language produced by a test taker.

graded objectives

A system, most commonly used in the UK, of describing increasing levels of attainment (or **achievement**) in language teaching programmes, designed to motivate language learners by breaking down language learning into small blocks, each of which should be achievable after a relatively short time. The objectives include statements describing both short-term goals for language learners and levels of **mastery** of language which learners may reach at the end of each period of study.

See also: **Council of Europe**

Further reading: Clarke 1987

grammar test

A test which aims to measure **knowledge** or control of grammatical structures, as compared with tests of **ability** to use the language, such as **performance tests**. Just as the focal place of grammar in language teaching has changed, in line with current views of the importance of communicative language teaching (and direct language testing), so has the emphasis on the testing of grammar declined in recent decades.

Although grammar tests, lacking a communicative focus, are often dismissed as **indirect tests** of language ability, there is evidence that the knowledge they tap underlies use of other language **skills**. This view receives support from the substantial **correlations** generally shown between tests of grammatical knowledge and most other kinds of language tests, whether direct or indirect. Large-scale tests of language ability still sometimes contain sections or at least individual items designed to test grammatical knowledge. An additional reason for the inclusion of grammar in language tests is that it is relatively easy to construct **objectively scored** items testing grammatical knowledge.

A grammar test may form a distinct section within a test, where a series of **test items** focuses on knowledge of a variety of grammatical forms. The advantage of this kind of **discrete-point** test is that knowledge of a wide range of grammatical forms may be systematically and reliably sampled. Alternatively, **grammatical competence** may be assessed in a **performance test** of writing or speaking. In this case, grammar may be explicitly identified as a category of **assessment** (if **analytic scoring** is used) or assessed implicitly, as a part of the whole **performance** (if **holistic scoring** is used); in this approach the ability to produce correct grammatical structures is generally assessed using a **scale** describing **levels** of grammatical competence.

See also: **pragmatic expectancy grammar**, **direct test**, **communicative language tests**

Further reading: Bachman 1990, Ch. 4; Hughes 1989, Ch. 13; Lado 1961

grammatical competence

A component of communicative language **ability**. Here, grammatical competence is a measure of control of the formal structure of language below the sentence (ie morphology, syntax, vocabulary, phonology and graphology), while textual competence refers to control of structures above the sentence.

Further reading: Bachman 1990

G-theory

See **generalisability theory**

guessing

Includes the apparently random selection of an answer (which may involve absolute randomness or may first involve elimination of those alternatives known to be wrong), or it may include a specific **criterion** for selection which is not related to the **trait** being assessed (such as always selecting the third alternative). Guessing is more of a problem in forced-choice tests than in other **formats** in the following ways:

- it introduces a random factor into test scores which lowers reliability and validity;
- where **candidates** guess correctly, their ability may be overestimated;
- candidates who are loath to guess are disadvantaged in relation to those who guess frequently or readily.

Where it is important to minimise guessing, **forced-choice** items should be avoided. Where this is not possible, in order to avoid advantaging some candidates, all candidates should be told either to guess or not to guess where they do not know the answer, according to the type of test (**norm-referenced** or **criterion-referenced**). Where candidates are advised to guess it is possible to undertake **correction for guessing**

See also: **constructed response**
Further reading: Anstey 1966

Guttman Procedure

A descriptive procedure used for testing the **distribution** of dichotomous **responses** for a series of **variables** to determine if they can be ordered for **difficulty**. A matrix of responses to items of varying degrees of difficulty is used. For example, if we wish to use a 5-item test to examine whether a group of ten students of different **abilities** could correctly use a set of five verbs of increasing difficulty, an idealised set of responses would look like this:

Learner	verb 1	verb 2	verb 3	verb 4	verb 5	score
1	0	0	0	0	0	0
2	1	0	0	0	0	1
3	1	1	0	0	0	2
4	1	1	0	0	0	2
5	1	1	1	0	0	3
6	1	1	1	0	0	3
7	1	1	1	1	0	4
8	1	1	1	1	0	4
9	1	1	1	1	1	5
10	1	1	1	1	1	5
total	9	8	6	4	2	

A general progression in difficulty may be observed from verb 1 to verb 5. In this case it appears that the **items** form a true or implicational scale (one where the items form a **scale** of reliably increasing difficulty and the learners show reliably increasing levels of ability, where a correct answer to one item implies that all easier items are also answered correctly) for this (hypothetical) group of learners. In practice, of course, learners will always produce unexpected answers: the extent to which it is possible to claim that the data from such a scale can be evaluated statistically using the Guttman Procedure.

See also: **implicational scaling**

Further reading: Hatch and Lazaraton 1991

h

halo effect

The distorting influence of early impressions on subsequent judgements of a subject's attributes or **performance**, or the tendency of a **rater** to let an overall judgement of the person influence judgements on more specific attributes. This is a common source of **response bias** in questionnaire data and in **subjectively-scored language tests**. For example, in **speaking tests** where raters are asked to assess a single performance according to a number of different **criteria** (eg **accuracy, fluency, intelligibility, appropriateness**) these ratings are often closely aligned. This may be due not to actual uniformity of language behaviour, but rather to raters' tendency to assign sets of **scores** on the basis of an initial decision about the **candidate**'s level of ability. The longer the test the more likely it is that this tendency will manifest itself.

It is possible to reduce or avoid the halo effect by varying the **format** of questions/**rating scales** so that raters are encouraged to consider each item independently of its predecessor, or by setting up the marking system so that **grades** assigned to candidates on the first **task** are concealed from raters when they come to rate performance on a subsequent task.

See also: **measurement error, method effect**

harshness

See **severity**

Hawthorne effect

The effect on research outcomes which can result from subjects' awareness that they are participants in an experiment. The term originates from a now disputed study conducted at the Western Electric Hawthorne Plant in Chicago in which the productivity of a group of workers appeared to rise independently of a series of positive and negative changes which were made to their working conditions. This increased productivity was therefore attributed not to the changes themselves but rather to the special interest taken in the subjects.

While it is often advocated that experiments be set up with a control and experimental group receiving equivalent treatments except with respect to **variables** which are deliberately being manipulated, in practice this may be difficult to achieve. For example, in **language programme evaluation** studies involving a comparison between two instructional methods, it is highly likely that the experimental group, where innovative methods are applied, will be the focus of greater public attention than is the case for the control group where no change is made to the teaching approach. This increased interest may boost the status of the experimental programme and the **motivation** of the staff and students involved. It is important to bear in mind that language gains amongst members of the experimental group may therefore be a function of the Hawthorne effect, rather than of the particular mode of instruction.

See also: **measurement error, method effect**

heterogeneity

See **homogeneity**

heuristics

Conscious or unconscious strategies or operating principles used to achieve particular goals (eg to aid language learning/acquisition, or to enhance test performance). These strategies may be rules of thumb which are explicitly taught or **hypotheses** applied by the learner to the solving of a problem. In language testing (as in other areas of linguistics) there are increasing numbers of **protocol** research studies which attempt to document the heuristics of test **task** performance (eg the processes involved in the selection of answers on **multiple-choice tests** of listening or reading comprehension).

See also: **hypothesis-testing (2)**

high stakes

See **stakes**

higher order skill

See **skill**

histogram

A graphic method of presenting statistical information about a quantitative or qualitative **variable**. For example if we wish to see at a glance the characteristics of the immigrant population in Australia presenting for a test of English for university entry we might present the information thus:

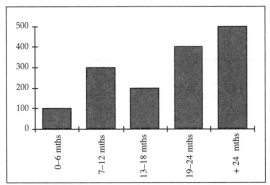

Fig 1. Time spent in Australia

Values of the qualitative variable (time spent) are set out along the (horizontal) x-axis. The frequency data (ie number of **test takers** in each category) are marked on the (vertical) y-axis and recorded by drawing a column above the relevant section of the x-axis. The information can be ordered in terms of time spent (as in the case in this diagram) or in terms of frequency (high to low or vice versa).

Strictly speaking the term histogram should be used only for diagrams in which the columns or bars are arranged in some meaningful order.

See also: **descriptive statistics**

Further reading: Hatch & Lazaraton 1991

holistic assessment

Also **global assessment**

1. A general approach to assessment which involves the awarding of one or more **scores** to a piece of writing or an oral performance on the basis of an overall impression, as distinct from making a count of specified **features** of the discourse. The scoring procedure may involve the use of detailed descriptive statements (**band descriptors**) for each level of **performance** and for each of a number of categories or features (such as grammatical control or coherence) or simple statements such as adequate/not adequate. The term holistic assessment thus includes **analytic** as well as **holistic scoring** methods.

2. A synonym for holistic scoring, where no more than a single score is given to any test performance. This narrower use is perhaps as common as the more general one described in (1).

Further reading: Cooper 1979; Hamp-Lyons 1991b

holistic scoring

Also **global assessment, global scoring, impressionistic assessment**
A type of marking procedure which is common in communicative language testing whereby **raters** judge a stretch of **discourse** (spoken or written) impressionistically according to its overall properties rather than providing separate **scores** for particular **features** of the language produced (eg **accuracy**, lexical range). The term is sometimes used synonymously with **holistic assessment (2)**.

In the **assessment** of writing, a major advantage of holistic scoring over **analytic scoring** is that each piece of writing can be scored quickly, enabling each to be assessed by more than one rater for the same cost as one rater using several analytic criteria, thus leading, it is claimed, to greater **reliability**. A problem with holistic judgements, however, is that different raters may choose to focus on different aspects of the **performance**, leading potentially to poor reliability if only one rater is used. For the sake of reliability, therefore, test performance is normally judged by several raters and their judgements pooled. A further drawback of holistic scoring is that it does not allow detailed diagnostic information to be reported.

Holistic scores should be treated as ordinal data because, when assigning candidates to **levels**, it is difficult to establish that the difference in quality between, say, an A and a B **grade** is of the same order as the difference between a B and a C grade. In other words, the various levels are unlikely to be situated at equal intervals from one another.

See also: **analytic scoring, criterion, ordinal scale, subjective scoring**
Further reading: Charney 1984; Hamp-Lyons 1991, Ch. 14; Williamson & Huot 1993

homogeneity

A property of tests which has to do with the similarity of their component **items** or **sub-tests** to one another in terms of what is being measured. Items on a **vocabulary** recognition test, for example, are more likely to be homogeneous than those on a test of reading which measures different **skills** such as inferencing, skimming and scanning as well as vocabulary knowledge. The narrower the focus of the behaviour **domain** sampled, the greater will be the homogeneity of the test.

Because it helps to characterise the behaviour domain or **trait** sampled by the test, the degree of homogeneity of a test has some relevance to its **construct validity**.

The various methods for estimating the **internal consistency** of a test such as the **Kuder-Richardson formulae**, the **split-half reliability** and the **alpha coefficient** are essentially measures of test homogeneity. Likewise in **IRT item analysis**, the **fit statistics** indicate the extent to which items can be regarded as belonging to a particular **construct** of **ability**.

Violations of homogeneity are usually dealt with at the test development stage by removing those items or parts of the test which do not fit within a single dimension of ability. An alternative approach is to set up reporting procedures which reflect the test's heterogeneity. For example, in a test such as **IELTS**, performance on listening, reading, writing and speaking **sub-tests** are reported separately to indicate instances of uneven **performance** across the four skills which would not be reflected in a single **global score**.

See also: **item characteristics**

hypothesis, hypotheses (pl.)

Also research hypothesis, statistical hypothesis

The process of advancing **knowledge** through the falsification of hypotheses is fundamental to positivist research.

A hypothesis is a speculative proposition about the presence or absence of a relationship or a treatment effect among phenomena. The basis for such speculation may initially derive from observation or experience.

For research purposes the proposition can be formulated in general terms as an experimental-alternate-positive hypothesis, eg,

H_1 *There is a relationship between gender and performance on **multiple-choice tests***.

or more specifically as a directional hypothesis

H_2 *Males perform better on M-C tests than do females.*

or

H_3 *Females perform better on M-C tests than do males.*

For every positive hypothesis positing a relationship between phenomena there is a corresponding null hypothesis which may or may not be stated. The null hypothesis for H_1 would be as follows:

H₀ *There is no relationship between gender and performance on multiple–choice tests.*

For H₂ it might be formulated thus:

H₀ *Males perform at the same level as females on M-C tests.*

Research studies should be designed in such a way as to determine whether the null hypothesis (H₀) can be retained or discarded. A non-significant result is described as a null finding. A significant result is taken as confirmation of the experimental hypothesis.

See also: **hypothesis testing, one-tailed test, significance test**
Further reading: Hatch & Lazaraton 1991

hypothesis testing

1. The branch of statistical inference concerned with deciding between two or more **hypotheses** about characteristics of the **population** of interest to the experimenter.

2. A cognitive process (identified by first and **second language acquisition** researchers) whereby learners test the tentative rules they have formulated about a language against environmental evidence and either reject or retain them according to whether they prove workable.

IELTS

IELTS (International English Language Testing System) is a **battery** of tests designed to assess the language **proficiency** of non-native speakers of English seeking entry to English-medium courses in institutions of higher or further education. Administered in over 100 countries, it competes with **TOEFL** as one of the most widely used measures of **EAP**. It was developed during the 1980s by a British–Australian team to replace its predecessor the **ELTS** test. IELTS is jointly managed by the British Council and IDP Education Australia: IELTS Australia. The British Council and IDP Education Australia are responsible for delivering the test. **Test maintenance** and development is now principally the responsibility of **UCLES** in the UK.

The IELTS test covers the four **skills** of listening, speaking, reading and writing. The listening and speaking sections measure general proficiency, while there are two modules for reading and writing: Academic (for degree courses) and General Training (for training and other sub-degree courses). The reading and writing sections originally contained modules relating to the following academic **domains**: Science and Technology, Arts and Social Sciences, Life and Medical Sciences as well as General (non-academic) Training. Candidates chose the module most closely related to their field of study. However, because of the difficulty of establishing **equivalence** of performance across domains, it was decided to do away with the subject-specific modules from April 1995.

Global proficiency and results on each of the four macroskills are reported on a 9-point **scale**, with native-speaker-like **competence** (Band 9) as the highest **level.** Institutions advocate different entry thresholds according to particular course demands.

IELTS has yielded data for research in a number of areas including native speaker vs non-native speaker **proficiency**, **rater** behaviour, text/topic specificity as a factor in test performance, **predictive validity**.

See also: **language for specific purposes**

Further reading: Clapham 1996; University of Cambridge Local Examinations Syndicate *et al.* 1996

ILR

See **Interagency Language Roundtable**

ILTA

See **International Language Testing Association**

impact

1. The effect of a test on individuals, on educational systems and on society in general. A test may have a significant impact on the career or life chances of individual **test takers**, particularly if it has a gatekeeping function. Other **stakeholders** (eg teachers, employers, course admissions officers) may also be affected by the introduction, administration or results of a test. A test may have a **washback** effect on the kinds of teaching offered as a preparation for it. A test can affect society on a larger scale when used to make decisions about, for example, immigration, **certification** for professional practice or the amount and kind of instruction to be given to school children.

Further reading: Bachman & Palmer 1996; Alderson & Wall 1993

2. *Also* **advantage**

Group difference in test **performance**. The differential impact of a test on particular groups of test takers is revealed by comparing the **mean** scores and **standard deviations** for various subgroups within the **population** (eg boys and girls, native and non-native speakers). Differences in performance may be caused by real differences in **ability** or by **bias** in the **measurement** instrument. For example, a difference in performance on a test of English between immigrant students of Asian and European background might be attributable to factors quite independent of the test, such as language distance or differences in the educational level of one or other group of candidates. If this is the case the test instrument itself should not be viewed pejoratively. The difference between the two groups, on the other hand, may be partly due to **test method effects**, such as the use of a role play rather than an **interview** format on the **speaking test**. The role play format may be unfamiliar to Asian candidates who may therefore be unable to display their true ability. If, as is common, a group difference in mean scores is attributable both to a real difference in ability and to systematic error or bias within the test, this score difference can be described as undifferentiated impact.

See also: **test fairness**, **culture-fair test**, **stakes**

Further reading: Holland & Thayer 1988

implicational scaling

A statistical technique involving the use of an implicational table (see matrix below). The technique assumes that successful **performance** at one **level** implies success at all lower levels.

The essential procedure in the development of such a **scale** is to identify a set of **items/traits** that fall into an ordered sequence in terms of the way people respond to them/manifest them in performance. Any items which do not fit the sequence are discarded.

The following matrix is offered as an example:

Student No.	Easy Item 1	Item 2	Item 3	Difficult Item 4	Item 5
1	0	0	0	0	0
2	1	0	0	0	0
3	1	1	0	0	0
4	1	1	1	0	0
5	1	1	1	1	0
6	1	1	1	1	1

According to this model any subject who gives the correct answer to Item 5 will know the answers to all other items in the set. On the other hand those who supply a wrong response to Item 3 will be unable to do Items 4 and 5.

The technique has been used to demonstrate that in foreign/second language learning there is a universal order in which particular features are acquired. From the presence of a particular morpheme in learners' output we can predict the other, simpler rules that are known.

The construction of **language tests** and **proficiency scales** is based on an analogous principle (which is however probabilistic rather than deterministic). **Scores** or **descriptors** of performance at a particular level can thus be taken to indicate that all previous levels have been mastered.

The building of an implicational scale is always an idealisation based on an assumption of **unidimensionality**. Such an assumption is open to criticism because any linear sequencing of data has the effect of disguising the complex and multifaceted nature of language performance.

See also: **Guttman Procedure**

impressionistic assessment

See **holistic scoring**

independent variable

See **variable**

indirect test

A test that does not require the **test taker** to perform **tasks** that directly reflect the kind of language use that is the target of **assessment**; rather, an **inference** is made from **performance** on more artificial tasks. For example, an indirect test of writing **ability** may include **items** requiring the test taker to identify grammatical or spelling **errors** in written sentences, rather than to produce a piece of writing; an indirect test of speaking might include **multiple-choice items** where the test taker has to select the most appropriate utterance for a particular situation.

Grammar tests and **vocabulary tests**, which test knowledge of a language, are commonly used as indirect tests of ability to use a language.

See also: **direct test, semi-direct test**

inference

The assumption that is made about a **candidate's ability** on the basis of his/her test **performance**.

See also: **inferential statistics**

inferential statistics

Methods used in making general probabilistic statements about the **population** under investigation on the basis of what is known about a **sample** of that population.

For example, it might be necessary to find out about the literacy levels of 10-year-olds in a particular school system. To administer reading tests to all relevant school children would be time-consuming and expensive. A short-cut approach to gathering this information would be to administer tests to a smaller sample of, say, 200 learners. **Descriptive statistics** are applied to calculate the **mean** of the sample. We cannot however be certain that the mean score obtained on the test by the sample group will be the same as that of the wider population of learners. Inferential statistics enable us, using **significance tests**, to estimate the degree of confidence with which we can use information about this particular sample of **test takers** as a basis for assumptions about the literacy level of the whole population of 10-year-olds. When learning differences are observed between group members, inferential statistics help us decide whether they are true differences or due to chance.

Examples of inferential statistics commonly used in language testing are **Chi-square**, *t*-**test** and **analysis of variance.**

See also: **hypothesis testing**

infit

A type of statistic used in **item response theory** analysis to indicate the extent of **score** variability in a given data set which remains after the extreme values (**outliers**) have been removed. An infit **mean** square value close to 0 indicates that the scores for the particular **item**, **rater** or **candidate** fall within the normal range. A standardised value (**z score**) equal to or exceeding +2 or –2 is usually taken to indicate that the behaviour of the candidate, rater or **item** (or other **facet** of the data set) shows an unacceptably high level of deviation from the norm, and hence that it does not fit within the dimension of **measurement** defined by the entire data set. Opinions differ concerning the range of acceptable infit mean square values, but one common view is that any value within the 0.7–1.3 range shows acceptable fit.

See also: **fit statistics, misfit**

information gap

A type of communication activity commonly used in language teaching in which the pieces of information required to complete a **task** or to solve a problem are divided between two or more participants. The process of reconstructing the complete set of information depends on verbal or written **input** from each of the participants. Information gap activities are claimed to be important generators of authentic communication because they involve meaningful negotiation between participants and because the focus is on task completion rather than on the mechanics of language production.

Role plays, in which each participant is given a different set of prompt materials, are a common form of information gap activity. A genuine information gap is difficult to achieve in language tests because the **interviewer** is usually privy to the information provided for the **candidate**. Some oral **proficiency tests** attempt to get around this difficulty by having two or more test candidates interact with one another.

information transfer

An **item** or **task** type used in tests of both **receptive** and **productive skills**. In tests of reading or listening comprehension, the **test taker** is typically required to transfer information from a **text** to graphic form (eg a table, chart, list, form or map). The information may take the form of a single word or number, or a phrase or sentence, and may be either subjectively or objectively marked. In **writing** or **speaking tests**, test takers may be required to produce a text presenting or describing information presented graphically or in some other **format**. The nature of test-taker **responses** for this kind of productive task is less predictable than for listening or reading, leading to a greater degree of subjectivity in the scoring.

See also: **constructed-response item**, **subjective scoring**
Further reading: Alderson *et al.* 1995, Ch. 3; Weir 1990, Ch. 4

input

In language teaching and learning, refers to the language (written or spoken) to which learners are exposed. If input is comprehensible, properly adjusted to a learner's stage of development, or somehow made salient to the learner it can be converted into intake (ie learners can process its meaning and learn from it).

In language testing the term is used differently, to denote the information or **stimulus** material contained in a given test **task**. The input may take the form of a language text ranging from a vocabulary item or single utterance to a piece of extended discourse, or it may be non-linguistic (eg a set of pictures or diagrams). It may be presented in printed form, on tape or via a 'live' **interlocutor**.

Further reading: Bachman 1990, Ch. 5

integrative

See **integrative test**

integrative test

A test in which learners are required to combine various **skills** in answering **test items** as opposed to a **discrete-point** test in which each item focuses on a single element of language. **Cloze** tests, which elicit both linguistic knowledge and the ability to predict meaning from a written **text** are one example of an integrative testing procedure. Further examples are **reading comprehension tests** in which candidates are required to decode meanings at both word and discourse level and **oral interviews** or **extended response** writing tests, which engage various language **abilities** such as grammatical, **discourse** and **strategic competence**. Test **tasks** which combine two macro-skills such as listening to and writing notes on a lecture are also described as integrative.

The term integrative test is sometimes used interchangeably with **pragmatic test** although there are greater constraints on the latter term, which has its theoretical basis in Oller's **'pragmatic expectancy grammar'**.

Because they come closer to reflecting the language processes required to perform real-world communicative tasks, integrative tests are generally regarded as being more **valid** measures of language ability than discrete-point tests in which language elements are decontextualised. For the same reason integrative tests are more commonly used in **proficiency testing** whereas discrete-point tests are more useful for diagnostic purposes. A limitation of integrative testing is that **scores** derived from tasks which combine different aspects of ability may be difficult to interpret.

Further reading: Oller 1979

intelligibility

The ease with which a **sample** of spoken language may be understood. It is influenced by a variety of **factors** including accent, intonation, speed of delivery, the location and duration of pauses, and the listener's ability to predict elements of the speaker's message.

In tests of spoken language, intelligibility may contribute (explicitly or implicitly) to holistic ratings given by **raters**, or may constitute a separate **assessment category** in analytically scored tests. It is sometimes the case that intelligibility ratings either conflict with other measures of language **ability** or are less reliable than other ratings, perhaps because intelligibility is hard to define as a single concept, because different elements dominate randomly in different individuals, or because of variations in the aural perception or tolerance of different listeners.

See also: **analytic scoring**, **holistic scoring**

interaction

1. In **applied linguistics** the term is normally used to refer to oral communication involving two or more speakers. For interaction to take place there has to be some negotiation of meaning between sender and receiver of the message. Interaction can also be used in relation to **receptive skills** to describe the process whereby listeners or readers construct meaning from written or oral texts.

A key requirement of **communicative language tests** is that they allow opportunities for interaction, hence the popularity of **tasks** such as **role play** and **information gap** which require some negotiation between **candidate** and

interlocutor.
See also: **interview**, **oral interview**, **direct test**

2. In statistics the term is used to denote the effect of one factor or **variable** on the magnitude of another.
Further reading: Hatch & Lazaraton 1991

Interagency Language Round Table (ILR)

A name given to a group of US government agencies which use the ILR Oral Interview, a variant of the **oral interview** associated with the original **FSI Scales**, to measure **proficiency** in speaking foreign languages. The **ACTFL Oral Proficiency Interview**, another offshoot of the FSI interview, is widely used in secondary and tertiary institutions in the USA.
Further reading: Bachman 1990; Clark & Gifford 1988

interlocutor

Also **interviewer**

1. Any person who makes an active spoken contribution to a conversation or some other form of oral **interaction**.

2. In language testing the term is used to refer to the interviewer or facilitator of communication in an **oral interview.** The interlocutor may also be the **assessor**. In some tests with **tasks** designed to elicit **interaction** between peers, each **candidate** may take on the role of interlocutor for other candidates.
See also: **interlocutor effect**, **test method effect**

interlocutor effect

The effect of **interlocutor** behaviour in an **oral interview** test. Variability in interlocutor behaviour is a potential source of **measurement error**.

Below are examples of different aspects of interlocutor **input** which may have an effect on either the language behaviour of the **candidate** or on the way in which this behaviour is assessed by **raters**:

- the complexity/formality of the language produced by the interlocutor;
- the number of turns initiated or allocated by him/her;
- the degree of empathy established with the candidate;
- the extent to which the interlocutor adheres to the script/guidelines provided.

Although interlocutor effect can be minimised by standardisation of test instructions and thorough briefing of those involved, factors such as the **proficiency** level or gender of candidates may influence the behaviour of interlocutors (eg their willingness to accommodate to the candidate) and these may be more difficult to monitor.

One criticism of oral tests involving group **interaction** is that there is no possibility of either predicting or controlling for interlocutor effect. For example, a candidate's opportunities to display his/her level of proficiency may be limited by the fact that he/she is paired with a forceful interlocutor who seizes a disproportionate number of turns in the conversation.

See also: **interview**, **test method effect**
Further reading: Lumley & Brown 1996; Ross 1992

interlocutor training

A process designed to ensure that, insofar as it is possible, test conditions pertaining to the conduct of an **oral interview** are the same for each **candidate**. **Interlocutors** are usually issued with detailed information about how to word test instructions, how much time to allow the candidate for preparation and performance of test **tasks**, etc. They may also be made aware of common sources of variability in interlocutor behaviour. The training programme usually involves a briefing session followed by practice in conducting the test.

See also: **interlocutor effect**, **interview**, **test method effect**

internal consistency

The degree to which **scores** on individual **items** or groups of items on a test correlate with one another.

Measures of internal consistency are an efficient alternative to repeated testing of candidates' **performance** on separate occasions. Statistical measures of internal consistency, such as the **split-half reliability** estimate, the **odd–even method** and the **Kuder-Richardson formulae**, obviate the need for repeated testing by treating a single test as a number of smaller tests and comparing scores on the component parts. A high **correlation** can be interpreted as an indication that the same **abilities** are being measured on each part of the test. Low correlations may be due to faulty scoring procedures or to sources of **measurement error** from within the test.

Internal consistency is commonly accepted as a measure of a test's **reliability** but is an insufficient basis for **validity** claims.

Further reading: Henning 1987

internal consistency measures

See **internal consistency**

International English Language Testing System (IELTS)

See **IELTS**

International Language Testing Association (ILTA)

The professional body representing language testers worldwide, set up on 28 February 1992 at the Language Testing Research Colloquium in Vancouver, British Columbia. The association's purpose is to promote the improvement of language testing throughout the world.

See also: **Language Testing Update**, **Language Testing**

International Second Language Proficiency Ratings (ISLPR)

Formerly Australian Second Language Proficiency Ratings (**ASLPR**). A **scale** (with subscales for speaking, listening, reading and writing) with twelve **levels**, ranging from zero to native-like **ability**. Most levels include detailed descriptions of language behaviour characteristic of the level. The first (1979) version of the ASLPR was a general **proficiency** version for English, based on the US **Foreign Service Institute** scale. It was refined through formal and field **trialling,** and versions for other languages (French, Italian, Chinese and Japanese) were developed. A major revision of the general proficiency model led to the publication in 1995 of a new English version, an Indonesian version and a generic version. A version of a specific purpose model, the ALSPR for second language teachers, was also published in 1995. A version for teachers of Indonesian followed. Versions for Academic Purposes, Business/Commerce and Engineering are due in 1998.

The ISLPR is used to specify **proficiency** in government legislation, and in a wide range of educational contexts (eg as a framework for curriculum development, as a means of determining entry requirements for particular courses) and other contexts (eg determining eligibility for professional registration or need for interpreters in legal situations).

The 'orthodox' means of rating an individual is an adaptative testing process. Trained testers select **tasks** according to the proficiency level of the **candidate** and, particularly with general proficiency versions, the person's experiences and interests. Tester registration has been introduced to provide assurance of **reliability** in **high-stakes** situations. Judgements can also be made by means of **self-assessment** or **observation** in naturalistic settings, and benchmarking processes have followed some **standardised tests** to be reported in terms of ISLPR levels.

See also: **ceiling effect**

inter-rater reliability

The level of consensus between two or more independent **raters** in their judgements of **candidates' performance**. This is a major concern in tests of writing and speaking **proficiency** which are **subjectively scored**. In the example below the **scores** are on a **scale** of 1–6 (with 6 representing the highest level of proficiency) and the **pass mark** is 4.

Candidate No.	Rater A Score	Rater B Score	Rater C Score
1	6	6	5
2	3	4	2
3	2	2	1
4	4	4	3
5	5	3	4
6	6	6	6
7	4	3	3
8	1	1	1
Total score	**31**	**29**	**25**

From this example it can be seen that the raters differ from one another in the way they rank the candidates. Agreement is greater at the extremes of the proficiency continuum but there is, as is often the case, considerable variability of scores around the mid-point of the scale. This can have serious consequences for the candidates concerned: in this instance candidate 4 will fail if he/she has the misfortune to be assessed by Rater C, who is harsher than the other two. In the interests of **fairness**, subjectively scored tests should be marked by two or more raters, in any **high-stakes** test. The more raters there are, the smaller will be the **error** associated with candidates' scores.

The extent of alignment among pairs of raters is typically calculated using the **Pearson product–moment correlation** or **Spearman's rho** (depending on the nature of the scale). A coefficient of less than 0.8 generally indicates a need for refinement of the test's scoring system or for further training of raters, in any test involving high stakes for the test taker.

Where more than two raters are involved, an average **correlation coefficient** is calculated. There are at least three ways of doing this:

- A Fisher z transformation is applied to convert the correlation coefficients derived from each pair of raters (raters A and B, raters A and C, raters B and C and so on) to an interval score so that all **correlations** can be summed and then averaged. The reliability **estimate** obtained is then adjusted to take into account the numbers of raters involved in the assessment using the Spearman Brown Prophecy formula;
- Each rater's scores are summed and the reliability is calculated using an alpha coefficient which takes into account the **variance** of scores for different raters;
- Raters' scores are compared by applying an intraclass correlation statistic, which like the **alpha coefficient**, takes account of the variance within and between raters in terms of **harshness**.

The latter two methods are more appropriate for research involving large numbers of raters and for high-stakes tests where important decisions hinge on the actual score that is assigned to each candidate.

Recent advances in multi-faceted **Rasch analysis** build in some adjustments for rater harshness in calculating **ability estimates**. Other **probabilistic models**, such as **generalisability theory**, make it possible to calculate the relative effects on test reliability of increasing or reducing the number of raters.

See also: **intra-rater reliability**

Further reading: Anastasi 1990; Hatch & Lazaraton 1991; Henning 1987

interval scale

A **scale** where the points or units of **measurement** are spaced at equal intervals, as in scales describing physical properties such as height or temperature. It is essential to differentiate the psychological **construct** (language **skills** or **ability**) we are interested in from the scale we use to measure it. Regardless of the nature of the psychological construct of language ability, and the rate at which it develops, it is sometimes possible to construct a scale consisting of equal intervals which provides a mathematical representation of differences between **performances** or **difficulty** of **items**. For example, **item response theory** uses probability to construct an interval scale, which measures both the difficulty of test items and the ability of **test takers** on the same scale.

Raw scores, on the other hand, whether derived from individual items on a test or from a **rating scale**, are unlikely to form an interval scale, because it is improbable that the difference in ability required on a test of 50 items to move from a score of 40 to 45 is the same as that required to move from 35 to 40.

In the case of a 5-point proficiency rating scale, the mathematical difference in proficiency between two people, one obtaining a score of 2 and the other a score of 3 is unlikely to be the same as that between two people obtaining scores of 3 and 4. An additional complication with scores derived from rating scales is the variations in the interpretations of **level** descriptions by different **raters**.

See also: **logit, ordinal scale**
Further reading: Hatch & Lazaraton 1991

interview

1. A formal oral exchange between two or more **interlocutors**. The purpose of the exchange is for the **interviewer(s)** to find out something about the attributes, experience or **ability** of the interviewee(s).

2. In language testing the term is often used to refer to the oral test encounter, regardless of whether the test consists of a series of 'interview-like' tasks, in which the interviewer elicits information from the **candidate**, or whether it is set up to measure other aspects of communication, such as the ability to initiate a conversation, to give instructions or to tell a story.

Whatever form it takes, the test interview arguably constitutes a particular kind of **register** which, because of its fundamental evaluative purpose, has its own particular norms/social constraints. This view of the test interview calls into question the possibility of eliciting **'authentic'** or 'natural' **discourse** in the context of an **Oral Proficiency Interview**.

See also: **oral interview**
Further reading: Griffin *et al.* 1986; Van Lier 1989; Berwick & Ross 1996

interviewer

See **interlocutor**

intonation test

A test which assesses the ability to distinguish (in a listening test) or produce (in a **speaking test**) differences in intonation patterns. **Discrete-point items** are generally used in these tests, and focus on clearly defined aspects of spoken language such as **discrimination** between the same and different patterns, recognition of particular patterns, and ability to mimic or retain intonation patterns.

Further reading: Valette 1967

intra-rater reliability

The extent to which a particular **rater** is consistent in using a **proficiency scale**. This is an issue with **subjectively scored** tests involving open-ended or **extended responses**.

In **classical test theory** the calculation of intra-rater reliability requires a comparison to be made between two independent **assessments** of the same test **performance** by a single rater. The order in which the papers/performances are assessed should be changed on each occasion and the rater should not have access to the original set of **scores**. The level of consistency between the two sets of scores can be computed using the statistics described under **inter-rater reliability**.

In the example below a rater has been asked to make two separate assessments (a month apart) of a set of oral proficiency tapes. There are only two **candidates** who receive the same score on each occasion which is an indication that this rater is not to be relied upon.

Candidate	1st Marking	2nd Marking
1	6	6
2	5	6
3	3	3
4	4	3
5	3	5
6	4	2

In **multi-faceted Rasch analysis**, intra-rater consistency can be calculated from a single set of ratings provided that the **sample** is large enough and that there are multiple ratings of each candidate. The model builds up a picture of a particular rater's marking patterns in relation to the assessment **scale** by comparing the scores that he/she assigns to particular candidates with those of other raters. Thus for any given candidate whose **ability** level is known (on the basis of other raters' scores) the programme can estimate the probable score or set of scores which that rater will assign. **Fit statistics** indicate the extent to which the rater's behaviour can be predicted by the model. Major inconsistencies between observed and expected ratings are classified as misfitting responses.

The consistency of a particular rater can be affected by such factors as:

- the nature of the scale (inadequately defined scales may cause rater uncertainty which leads to random assignment of scores);
- the order in which candidates/test papers are assessed (raters may be normative in their behaviour and each new performance may therefore

be assessed in relation to the previous one rather than according to the standards defined by the scale);

- the 'stability' of the rater (raters' interpretation of the scale may change either because they are tired or distracted after successive marking of a number of test performances or because considerable time has elapsed since their training session or since the previous test **administration**).

Intra-rater reliability is of particular concern in the case of tests which are frequently administered. It cannot be assumed that the effect of rater training will last from one administration to another. Erratic behaviour from an individual rater will in turn lead to low **inter-rater reliability**. The reduction of individual inconsistencies (by means of individualised **feedback** to raters) is important since it minimises the **measurement error** associated with test scores.

Further reading: Bachman 1990; Henning 1987; McNamara 1996

IRT

See **item response theory**

ISLPR

See **International Second Language Proficiency Ratings**

item

1. A component of language (eg grammar item, vocabulary item).

2. That part of a test from which scores are derived.
   See also: **test item**

item analysis

An aspect of **test analysis** which involves examination of the characteristics of **test items.**

The term is used more specifically in the context of classical measurement to refer to the application of statistical techniques to determine the properties of test items, principally **item difficulty** and **item discrimination**. (Item analysis is also undertaken in the context of **IRT** measurement, but different techniques are applied.)

In **norm-referenced testing**, items are typically evaluated in terms of their

homogeneity. Since a test is expected to discriminate between various degrees of a single attribute, the more similar items are to one another (without being identical) in terms of what they are measuring the more likely they are to make useful and consistent distinctions among **candidates** (provided of course that these items are sufficiently difficult to ensure that not all candidates get them right).

In **criterion-referenced testing** items should be evaluated in terms of their capacity to divide individuals into discontinuous groups, representing **mastery** or non-mastery of a specified objective or behaviour **domain**. While there are techniques available for this purpose, they are not widely used by language testers.

The results of item analysis are used to shorten or modify a test. The revision or removal of items identified as less than satisfactory will increase the test's **reliability** and **validity**.

See also: **item characteristics**

item bank

A relatively large and accessible collection of test items with known properties.

Item banks are commonly used:
- for the construction of equivalent or **alternate forms** of frequently administered **standardised tests** (different combinations of homogeneous items are drawn from the bank); and
- as the basis for **computer adaptive tests** (items at a suitable level of difficulty for individual **candidates** are retrieved from the computer bank as required).

The requirements for an item bank are:
- an adequate pool of test items;
- an inventory of the **abilities** and content which each item purports to measure;
- statistical data indicating the characteristics of each item as evidenced in test **trialling** (eg **item difficulty** and **item discrimination** indices);
- a theory or **construct** of ability which enables the meaning of **scores** on any test which may be constructed from the banked items to be interpreted.

Latent trait models are particularly useful in item banking because they have the advantage of allowing item **scores** to be translated into estimates of ability on a common **scale**. Thus, all tests deriving from a **logit** scale item bank are automatically equated since a person's score on any combination of test items can be converted into an **ability estimate** on the common bank scale. This means that any group of people can be given a test made up of items particularly suitable for them, yet all the results can be compared to one another.

See also: **item characteristics, item response theory**
Further reading: Pollitt 1984; Henning 1987

item bias

See **differential item functioning**

item calibration

A term used in **item response theory.** Item calibration is the process of estimating the position of the **test item** on the line of the **variable** along which persons are being measured. If the variable is language **ability**, statistical techniques will be applied to allocate each of the items to an abstract continuum one direction of which represents low (or less) language ability and the other high (or more) language ability. Items at one end will be more difficult than those at the other end.

item characteristic curve

In the case of a **dichotomously scored test item**, a curve showing the relationship between the probability of a correct response and a person's **ability**. The figure below shows an item characteristic curve (ICC) for one dichotomous item.

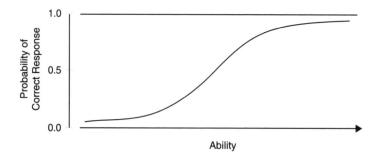

The probability of a correct response on the item, represented on the *y*-axis, is a function of the ability of the individual taking the item, represented on the *x*-axis. The discrimination of the item is represented by the slope of the curve. This means that the steeper the slope of the ICC for an item, the higher the **discrimination** of that item.

See also: **dichotomous scoring**
Further reading: Wright & Stone 1979

item characteristic function

See **item characteristic curve**

item characteristics

Stable characteristics of items, including **item difficulty** or **facility**, and **item discrimination**. These characteristics are directly or indirectly the focus of both **classical test theory** and **item response theory** analyses.

item dependence

See **item independence**

item difficulty

Also **item facility**
The degree of difficulty (or facility) of a **test item** which is calculated on the basis of a group's test performance.

Item difficulty is an important aspect of both **classical test theory** and **IRT**. The IRT method of computing item difficulty is discussed under **one-parameter model**. In classical test theory item difficulty can be determined by calculating the percentage of the trial group who answered the item correctly. Thus, if in a sample of 50 **candidates**, 43 responded correctly then the item has a difficulty/facility index of 86%. The higher the index the easier the item. The closer the index is to 100% or 0% the less differential information it can provide about candidates. (If all candidates get an item right, or alternatively, if no candidates answer the item correctly, we have gained no useful information about candidate **ability**.) Items that are excessively easy or difficult are usually removed because they do not contribute to the test's **discriminability**.

Standardised tests generally aim for a set of items with a moderate spread of difficulty values within the range of 30%–70% (averaging out at approximately 50%). This allows for maximum differentiation amongst individuals. For **multiple-choice tests** however, the average item difficulty index is set higher than is the case for tests composed of **constructed-response items** to compensate for the probability that candidates will guess some of the answers.

Item difficulty requirements vary according to **test purpose**. In a **selection test**, for example, there may be no need for fine-graded **assessment** within the 'pass' or 'fail' groups so that the most efficient test design will have a majority of items clustering near the critical **cut-score**. In a pre-course **diagnostic** or **placement test** for newly-arrived immigrants, difficult items may be tolerated because they tell us what needs to be taught and where to direct students. If the same test were to be administered on completion of the course we would expect the items to be significantly easier. In **achievement tests** when a high pass rate is expected it is common to find items in the 80%–90% range; such items would normally be discarded from a **standardised norm-referenced test**.

Information about item difficulty is also useful in determining the order of items on a test. Tests tend to begin with easy items in order to boost confidence and to ensure that weaker candidates do not waste valuable time on items which are too difficult for them. In **adaptive testing** information about the difficulty level of items determines the sequence which is followed by particular candidates. If a candidate gives the wrong answer to an item or items at a particular difficulty level he/she will be directed to easier items. A series of correct answers will lead to the presentation of the next most difficult item until there is no further score gain on the **trait** under test and a sufficiently accurate ability **estimate** has been obtained.

See also: **item discrimination**
Further reading: Henning 1987

item discrimination

Also **discriminability**

The capacity of **test items** to differentiate among **candidates** possessing more or less of the **trait** that the test is designed to measure. **Discrimination** is an essential feature of a test's **measurement** function. A test with consistently high levels of item discriminability is considered to be **reliable** (on the grounds that if these items have the capacity to spread individuals of differing ability along a single **scale** they must be repeatedly measuring the same underlying **ability**). For **norm-referenced** measurement decisions items should be designed in such as way as to produce a relatively large spread of **scores** and a fairly even **distribution** across the **ability** range. For **criterion-referenced** measurement purposes, discrimination is best thought of as the test's capacity to distinguish between masters and non-masters (or instructed and uninstructed students) on the **criterion** behaviour.

In **classical analysis** there are several statistical techniques (eg **phi correlation**, **biserial correlation**, **point-biserial correlation**, sample separation) which can be used to calculate item discrimination.

The **distractors** of **multiple-choice items** should have low or negative discrimination values because only the right answer is supposed to discriminate among candidates.

There are a number of possible explanations for poor item discriminability:

- the item may be too easy or too difficult for the sample **population**;
- the item may be measuring a different kind of ability (eg **background knowledge** instead of reading skills) and therefore does not rank candidates in the same way as other items on the test;
- there may be features of item design which interfere with test performance or which boost it for the wrong reasons (eg confusing instructions or implausible **distractors** which make it easy to guess the right answer);
- the sample that is chosen for test trials may not be truly representative of the range of abilities which characterise the target population.

Items showing negative discrimination or low discriminability are typically revised or discarded from a test because they do not provide useful information about candidates. The practice of rejecting such items will have the effect of homogenising the test. It should be noted that this method of selecting items will only increase **validity** if the **criterion** behaviour is itself unitary. A test designed for the certification of language teachers, for example, will require mastery of a broad **proficiency domain** covering both metalinguistic knowledge and ability for use. Excessive homogenising of such a test may reduce its criterion coverage and hence its **content** and **construct validity**.

See also: **item characteristics**, **item analysis**
Further reading: Henning 1987; McNamara 1996

item equating

See **equate**

item facility

See **item difficulty**

item independence

Independence of the content of one item from others in the same test, so that each item can be answered whether or not any earlier items have been attempted. It is important for items to remain independent, in order that each contributes as much information about **test-taker ability** as possible.

Item dependence or lack of independence means that a test taker only gets item $x+1$ correct if item x has been answered correctly, as answering item $x+1$ depends in some way on having understood the answer to item x. This means that item $x+1$ contributes no independent information on candidate ability, and is thus redundant and inefficient as an item.

An example of a test where items are not independent is a **cloze test**.

See also: **local independence**, **overfit**

item ordering

See **ordering**

item pool

A set of **test items** which act as exemplars for teachers or examiners in different institutions in developing their own tests. The items in the pool may not have been pre-tested on **candidates**.

item response theory (IRT)

Also **latent trait theory**, **latent trait models**

A general **measurement** theory developed independently by Birnbaum in the United States and by Rasch in Denmark; the ideas of the latter were popularised by Wright. Two main branches of IRT, differing theoretically and practically, stem from these two developmental traditions. The essential feature of both is that they attempt to generalise from test data to form estimates of:

- **candidate ability** which have taken into account the particular test **tasks** set; and
- **item characteristics** which take into account the characteristics of the particular **test takers** involved in the generation of the data.

By contrast, traditional reports of candidate ability (**raw scores**) and item characteristics (**item facility**, **item discrimination**) are potentially unstable, more susceptible to change if different **test items** and test subjects with differing **levels** of achievement are involved. The achievement of more stable estimates allows important applications such as **test equating**, test linking and computer adaptive testing, among others. The branches of IRT differ mainly in the number of item **parameters** (characteristics of the interaction between a test taker and a test item) being estimated in the analysis: **Rasch analysis** considers one item parameter (**item difficulty**), while other models consider one or more additional parameters (item discrimination, and a guessing factor). There is ongoing dispute over the relative merits of the two traditions, especially in relation to the analysis of dichotomous data, for example over the need to incorporate the discrimination and guessing parameters, and over the property of **specific objectivity** in the Rasch model, that is, the invariance of item parameters for subjects of differing ability levels. Where test scores are the result of a subjective judging process involving **partial credit** and **rating scale** data, as is typically the case in **performance testing**, the issue does not arise so sharply as only the **one-parameter model** can deal operationally with judge-mediated data at this time.

Further reading: McNamara 1996; Henning 1987

item writing

The stage of test development in which **test items** are produced, according to a set of **test specifications**. When a new test is being developed, item writing normally takes place once initial decisions have been made (such as **test purpose**, **target test population**), and after some consideration has been given to the design and content of the test (for example, after a **needs analysis** has been conducted and/or a theoretical framework for the test has been put forward). For most tests more items or **tasks** will be written than will ultimately be used in the test, to allow for rejection of those which prove during **trialling** and **test analysis** to be unsatisfactory. Items may be written by professional item writers, by language teachers, or (for some **LSP tests**) by occupational experts; or by a team of people combining different kinds of relevant experience.

See also: **content validity, construct validity**

Further reading: Alderson *et al.* 1995, Ch. 3; Bachman & Palmer 1996; Weir 1993

j, k

judge

See **rate, rater**

Kendall's coefficient of concordance

Also Kendall's W

A non-parametric statistical procedure used to examine the relationship between more than two **variables**. It is suitable for use with **ordinal data** only.

Kendall's W is often used for the calculation of levels of agreement in situations where more than two **raters** are ranking the same group of subjects or attributes.

Further reading: Hatch & Lazaraton 1991

Kendall's tau

A non-parametric statistical procedure used to calculate the degree of relationship between two **variables**, for example a) students' language **aptitude** measured before undertaking foreign language study and b) their subsequent level of attainment on a foreign language **achievement test**.

Kendall's tau is used in preference to **Spearman's rho** when there are a number of tied ranks in the data.

See also: **correlation**

Further reading: Hatch & Lazaraton 1991

key

1. In linguistics this term is used to refer to the tone, manner or spirit in which utterances are delivered by a speaker. The key may be signalled verbally (eg through pitch and intonation) or non-verbally (by means of gesture).

2. In language testing the term refers either to:
- a **marking scheme** containing information about acceptable and unacceptable answers to short-answer **test items**. The key is usually

developed on the basis of preliminary marking of a number of trial scripts and is then issued to assessors to ensure consistent rating behaviour in subsequent **test administrations**; or to

- the correct answer amongst the range of options offered in a **forced-** or **multiple-choice** item. In a well designed item, the key should have higher **discriminability** than the accompanying **distractors**.

Key English Test (KET)

KET was introduced by **UCLES** in 1994. It is based on the **Council of Europe's** *Waystage 1990* specification. KET provides an initial learning objective and enables learners to meet their basic communication needs in English. KET is part of a coherent suite of UCLES examinations in English as a Foreign Language, which, in addition to the KET, include the **Preliminary English Test**, the **First Certificate in English**, the **Certificate in Advanced English**, the **Certificate of Proficiency in English**, the Cambridge Examination in English for Language Teachers and several examinations in English for business.

The present components of the KET are a Reading/Writing and a Listening paper, as well as a Speaking test. In determining the **score**, the Reading/Writing paper carries 50% of the total marks and the Listening and Speaking each carrying 25% of the total marks.

knowledge

In the field of language testing the term knowledge is generally used synonymously with **linguistic competence** to denote command of the formal linguistic system (ie grammar and phonology) as distinct from the application of this knowledge in language **performance**.

Discrete-point tests of grammar or vocabulary are designed to tap this underlying knowledge of the language system, rather than being concerned with **communicative competence** or an individual's **ability** to harness his/her knowledge of language for communicative purposes (which is the focus of **performance testing** or **communicative language testing**).

The justification for tests of language knowledge is that from them we can draw inferences about potential performance in a range of different situations. The argument against this kind of testing is that knowledge of the language system is not always translatable into actual communicative performance.

The term knowledge is also used to refer to knowledge about language, also called language awareness and metalinguistic knowledge. Research into language aptitude has sometimes made use of metalinguistic tests.

See also: **background knowledge**

K-R 20/21
See **Kuder-Richardson formulae**

Kuder-Richardson formulae

Statistical formulae used to estimate the **internal consistency** of a test. These formulae provide a short cut alternative to retesting. Like the **split-half reliability** method these formulae are based on total score **variance** but are more sophisticated in that they give the average **correlation** between all possible divisions of a test's **items**. They serve to determine whether **candidates**' performance on any half of a given test is equivalent to performance on any other half and thus give an indication of item consistency.

There are two formulae, **K-R20**, which is based on the ratio of the sum of item variances to the total test **score** variance, and **K-R21**, which is easier to compute but slightly less accurate.

The K coefficient has a value between 0 and 1. The higher the value the greater is the test's **reliability**.

The K-R formulae should only be used when the number of **test items** is fairly large and when these items are **dichotomously scored**. For **partial credit** or scaled **responses** a more general method known as **Cronbach's alpha** is commonly used.

See also: **test consistency**
Further reading: Henning 1987

kurtosis

A property of **distribution** curves which has to do with the degree of peaking; if the distribution of the data forms a very flat curve, the curve is said to be **platokurtic**; if it forms a very sharp peak it is **leptokurtic** (see diagram on next page).

Neither of the shown distributions corresponds to the normal curve. This indicates that there is something unusual about the nature of this particular **population** or the instrument used to describe it.

A 'flat' platokurtic distribution of scores is an indication that there is both large spread of scores and an even distribution across the **ability** range. This kind of distribution is most likely to occur with a language test which is finely honed to make **norm-referenced measurement** decisions. A leptokurtic distribution is more likely to occur in a **criterion-referenced test** in which students are all of similar **ability** with the **mastery** decision point being located near the **mean** of the distribution.

In naturally occurring data kurtosis characteristics tend to be combined with skewness. Whereas information about skewness of a distribution curve can be obtained from the various measures of **central tendency**, information about its shape or degree of peaking is derived by calculating the range, **variance** and **standard deviation** of **test scores.**

See also: **normal distribution, skewed distribution**

Further reading: Butler 1985; Hatch & Lazaraton 1991

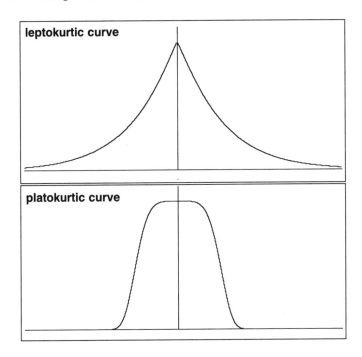

1

language ability

See **ability**

Language Aptitude Battery (LAB)

A language aptitude test battery designed by Paul Pimsleur and colleagues and published in 1966 to provide a diagnosis of underachievement problems in foreign language learning in the US junior high school. The battery consists of four **sub-tests** (vocabulary of the first language; language analysis of Kabardian; sound discrimination of the tone language, Ewe; sound-symbol association) plus measures of grade-point average and interest in language learning. Pimsleur's early death terminated his project before it became widely known.

See also: **aptitude, Modern Language Aptitude Test**

language(s) for specific purposes (LSP)

Also language(s) for special purposes

An approach to language teaching/testing which has arisen from the notion that the lexical, syntactical, discoursal and pragmatic features of language use vary according to context. Context is usually defined either in terms of **domain** (eg science vs politics), occupational use (eg the practice of medicine vs teaching) or in terms of genre (eg report writing vs narrative). The recognition of these variations in language use has led to the development of second/foreign language courses and tests (eg of English for Academic Purposes; of Japanese for Tourism) which are tailored to the needs of particular groups.

A major attraction of LSP is that, unlike general **proficiency**, it offers the prospect of exact specification of the language features which make up a particular domain and, by delimiting the range of target behaviours, it goes some way towards solving the problem of **sampling**, which is of importance to language testing.

Critics of **LSP testing** raise two major problems with this approach. The first is practical: once the need to be specific is acknowledged, it is difficult to know where to stop. English for Health Professionals, for example, can be further subdivided into English for Pharmacists, for Doctors, for Neurosurgeons and so on. The path to specificity ends logically with the individual whereas tests are necessarily concerned with groups. The second is theoretical: attempts to make principled distinctions between major dimensions of language use in particular contexts have proved problematic. The boundary between academic and non-academic journal articles, for example, is not easy to draw. LSP tests are thus easier to justify in terms of **face validity** rather than **content validity**.

See also: **background knowledge**, **performance testing**, **needs analysis**, **register**

Further reading: Swales 1985, 1990

language impairment

Weakness in language development by comparison with 'normal' development. In making assessments of development, speech and language therapists consider both receptive language and expressive language, including pre-linguistic development, age- or skills-related models and the concept of critical period in language development.

Sub-categories of language impairment that are commonly assessed or identified include:

- articulation and phonology (anatomical and physiological, phonetic, phonological and developmental dimensions);
- voice disorders (loudness, pitch, voice projection, prosody);
- stammering;
- acquired language problems (also usually 'aphasia': difficulty in speech output, auditory comprehension, reading comprehension and writing, resulting from acquired brain damage);
- special needs of children (arising from physical or sensory disabilities, learning difficulties, or emotional or behavioural problems);
- communication problems of elderly people;
- language disorders arising from mental illness.

A wide range of tests and other assessment procedures are used in speech therapy to identify these problems.

Further reading: Beech *et al.* 1993

language norms

See **norms**

language proficiency
See **proficiency**

language proficiency test
See **proficiency test**

language program(me) evaluation
The assigning of value to an abstract entity such as a language program (or curriculum), often by means of comparison to other programs or curricula. Although **evaluation** and **assessment** are often used synonymously, it is useful to keep them separate, reserving assessment for application to people. While assessment is an activity most language teachers engage in, language program evaluation is more likely to be an activity for applied linguists working in research and development.

Further reading: Lynch 1996; Walberg & Haertel 1990

language testers
Those involved in the activity of language **assessment**. Their work is concerned with the development of language assessment procedures or with research. Research in language testing tends to focus on the **validity**, **reliability** and use of existing tests, improving techniques of testing and **test analysis** through understanding of the assessment process and its consequences.

Language Testing
The principal academic journal in the field of language testing, published twice annually from 1984–92 and three times a year since then, by Arnold. Since 1993 *Language Testing* has been the official journal of the **International Language Testing Association**.

Language Testing Update (LTU)
The official newsletter of the **International Language Testing Association**, produced at the Centre for Research in Language Education, Lancaster University, UK.

language tests

Instruments used to measure language **ability** or **aptitude.** A defining feature of language tests is that they consist of specified **tasks** through which language abilities are elicited. They are thus distinguished from **scales**, which represent (only) the means of describing or reporting the results of the test.

See **measurement, test purpose, test type**

latent trait models, latent trait theory

See **item response theory**

LD

See **lexical density**

leniency

A facet of rater behaviour: the attitude shown by a **rater** towards a **performance** by a **test taker**.

See also: **severity**

leptokurtic distribution

See **kurtosis**

level

Also **band**

1. A measure (eg 1 to 9, or A to E) or description of the **proficiency** or **ability** of a **test taker**, normally as described on some kind of **scale** and determined on the basis of test **performance**.

2. An indication or description of the **difficulty** of a test or **examination** (eg Beginner, Intermediate, Advanced), or of the **tasks** or **texts** it contains.

3. A conflation of level of ability and test or task: an idealised view of the proficiency or ability of a language learner, where success on a task or test is equated with ability to use a language at the level of difficulty that task or test is considered to represent. This view rests on a circular argument requiring subjective judgements by the test developers or administrators. This view is circular because it is impossible to describe the performance without assuming that the task is at the same level. At the same time it is equally impossible to describe the difficulty level of the task without first establishing the ability level of test takers who can perform it successfully. In either case, it would be necessary to establish the difficulty level of tasks, and to confirm the ability level of a **sample** of test takers, by other, empirical means.

See also: **grade**, **ceiling effect**, **proficiency scale**

Further reading: Pollitt 1991; Alderson 1991; Bachman 1988

lexical density

Also **LD**

The relationship between the total number of words in a given **text** and lexical words (ie those which have semantic content as distinct from grammatical words such as *of, to, and, the*, whose sole function is to signal grammatical relationships). The ratio of lexical words to total words is usually expressed as a percentage. Thus, the lexical density of the previous sentence in this entry is 8 (lexical words) : 14 (total words) or 55%.

Lexical density has been used as an indicator of text type. In English, for example, written monologue tends to have a higher LD than does written or spoken dialogue. Estimates of lexical density can therefore be a useful measure of the registral **appropriateness** of learners' writing. These estimates can also serve as a basis for selecting passages for reading comprehension, random **cloze tests** and for ordering **test items** according to **difficulty**: the higher the lexical density of a text the greater its demands on **candidates'** reading or listening ability.

See also: **register**, **readability**

Further reading: Ure 1971; O'Loughlin 1995

Likert Scale

Named after its inventor, this is a particular kind of **ordinal scale** typically used in questionnaires to gauge the comparative magnitude of respondents' attitudes or attributes. Respondents are asked to indicate the strength of their agreement with a series of assertions such as:

> *The test was a fair measure of reading ability.*
>
> *There was enough time allowed.*
>
> *The instructions were confusing.*
>
> *The text was difficult.*

The statements which are selected for the questionnaire should be based on points raised repeatedly by a **trial sample** of respondents who have been asked to express their views on the issue under study.

The **response** to each statement is usually, but not necessarily, expressed in terms of the following five categories: strongly agree (SA); agree (A); undecided (U); disagree (D); and strongly disagree (SD) with a **score** of 5, 4, 3, 2, or 1 (from the favourable to the unfavourable end) assigned to each response. For example a 'strongly agree' response to the first two statements above would receive a score of 5 as would a 'strongly disagree' response to the last two statements. Favourable and unfavourable statements are often interspersed to avoid the risk of a **halo effect.**

The number of points on the **scale** may vary (there are usually between five and nine of them) according to the amount of **discrimination** required of respondents. Scores for each questionnaire item are summed to produce a total score for each respondent which is interpreted according to empirically established **norms**.

This method of data collection has become popular because it circumvents the elaborate construction procedures of the **Thurstone Scale** and the stringent conditions associated with the Guttman scale. It is commonly used in **language programme evaluation** studies.

linearity

An abstract concept implied in all **measurement**. When people are described according to an **attribute** such as height any measurement of this attribute will require that it be restated in a linear or scalar fashion (eg as inches on a ruler) so that various people can be allocated to this **scale** according to whether they possess greater or lesser degrees of the attribute. The prime function of language tests is to allocate **candidates** to various points on a linear scale on the basis of the amounts of language **ability**, or some component of language ability, that they demonstrate in test **performance**.

linear regression

See **regression**

linear structural equation modelling

See **structural equation modelling**

linguistic competence

Also language competence

Normally refers to **knowledge** of the formal linguistic system (ie sentence level grammar) as opposed to the application of this knowledge in language **performance** or language in actual use. In language testing an increased concern with the context of language use rather than with its cognitive basis has led to a broadening of the definition of linguistic competence. In recent models of **communicative competence** linguistic competence encompasses not only grammatical **knowledge** but also discourse and **pragmatic competence**. It nevertheless remains distinct from **strategic competence**, which has to do with language processing or the harnessing of various aspects of language knowledge to accomplish particular communicative goals.

Further reading: Hymes 1972; Canale & Swain 1980; Bachman 1990

LISREL
A statistical software package allowing modelling of structural relationships between **variables**.
See also: **structural equation modelling, path analysis**

Listening Comprehension Test (LCT)
A 45-item, tape-recorded multiple-choice aural grammar test. A retired component of the old Michigan Battery, the LCT was developed by the English Language Institute at the University of Michigan. Multiple forms are commercially available to *bona fide* educational institutions. Some institutions that purchase the LCT administer it in conjunction with the **Michigan Test of English Language Proficiency (MTELP)** and an in-house written essay for an overall proficiency **assessment**. Further information available at www.lsa.umich.edu/eli/.
See also: **English Placement Test, MELAB**

listening comprehension test
A test of **ability** to understand spoken language. Listening is a process that we are unable to observe directly, and the **construct** of listening comprehension is therefore highly elusive. In addition, contextual **variables** (eg number and background of speakers; speed and clarity of speech; purpose, topic and complexity of discourse; reason for listening) affect the ability of individuals to comprehend spoken language. It is thus very difficult to make statements about the listening ability of **test takers** on the basis of their test **performance**; in other words, it is hard both to describe different **levels** of listening comprehension ability and to link test **scores** to levels of ability with confidence. A variety of **item** types or **tasks** are used in tests of listening

comprehension, including **multiple-choice items**, **short-answer questions**, **dictation**, **information transfer** items, **summary cloze** and written **summaries**.

Listening ability was formerly considered to depend principally on aural abilities including phoneme discrimination, recognition of stress and intonation patterns, and retention of what has been heard. Listening tests thus typically included **discrete-point** items designed to test these abilities, based on short spoken **texts**. Since the 1970s there has been a shift towards the use of longer passages of contextualised discourse such as mini-lectures or extended stretches of dialogue, taking account of greater interest in sociolinguistics, integration of language skills and concentration on the message conveyed in the discourse.

Listening comprehension is also sometimes assessed during tests of spoken interaction. This is done indirectly, by assessors making inferences about what the test taker has understood on the basis of what he/she says.

Attempts are now being made to expand the notion of listening comprehension to include other modes of communication, including interactive modes and visual elements.

See also: **sound discrimination test**, **receptive test**, **test administration**
Further reading: Weir 1990; Buck 1994

live test

1. An operational version of a test; one that is currently in use or that may be used in future administrations. Operational tests have normally undergone **trialling** and **revision** procedures to establish their **reliability** and **validity**, although sometimes these are investigated **a posteriori**.

See also: **operationalise**, **test security**, **retired test**

2. Sometimes used to refer to a **direct test** of speaking, involving face-to-face interaction between one or more **candidates** and/or other **interlocutors**.

See also: **semi-direct test**, **tape-mediated test**

local independence

A **measurement** assumption, to the effect that all **items** in a given test are statistically independent of one another or, in other words, that a **candidate's response** to any given item does not influence his/her **performance** on any other item, once the candidate's level of **ability** has been controlled for. If this is true, all candidates of equal ability have the same **probability** of producing the right answer to each item and from this it can be inferred that all items are measuring a single ability. If the assumption of local independence is not sustained, or if candidates of equal ability have different probabilities of producing the right answer to a particular item, the reason must be that some other ability, other than what is tested by the item, is accounting for the performance of some of the candidates. This would be a violation of the assumption of **unidimensionality** which underlies the most popular **IRT** models.

Thus tests which involve the integration of different **skills**, such as reading and writing, while arguably more **authentic**, are suspect in pure measurement terms, because **scores** on the writing component may, for some candidates, have less to do with writing per se than with the ability to read and interpret the written prompts. Scores will therefore be difficult to interpret, because any given score may have different meaning for different candidates.

It is generally agreed, however, that the responses to test items are always multiply determined, and that, in practical terms, it is sufficient to demonstrate that there is one dominant ability underlying responses to a set of items.

See also: **item independence**, **dimensionality**, **integrative tests**
Further reading: Eells *et al.* 1951

logistic curve

A type of curve with a typical s-shape, as in the **item characteristic curve**; technically, the curve is defined mathematically, as that which results when $a/a+b$ is plotted, where a and b are positive real numbers. Other apparently s-shaped curves, for example the cumulative form of the **normal distribution**, are not logistic as they do not meet this technical criterion.

logit

In **measurement**, a way of expressing the probability or odds of a particular event, outcome or **response**; short for 'logistic probability unit' or 'log odds unit'; pronounced 'LOH-jit' with stress on the first syllable. In non-measurement contexts, probabilities or odds are more familiarly expressed as '5 to 1', '1 in 5', 'a 30% chance of such-and-such an event happening'; in measurement, particularly in **Rasch** and other **IRT**-based measurement, odds are expressed in a form that is more tractable mathematically, as a logarithm (or 'log') of the naturally occurring constant e. Thus, rather than speaking of the odds of a response, we speak of the 'log odds' of a response; conceptually, these are the same thing. The units on the scale of probability used in reporting the results of IRT analyses are called 'log odds units' or logits.

The logit **scale** has the advantage that it is an equal **interval scale** - that is, it can tell us not only that one **item** is more difficult than another, but also how much more difficult it is. The equal interval nature of the **ability** measurements means that growth in ability over time can be plotted on the **scale**; this has attractive implications for the **evaluation** of the effectiveness of teaching.

By convention, the average **difficulty** of **items** in a test is set at zero logits. Items of above average difficulty will thus be positive in sign, those of below average difficulty negative in sign. Ability **estimates** in turn are related to **item difficulty** estimates, so that a person of an ability expressed as 0 logits will conventionally have a 50% chance of getting right an item of average difficulty. **Candidates** more able than that will have positive logit values; candidates less able than that will have negative logit values.

See also: **item response theory**
Further reading: Ludlow 1995; McNamara 1996; Wright & Stone 1979

low stakes
See **stakes**

lower order skill
See **skill**

LSP test(ing)
Also **EAP test, ESP test, EOP test, field-specific testing, occupation-specific testing**

A test designed for language learners in specific academic, professional or vocational fields, such as tertiary students, language teachers, doctors and tour guides. Such tests rest on the assumption that language **performance** varies with both context and test **task**. While LSP tests typically claim to be testing language alone rather than content or non-language **skills**, in practice the boundary between language and these other skills is somewhat blurred.

Test content and **format** typically draw on a **needs analysis** carried out as the first stage of test development. Such tests are typically **performance tests**, requiring simulation of occupational tasks in order to facilitate inferences about **test-takers' ability** to cope in the target context. However, it is also possible for an LSP test to have a **knowledge** component, such as a test of field-specific vocabulary.

Because of their content specificity, LSP tests typically enjoy high **face validity**. It is also claimed that they generate positive **washback** on courses preparing language learners for the particular context. On the negative side, their performance testing format and their limited target **population** means that they are often costly to produce and administer.

See also: **language(s) for specific purposes**

Further reading: Lumley 1993; Douglas 1996; McNamara 1996

LTU

*See **Language Testing Update***

macro-skill
See **skill**

Mann Whitney U
The non-parametric equivalent of the *t*-**test** statistic, used for comparing differences between sets of **scores**.
Further reading: Hatch & Lazaraton 1991

MANOVA
Stands for 'multivariate analysis of variance'; a type of Analysis of Variance (**ANOVA**) procedure, this is a complex statistical procedure, used when more than one dependent **variable** is to be analysed. For example, a MANOVA might be used to analyse test data from a **sample** of 100 language learners (50 female and 50 male, of two different language backgrounds), each taking a test with three sections (vocabulary, speaking, writing). The MANOVA procedure could help to determine whether, for this sample, differences in **scores** on particular **sub-tests** (the three dependent variables) were influenced by the sex or language background (the two independent variables) of the **test takers**.

MANOVA enables multiple comparisons to be conducted within a single study, while avoiding the erroneous interpretations which often arise from separate analyses (eg doing multiple ANOVAs) of variables which are in fact related. MANOVA first establishes whether the differences between groups formed by the independent variables are likely to be due to chance, across all dependent variables; in other words, whether it is reasonable to proceed with investigating group differences on any of the dependent variables. Then it allows for judgements about the significance of interactions between the groups and the dependent variables, and lastly (if there are no significant interactions) between the groups and particular dependent variables.
See also: **interaction (2)**

Mantel-Haenszel

A statistical procedure used as a tool for studying **differential item functioning** (DIF) in relation to different groups of **test takers**. In common with most other methods used to identify DIF, the Mantel-Haenszel technique draws on groups of equivalent **ability** (who are matched on the same **construct** or **criterion** measured by the **items**, usually the total test **score**). The basic data used by the Mantel-Haenszel method is in the form of two-by-two contingency tables for each item being studied. There are two groups (the **focal group** and the **reference group**) and two levels for item response (right or wrong). There is also a range of **score** levels on the matching **variable**. The Mantel-Haenszel procedure is basically a **Chi-square** test of the null DIF **hypothesis**, namely, that the odds of getting the item correct at a given level of ability is the same in both groups. The Chi-square test is applied repeatedly for candidates at each score **level** to determine whether the null hypothesis holds across all levels of ability.

Further reading: Holland & Thayer 1988

many-faceted Rasch measurement

See **multi-faceted Rasch measurement**

marker

See **rater**

marking scheme

A **key** containing information about acceptable and unacceptable answers to **short-answer questions** or **cloze** items. It generally includes a comprehensive list of acceptable answers, although sometimes less strict guidelines are provided for the content of the expected answers. A marking scheme normally contains as much information as possible to guide **raters**, to ensure adequate **reliability**. For example, in addition to specifying content required in the answer, it may contain guidelines about how raters of a comprehension test are to treat answers containing spelling or grammatical **errors**. Marking schemes are commonly devised following examination of a range of **responses** elicited from **test takers** during the **pilot testing** of a **trial** version of a test, during a formal trial, or during the first live administration of the test; sometimes a draft marking scheme is progressively refined at each of these stages.

See also: **proficiency scale**
Further reading: Alderson *et al.* 1995, Ch. 5

mastery

A term derived from criterion-referenced **measurement** (CRM), denoting a sufficient level of **competence** (the **criterion**) shown by a **test taker** on some well-defined **domain**, such as the content of a course of instruction. The competence may be either **knowledge** (eg of particular lexical items, or of a grammatical system), or **ability** to use **language for specified purposes** or in specified ways.

Mastery decisions are made using a **cut-score**: those test takers scoring at or above this **level** are deemed to have acquired the specified language or knowledge or **skills**, while those below it are considered to lack the required knowledge or skills or to have an insufficient degree of competence in them. The primary concern is thus not with the standing of test takers relative to each other or to some established **norm**, but with their absolute standing (pass/fail) with regard to target behaviours within the specified domain.

The **validity** of the cut-score used determines the value of mastery testing. Issues of **construct** and **content validity** are central here. It is thus necessary both to define clearly the content (the **trait** or language behaviour that is of interest) to be tested as well as to develop a notion of how this is to be judged. Careful deliberation and well-informed decisions should then be used as the basis for determining the cut-score or standard.

The **reliability** (or consistency) of decisions based on a cut-score is also crucial. The term 'reliability' derives from **classical test theory** (and thus uses score **variance** to rank individuals for relative decisions). The term 'dependability' (or agreement) is generally preferred in CRM to refer to the notion of confidence in the decisions made using the cut-score. Although mastery decisions involve absolute judgements, the notion of relative mastery is still relevant, since it is easiest to classify those furthest from the cut-score, and much more difficult to make dependable decisions close to this score.

See also: **criterion-referenced test**, **achievement test**, **generalisability theory**, **standard setting**

Further reading: Berk 1980; Hudson 1989; Popham 1990

MCQ

See **multiple-choice item**

M-C tests

See: **multiple-choice test**

mean

Also arithmetical average

A **descriptive statistic**, measuring **central tendency**. The mean is calculated by dividing the sum of a set of **scores** by the number of scores. It is represented by the symbol $\overline{X}$

Like other measures of central tendency, the mean gives an indication of the trend or the score which is typical of the whole group. In **normal distributions** the mean is closely aligned to the **median** and the **mode**.

Of the three measures of central tendency, the mean is by far the most commonly used. It is the basis of a number of statistical tests of comparison between groups commonly used in language testing (eg *t*-**test**, **ANOVA**).

measurement

The process of quantifying the **performances** of **test takers**. It thus involves both the production and the use of an instrument (a language test), calibrated on some kind of **scale**, the purpose of which is to differentiate among test takers on the basis of **ability** or **knowledge**.

Measurement should be distinguished from **reporting** of **test results**, which takes place following measurement, and is a separate activity. Measurement can also be contrasted with purely qualitative descriptions of performance, in which the focus of attention is not comparison between learners.

The principal concerns in measurement are the **validity**, **reliability** and **practicality** of the procedures used and the measures produced. Related issues include the **test purpose**, method of **test analysis** used, and whether we are concerned with a **norm-referenced test** (comparing individuals to a **population**) or a **criterion-referenced test** (stating whether or not, or how well, specified skills or abilities have been mastered).

See also: **construct**, **score**

Further reading: Linn 1993

measurement error

Error is associated with all measurement of language, and interferes with the attempt to determine the **true score** of the **test taker**. It is the result of a combination of factors. The level of error attached to results will affect the **reliability** and **validity** of the measure.

Error may be random or systematic.

1. Unsystematic or **random error**. This is the portion of error that is relevant to judgement of the reliability of a test. Although random error may be

estimated, using a statistic called the **standard error of measurement**, it cannot be entirely eliminated.

There are a number of major sources of measurement error that may reduce the reliability of a test. The most important are:

- random variation associated with **candidate** behaviour such as **motivation, anxiety,** illness, **guessing,** etc.;
- factors associated with the testing situation, including the test environment, problems with **test administration** (such as faulty equipment or illegible texts) and the amount of preparation each test taker has had for the test;
- differences within and between **raters** in their application of **rating scales** or **marking schemes;**
- variables associated with the testing instrument used and the **sample** of test takers involved, including variations in **task difficulty** and such variables as the influence of **background knowledge** on test takers' performance;
- factors associated with recording and reporting of **scores,** including coding error (where **responses** are incorrectly recorded or reported).

2. Systematic error, or **bias,** occurs when one subgroup is consistently mismeasured or when a biased sample is used to obtain test results. Such variability is due in part to the fact that something other than the intended **trait** is being measured (for example, cultural knowledge may interfere with measurement in a test of **reading comprehension**). **Sampling error** can add bias to the measurement (for example, when the test **population** is not systematically represented).

This type of error affects the validity of a test. Test **validation,** therefore, may include processes to identify and evaluate potential sources of systematic error, and hence possibly to reduce or eliminate them.

Further reading: Feldt & Brennan 1993; Anastasi 1990, Ch. 5

median

A **descriptive statistic,** measuring **central tendency**: the middle **score** or value (the 50th **percentile**) in a set. If the **distribution** contains an even number of scores, the median is the average of the middle two. Half of the scores in the set are higher than the median, and half are lower.

Although the median is more subject to chance variations than the **mean,** it may be appropriate to use the median in preference to the mean when the set of scores includes a small number of **outliers** (atypically high or low scores) which would distort the mean.

See also: **mode**

MELAB
See **Michigan English Language Assessment Battery**

method effect
See **test method effect**

Michigan English Language Assessment Battery (MELAB)

A secure English-as-a-second-language **proficiency test** battery administered only by the University of Michigan English Language Institute (ELI-UM) and by its authorised examiners world-wide. The MELAB is an alternative to the **TOEFL** and **IELTS**. It is used primarily to assess the English language proficiency of students applying to post-secondary institutions where English is the medium of instruction. It is also used to assess the general language **proficiency** of professionals such as medical personnel, engineers, managers, and government officials who need to use English in their work or in special training programmes. The MELAB includes a written composition, a listening test, a grammar/**cloze**/vocabulary/reading test and an optional **speaking test**. Official **score** reports are issued by ELI-UM, where all MELABs are scored. Technical Manual available. Further information available at www.lsa.umich.edu/eli/.

See also: **Listening Comprehension Test, English Placement Test, MTELP**

Michigan Test of English Language Proficiency (MTELP)

An 100-item **multiple-choice test** of grammar, vocabulary and reading comprehension for advanced-level speakers of English as a second language. A retired component of the old Michigan Battery, the MTELP was developed by the English Language Institute at the University of Michigan. Multiple forms are commercially available to *bona fide* educational institutions. Some institutions that purchase the MTELP administer it in conjunction with the **Listening Comprehension Test** (LCT) and an in-house written essay for an overall **proficiency** assessment. Further information available at www.lsa.umich.edu/eli/.

See also: **English Placement Test, MELAB**
Further reading: Jenks 1987

micro-skill
See **skill**

minimum competence testing

A type of **assessment** which distinguishes those who are minimally competent in a particular language **ability** from those who are not. This level of **mastery** is normally defined as a **cut-score** on a **criterion-referenced** test. Minimum competence tests are often tied to survival or workplace skills, ie they focus on **candidates'** ability to use the **language for specific purposes** rather than their **knowledge** of the language. They aim to predict which candidates will be able to cope (albeit minimally) within the target **domain** and are thus frequently used as **screening** or **selection** tests, or for **certification**.

See also: **LSP testing, predictive validity, competency-based assessment**

misfit
Also **underfit**

In **Rasch analysis**, a type of **model data fit**, reported in **fit statistics** for estimates of test **item difficulty**, **candidate ability**, **rater severity** and other **facets** of the **assessment** context and their interactions. Misfit indicates a lack of consistency in the **score** patterns associated with the **facet** concerned. Misfitting items suggest that the items are either poorly designed, or are measuring something other than is being measured in the rest of the test; misfitting person **responses** mean that the candidate's responses to the **test items** are inconsistent, suggesting a pattern of **guessing**, or inattention, or that the person's abilities are not being appropriately measured by the test. If the responses of more than a handful of persons show misfit and the response patterns of these individuals cannot be explained appropriately, then the test is unsuitable for use with the given **population**. Rater misfit suggests lack of consistency in judgements by the rater, who may need re-training or in the worst case, if the misfit persists, ultimate exclusion from the rating process.

See also: **overfit**
Further reading: McNamara 1996

MLAT
See **Modern Language Aptitude Test**

mode

A **descriptive statistic**, measuring **central tendency**: the most frequently occurring score or score interval in a **distribution**. The mode is the easiest measure of central tendency to locate, but it is also the least stable (and least used), since a chance variation of a single mark might make a considerable difference to the mode. Unlike the **mean** and the **median**, it must of necessity be an actually occurring score.

The mode is useful for requirements such as reporting the most common **score** amongst members of a particular group, for example, scores on the **IELTS** test obtained by members of a class, following a course of English for Academic Purposes.

See also: **normal distribution**

model data fit

The extent to which a data set is predictable by the application of a statistical model; a necessary condition for the meaningful interpretation of the results of such modelling. Statistical tests for goodness of fit which summarise the extent of model data fit are routinely reported in statistical analyses of test data. These summaries will either be at the global level for the data set as a whole (as in the output from **two-parameter IRT** analyses executed by the program BILOG), or more locally, in the form of **fit statistics** for **items**, **candidates** or **raters**, as in **Rasch analysis**.

See also: **misfit, overfit**
Further reading: Hambleton *et al.* 1991

moderation

A process of review, discussion and **evaluation** of test materials or performance by a group or committee of **language testers**, **raters**, teachers and/or other experts. There are two types of moderation:

- Moderation may focus during the process of test development on **test content** (eg on particular **tasks** or **items**). The aim is to consider the quality of **test items** or tasks and issues of **content validity** (for example, **domain** coverage, or the equivalence of alternative **test forms**);
- Moderation is used in relation to judgements made about **test takers**. It focuses upon both the scoring **criteria** used and individual **samples** of **test-taker** performance. Here, moderation assists in establishing common interpretations of the **criteria** and **levels** used as they relate to test-taker **performance**, thus contributing to improved **reliability** of the test.

See also: **content analysis, rater training, scale, item writing, test equivalence**
Further reading: Weir 1993, Ch. 1; Alderson *et al.* 1995, Chs. 3, 6

Modern Language Aptitude Test (MLAT)

First published in 1959 by the Psychological Corporation, this is a commercial form of a **battery** of tests of language **aptitude** developed by Carroll and Sapon for the US Foreign Service and language training selection. It comprised five tests of reading and listening, which Carroll considered, on the basis of a **factor analysis**, to test a number of distinct **abilities** (indicated in the brackets below).

The five tests are:

- number learning (testing rote memory for recall of numbers);
- phonetic script (measuring ability to associate sounds with symbols);
- spelling clues: the student is given clues about the pronunciation of a stimulus**, and selects a synonym from a set of choices** (**verbal knowledge** is tested here);
- words in sentences (testing grammatical sensitivity/knowledge);
- paired associates (testing rote memory of visual stimuli).

See also: **aptitude**, **Language Aptitude Battery**
Further reading: Carroll & Sapon 1958; Buros 1975; Spolsky 1995, Ch. 7

motivation

Generally used in language testing to refer to the force that drives an individual to perform as well as possible in a test.

A test may in itself constitute a motivating influence on students to study hard (see **washback**). There is also evidence that increased motivation will lead to better test **performance**. This motivation may be influenced by the consequences for the **test taker** of the test: if, for example, the test has a selection purpose for a course of study, or entry to a profession, then it is likely that motivation will be high; if, on the other hand, results on the test hold little consequence for the test taker, as in some routine classroom tests, or in test **trials**, then motivation is more likely to be low. Generally, it is considered that the higher the test taker's level of motivation, the truer the reflection of **ability** shown by the performance, and hence the lower the amount of **error** (caused, for example, by lack of effort). Clearly, results from tests where test takers are not motivated are likely to be less reliable than those where they are strongly motivated.

See also: **reliability**, **test anxiety**, **affective reaction**
Further reading: Wolf & Smith 1995

MTELP

See **Michigan Test of English Language Proficiency**

multichotomous

See **polytomous scoring**

multidimensionality

See **dimensionality**

multi-faceted Rasch measurement

Also multi-facet Rasch measurement, **many-faceted Rasch measurement**
A type of **Rasch analysis** particularly suited for the analysis of judge-mediated data from **performance** assessments, for example the **assessment** of speaking or writing **skills**. Developed by Michael Linacre, it represents a further extension of the basic Rasch model to enable us to investigate the characteristics of **raters** or other facets of the assessment setting (**task**, **interlocutor**, etc.), and their impact on estimates of **candidate ability**. It also permits analysis of the interaction between these facets (the way particular **judges** are affected by particular tasks, for example) through the feature known as **bias analysis**.

See also: **facet**, **item response theory**
Further reading: Linacre 1989; McNamara 1996

multiple-choice item

Also **multiple-choice question**, **MCQ**
A **test item** where the **test taker** is required to choose the correct option (the **key**) from several given. Most commonly, multiple-choice items include an instruction to the test taker and a **stem** (typically either a phrase or sentence to be completed, or a question). The key and several **distractors**, usually three, then follow in random order. **Stimulus** material, in the form of an **input text** (written or spoken) may be provided (as in a **reading comprehension test**), or the item may stand alone (for example, in a **grammar test**), as in the example below.

Select the best answer:
Paris .... the capital of France.
  A) being   B) is   C) be   D) are
Multiple-choice items have a number of advantages compared to other types of test item. No special expertise is required to score them, because there is only one possible correct answer for each item. A large number of such items may be included in a language test, ensuring wide **sampling** of the **domain** of interest. **Scores** derived from them may easily be analysed, giving a clear idea

of the **difficulty** and **reliability** of each item, as well as the test as a whole. Analysis can also identify successful and unsuccessful distractors, assisting in revision of items, if necessary. A careful process of reviewing, **pre-testing**, **trialling**, analysis and revision, in combination with the fact that they are objectively scored, means that the reliability of multiple-choice tests produced by large testing agencies tends to be higher than that of other forms of test. As a result, multiple-choice items have been widely used, particularly in **standardised tests**, over the last 50 years or so. It is also contended that the high **correlations** sometimes found between multiple-choice tests and tests of **productive skills** provide evidence that they are tapping some underlying **ability** common to many kinds of language use.

However, the **validity** of multiple-choice items has been criticised in recent decades, partly because they appear able only to assess test takers' ability to recognise correct forms, and not to produce language. As with many test methods, a further criticism of their validity is that however carefully multiple-choice items may have been constructed, it remains uncertain exactly what they are testing. For example, it has been suggested that the principal **trait** required to answer them correctly is not knowledge of the target language, but some other, irrelevant construct such as ability to reject obviously incorrect distractors. This claim is supported by studies showing that test takers can significantly improve their score on multiple-choice tests with practice.

A drawback of multiple-choice items which may not initially be apparent is that the writing of reliable items is a difficult and time-consuming process, as well as requiring expertise and substantial resources.

See also: **objective scoring**, **forced-choice item**, **test method**, **method effect**

Further reading: Henning 1987; Spolsky 1995

multiple-choice question (MCQ)

See **multiple-choice item**

multiple-choice test

A test consisting of **multiple-choice items**.

multiple regression analysis

See **regression**

multiple-trait scoring

An approach to the scoring of writing (or speaking) **performance** in which **raters** are required to provide separate **scores** for each of several (generally three or four) **facets** or **traits** of the performance. It may be contrasted with scoring methods where a single score is produced, either to describe a single trait or when an overall judgement is made. Multiple-trait scoring procedures aim to focus on the most salient **criteria** or traits relevant to the **task**, as identified during a careful process of test development, and in which the raters are normally involved. The same multiple-trait scoring procedure may be used for a variety of task **prompts** if they share the same **test specifications**. Examples of criteria used in multiple-trait scoring of writing include: content, **cohesion**, **coherence**, control of grammar and range of vocabulary.

Advantages of multiple-trait scoring procedures include: they provide more information (eg for diagnostic purposes) than **global scoring** methods, and, when accompanied by proper **rater training** and multiple **rating**, they have the potential to improve the **reliability** of scores; they are also less costly than primary-trait instruments, although more expensive than holistic scoring. Multiple-trait scoring is nowadays sometimes considered synonymous with **analytic scoring**.

See also: **primary-trait scoring, holistic scoring, holistic assessment**
Further reading: Hamp-Lyons 1991a

multi-trait multi-method analysis

An experimental design to determine to what extent **test results** are attributable either to **candidate abilities** (**trait**) or to **method effects**.

The Campbell and Fiske statistical method of **construct validation** involves investigation of the relevant contributions of method and trait to **observed scores**. To indicate that candidate abilities are determining test scores, the **correlations** between different measures of the same trait should be high positive (convergent) while those between different traits measured by the same method should be low or zero (discriminant).

For example, two traits, reading and listening, are both measured by two methods, multiple choice and **self-assessment**. If reading and listening are being tested differently (and therefore validly), the correlation between multiple choice and self-assessment of reading should be higher than between reading and listening both measured by multiple choice.

See also: **validity**
Further reading: Bachman 1990; Campbell & Fiske 1959

multivariate analysis of variance (MANOVA)

See **MANOVA**

n

native speaker norms

Native speaker ability is commonly appealed to as a **criterion** of perfect
mastery on a **language proficiency test** and therefore as influencing both
choice of content and definition of success. Educated native speaker ability
was adopted as a criterion by the Foreign Service Institute (FSI) for their
highest **FSI Scale** levels in 1968, but absolute **rating scales** such as the FSI
are now regarded with a certain scepticism. In addition, growing recognition
that native speakers vary in their own language proficiency and that all
definitions of the native speaker are elusive indicate that native speaker norms
themselves need to be relative to the norming group and cannot be absolute.
Furthermore, the highly proficient second language speaker may be a more
appropriate criterion for a second language proficiency test. Nevertheless, the
educated native speaker as an ideal type remains a useful model for test
constructors to have in mind (especially with regard to grammar and
vocabulary) in the first stages of test construction.

See also: **norms**

Further reading: Bachman 1990; Davies 1991; Hamilton *et al.* 1993

needs analysis

An analysis of a specified area, or **domain**, of endeavour (eg a particular
occupation, or a field of study) and of the communicative demands placed
upon participants in such an area. Needs analysis is conducted in order to
determine the content of a test or programme of instruction.

The process was originally conceived as a means of determining the
content of a communicatively oriented **ESP syllabus** where the target
communicative context could be clearly defined, but has since also been
widely used in the development of ESP **performance tests**.

A needs analysis of some kind is a common stage in the development of
language tests, as it provides justification for the choice of content and **tasks**
(cf. **content validity**). Choices about content and task type must inevitably be
made in constructing any test, and rather than the test developer relying on
intuition, it may be much more satisfactory to base such decisions on a review
of **input** provided by experts in the field of interest. There are, however,
drawbacks to the establishing of content validity by needs analysis. These

drawbacks involve both practicality and **sampling** of the domain of interest. They can be summarised as follows:

- the complexity of a domain may lead to problems in specifying or predicting its components;
- the results of a needs analysis, often based for practical reasons on very limited data, may be of limited generalisability, or provide only information of the most general nature;
- the subjective nature of a needs analysis conducted by a single researcher leaves its findings open to dispute;
- the lack of an empirical framework for deciding which elements of the domain it is critical to test creates problems of sampling and coverage in test construction.

Further reading: Munby 1978; Carroll 1981; Weir 1988

negatively skewed distribution

See **skewed distribution**

nominal scale

Also categorical scale

One which consists of counts of occurrence of mutually exclusive attributes. Thus it is a measure of frequency of occurrence of an attribute rather than of how much of it is present. Examples may include counts (which are entered as frequency tallies) of the number of people of particular language backgrounds, the number of people at different **levels** of **ability** (beginner, intermediate, etc.) or the number of non-native speakers studying in particular university faculties. In language testing such data are often gathered to provide background information on test **candidates** or the prospective target **population** of a test (for purposes of establishing a representative trial group, for example).

A nominal scale consisting of only two categories, such as 'male/female', 'right/wrong', or monolingual/bilingual, is known as a **dichotomous scale**.

See also: **interval scale**, **ordinal scale**, **scales**

Further reading: Hatch & Lazaraton 1991; Woods *et al.* 1986

nomothetic span

The empirical network of relationships of a **test** to other measures of the same **construct** which may be obtained under different conditions. A test cannot truly be considered to have **construct validity** without corroborative evidence from external sources. As an example, the **validity** of a test of verbal **aptitude** may be established by relating it to other measures such as **vocabulary knowledge** and **writing ability** as well as to **candidates' performance** in other situations which are deemed to require this kind of aptitude. The stronger a test's **correlations** with other **variables** which theory suggests should be related to the test construct, the wider its nomothetic span.

See also: **convergent validity**
Further reading: Messick 1993

normal curve
See **normal distribution**

normal distribution
Also normal distribution curve, Gaussian curve, normal probability curve
A theoretical concept central to most statistical thinking, based on the common observation that events (such as annual rainfall) or physical characteristics (such as height) show a similar symmetrical pattern or distribution. This distribution is bell-shaped, with most rainfall or height being average, and extremes, both low and high, being few. In language tests, the distribution of **scores** in a **population** is similarly normally distributed (see diagram) with most **test takers** scoring around the average (or mean) and progressively fewer scoring towards the extremes.

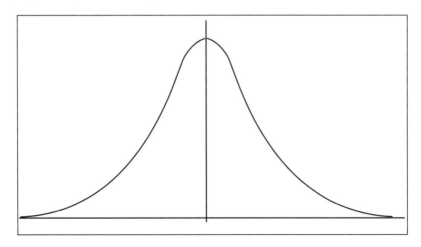

The mid-point of the normal curve is both **median** and **mode** as well as the mean. The distribution on either side of the mean is indicated by the **standard**

deviation. The assumption that the data are normally distributed underlies the application of **parametric** statistical tests.

Standardised language tests make the assumption of normality. Nevertheless, it seems unlikely that language **ability** is normally distributed in a population, and in **achievement** testing and **mastery** testing no such assumption can be made. Many language test distributions depart from normality, showing skewedness. Severe skewedness affects the type of **significance test** that should be used.

Note that 'normal' and 'normality' refer simply to the symmetrical properties of this type of curve and carry no judgemental meaning.

See also: **kurtosis, norm-referenced test, skewed distribution**
Further reading: Hatch & Lazaraton 1991; Woods *et al.* 1986

norm-referenced test(ing)

Also norm-referenced measurement

A type of test whereby a **candidate**'s scores are interpreted with reference to the **performance** of the other candidates. Thus the quality of each performance is judged not in its own right, or with reference to some external **criterion**, but according to the standard of the group as a whole. In other words, norm-referenced tests are more concerned with spreading individuals along an **ability** continuum, the **normal curve**, than with the nature of the task to be attained, which is the focus of **criterion-referenced tests**.

Where an **alternate** version of a norm-referenced test is being developed, interpretation of **raw scores** on the new version of the test may be made in the light of normative performance (ie the **mean** and **standard deviation**) on the previous version, as is the case for widely administered tests such as **TOEFL**. For norm-referencing to be effective, it is important that there be a large number of subjects, and a wide range of normally-distributed scores.

The ranking capacity of norm-referenced tests is sometimes used to set **cut-off scores**, so that, for example, only 60% of the test **population** are allowed to pass.

See also: **normal distribution, criterion-referenced test, standardised test**
Further reading: Popham 1990

norms

Standards of behaviour, including language behaviour. Language norms are variable and describe the customary or conventional choices groups and individuals make among alternative ways of speaking and writing. At the macro level what is typically chosen is a standard language or code. At the micro level it is customary to choose situationally-appropriate forms and expressions. Norms are also prescriptive, indicating language uses preferred by elite groups. It is natural for norms to change and for there to be resistance to change; such resistance is often reflected in disputes about 'correctness'.

Language tests are doubly normative, first because they are necessarily based on a standard of speaking or writing (often the native speaker); and second because they impose that standard on **test takers** and, through them, on the community.

See also: **appropriateness**, **rules**, **native speaker norms**, **norm-referenced test**

Further reading: Bartsch 1987; Davies 1991; Milroy & Milroy 1985

null finding
See **hypothesis**

O

objective item

Objective items (or questions) are traditionally distinguished from **subjective items** on the basis of their **response** format. Objective items are those with a choice **format** (multiple-choice, **true–false**, matching) or a completion format (fill-in-the-blank, **cloze**). Subjective items (or questions) are those which require a **constructed response**.

An objective item calls for the choice of a correct answer out of several provided for each question, or one clearly specifiable correct response. Objective items typically contain a **stem**, which presents the problem clearly, and then two or more choices, only one of which is correct. In **multiple-choice items** there are three, four or five choices; binary choice items (also known as **yes–no questions**) contain only two choices.

Objective items have been criticised for trivialising **assessment** and for being amenable to **guessing**. However, there is good empirical evidence that objective items can provide broad subject-matter coverage, that they yield more reliable **scores** and that they are fairer. If there is serious concern about guessing, measures can be taken to minimise its effect. In addition objective items are economical with the **test taker's** time.

The objective–subjective distinction has been challenged on the grounds that response format alone does not determine objectivity. For example a so-called subjective item could be considered objective when there is a high degree of consensus among experts as to what may be expected from a constructed response.

See also: **subjective item**
Further reading: Anastasi 1990; Jacobs & Chase 1992; Heaton 1975/1987

objective scoring, objectively scored

Scoring procedures for **test items** which do not require markers to make subjective decisions. All acceptable answers are clearly specified in a **scoring key**, thus **inter-rater reliability** should be perfect. While many tests are distinguished as being objectively or subjectively scored, others may consist of a mix of both types of scoring, especially where **sub-tests** test different **skills**.

See also: **objective test, subjective scoring, test item**

objective test

A test in which all the **items** are **objectively scored**. In an objective test, correct **responses** are clearly specified, and markers are not required to make judgements. Thus the issue of **inter-** and **intra-rater reliability** does not arise.

Certain testing techniques and **test item** types are associated with objective tests, such as **multiple-choice** and **cloze**. Scoring **keys** specify which answers are acceptable. An advantage of **objectively scored** test items, as opposed to **constructed-response** items, is that they can allow for machine scoring.

In some contexts, particularly the assessment of **productive skills**, such tests, however, are often perceived as possessing less **validity** than subjective tests.

See also: **subjective scoring**

observation

1. A non-intrusive means of gathering data on **ability** outside the confines of formal testing. Often undertaken as one aspect of classroom-based **assessment**, the teacher records information on the ability of students based on their **performance** on one or more classroom activities. Depending on whether such information is gathered over a period of time or at the end of a period of instruction, it may be seen as contributing to **formative** or **summative assessment**. Observation for the purposes of making an assessment may also be undertaken in other settings, such as the workplace.

2. Each assessment made by a **rater** on the basis of a **candidate**'s test performance. During a single performance, several observations may be made which together contribute to the final **score** or **grade** awarded. These multiple observations may involve a single application of each of several **criteria**, or repeated applications of one or more criteria (by the same or different raters).

See also: **profile**

observed score

A test **candidate**'s actual test score. This observed **score** is assumed to imperfectly represent the **true score** (**ability**) due to **measurement error**. **Classical test theory** is based on the recognition of the fact that abilities, being abstract, can never be measured directly. It assumes that the observed score consists of two components, the true score and the error score (variation which is not due to ability and which is unsystematic). Thus the **variance** of a set of test scores consists of the observed score variance plus the measurement error.

If the observed scores from two tests which claim to measure the same ability are highly correlated, then the effect of measurement error must be small. This technique of comparing tests can consequently provide evidence of the **reliability** of the observed scores. This procedure is used in determining **parallel forms reliability**. Comparisons of observed scores are also used to determine **concurrent validity**.

See also: **error variance**

Further reading: Henning 1987

occupation-specific test

See **LSP testing**

odd–even method

A method for determining **split-half reliability** used with tests made up of more or less homogeneous items. The test is administered once to a group of **candidates** and then divided into halves, one half consisting of all the odd-numbered **items** and the other consisting of all the even-numbered items. If the items were originally ordered according to **difficulty**, such a division should yield very near equivalent half-scores. The scores for each set of items are then correlated with one another. The resultant **coefficient**, after it has been corrected with the **Spearman Brown Prophecy Formula** to produce an estimate for the whole test, will determine the extent to which the test has **internal consistency**.

See also: **reliability, Kuder-Richardson formulae**

Further reading: Anastasi 1990; Hatch & Lazaraton 1991

one-parameter model

Also Rasch model, Rasch one-parameter model

An **item response theory** (IRT) model developed by Georg Rasch, which states that the probability of a correct **response** is a function of the **difficulty** of the item and the **ability** of the **candidate**. The term 'one-parameter' refers to the item difficulty parameter. In this model all the items are assumed to have the same **discrimination**, and **guessing** is not quantified directly (but is included indirectly, along with other **error** sources, in the **fit** of the person to the model). The one-parameter model contrasts with the **two-parameter model** which does not provide an estimation for the effect of guessing, but does include a **discriminability** parameter, and the **three-parameter model** which incorporates information on all three **item** characteristics.

The Rasch one-parameter model is widely used in applications of IRT to language testing. Its advantage over the other models is that it can be applied to **rating scale** or **partial credit** data.

See also: **Rasch analysis**

Further reading: McNamara 1996; Henning 1987

one-tail(ed) test

Also one-tailed hypothesis

Used where a direction is specified for the hypothesised difference between two groups. A positive directional **hypothesis** predicts that the experimental group will perform better than the control group, while a negative directional hypothesis predicts that the experimental group will perform less well. A significant finding is more readily obtained where there is a one-tailed hypothesis than where there is a two-tailed hypothesis (where there is no hypothesis about the direction of any observed difference); consequently a one-tailed hypothesis should only be posited where previous research points strongly to the likelihood of such a difference between groups.

An example where a one-tailed hypothesis would be appropriate is in a comparison of girls learning French with boys learning French in high schools in a particular city. Previous research has shown that girls perform significantly better than boys on foreign/second language tests; it would, therefore, be appropriate to have a one-tailed hypothesis, ie that girls will outperform boys.

See also: **hypothesis testing**

Further reading: Hatch & Lazaraton 1991

open-ended question

See **constructed-response item**

operational definition

An operational definition of a **construct** (such as 'intelligence' or 'language ability') enables a test designer to relate the theoretical construct to the actual **observations** of behaviour. As a step in the test development process, this involves determining how to isolate the construct and make it observable in actual **test items**. Thus, such features of the testing procedure as the **test format**, **test length**, item types and **scoring** procedures need to be specified. Operational definitions are intended to minimise variation in **test method** and to ensure that the **performances** elicited provide adequate **samples** of the **abilities** being tested.

Further reading: Bachman 1990

operationalise

1. The act of implementing actual administrations of a test following the test development process of **trialling** and revision. During test development information is sought only on the characteristics of the test; during operational testing, information is sought on the **ability** or **proficiency** of individuals taking the test.

2. Tests themselves can be viewed as operationalisations of the test **construct**, the theoretical model of language proficiency underlying the test.
Further reading: Bachman 1990; Bachman & Palmer 1996

OPI

See **Oral Proficiency Interview**

oral interview

A term applied to direct **assessments** of oral language **proficiency** where each **candidate** interacts with one (or more) **interlocutors**. Oral interviews are subjectively assessed, normally either against specific **criteria** or using a holistic **proficiency scale**, and may be assessed immediately or from an audio recording or videotape of the **performance**.

Oral interviews may vary in length, in the elicitation procedures used, in the specific **tasks** and types of language elicited, and in the **assessment criteria** used.

The most widely known of the oral interview tests is the **Oral Proficiency Interview**.
See also: **FSI scale**, **proficiency scale**

Oral Proficiency Interview (OPI)

Also **OPI**

A procedure for the elicitation of oral language, used in conjunction with the **ACTFL** Proficiency Guidelines for the assessment of oral language **skills**. The test consists of a structured **interview** which leads **candidates** through activities requiring progressively higher levels of **proficiency**. The phases are characteristically a warm-up, a probe, a level check and a wind-down. The **performance** on each of the phases is evaluated against definitions for each band **level**.

The OPI derives from the **ILR** approach, which drew on the **FSI** Oral Interview and used the ILR **rating scale** to assess responses. This format has also been adapted to be used in conjunction with other rating scales, such as the **ASLPR** in Australia. All these techniques represent a view of language **ability** whereby proficiency is characterised through functional language skills and is measured by means of a **rating** (either **global** or **analytic**), generally assigned by the interviewer.

See also: **Simulated Oral Proficiency Interview, descriptors, scales**
Further reading: Wilds 1975; Alderson *et al.* 1987; Byrnes & Canale 1987

ordering

The sequencing of **test items** according to specific principles. Two commonly applied strategies are based on **item difficulty**:

- a few easy items are placed at the beginning of the test;
- the items in the test are sequenced from easiest to most difficult.

Both these strategies are intended to relieve **test anxiety** and to motivate weaker **candidates**. The second strategy in particular also aims to ensure that all candidates attempt the maximum number of items.

In **power tests** items are strictly ordered according to difficulty. In **adaptive tests** the selection and order of items is dependent on the candidate's **performance**.

The ordering of **items, tasks** and **sub-tests** is an important consideration in test development, as it may affect candidates' performances.

See also: **test anxiety, speed(ed) test**

ordinal scale

A **scale** which orders objects in terms of their relationship to one another. The points on the scale stand in 'more than' or 'less than' relationship to each other, the best known example being a rank-order scale.

Examples of ordinal scales are:

- teacher or test-based rankings – first, second, third, etc.;
- ratings based on subjective **assessment**, as in the assessment of oral proficiency;
- **measurement** of how much of a **variable** is present, such as when **candidates** are asked to rate the level of **difficulty** of a test using a **Likert scale**.

While an ordinal scale is able to order items in relation to each other, the size of the increments between any two adjacent points cannot be assumed to be the same. An ordinal scale, therefore, cannot provide information on the extent of difference between any two **items**, for example the difference in **ability** between candidates. Thus, we know that a candidate who gets an oral rating of 5 is more capable than a student who gets a rating of 4, but we cannot say that the difference in ability between these two students is the same as that between the student scoring 4 and another who scores 3. While test scores should theoretically be treated as ordinal data rather than interval data because test items cannot be assumed to be of equivalent **difficulty**, it is generally accepted that where the test is of a reasonable length (ie where the total **score** possible is suitably high), it is permissible to treat the data as interval data.

See also: **nominal scale, interval scale, scale**

Further reading: Hatch & Lazaraton 1991

outfit

A type of statistic used in **IRT** analysis to indicate the extent of **score** variability in a given data set. An outfit **mean** square value close to 0 indicates that the scores for the particular **item, rater** or **candidate** fall within the normal range expected. A value greater than +/– 2 is usually taken to indicate that the behaviour of the candidate, rater or item shows an unacceptably high level of deviation from the norm. It is, however, more common to use the **infit** values, from which the extreme values (**outliers**) have been removed.

See also: **model data fit, overfit**

outlier

An extreme **score** which can be considered not to 'belong' to the general pattern of behaviour. The **mean** score is very sensitive to outliers, so where there is justification for considering such scores to be aberrant in some way they may be removed from the data. Outliers may also skew the data, resulting in a **distribution** that is not normal, and this in turn limits the type of statistical procedure which may be performed.

One problem with the exclusion of outliers is the definition of what constitutes an outlier in any particular set of data.

In **item response theory** two types of **fit statistics** are given, **infit** and **outfit**. Outfit includes all the **observations** whereas infit excludes outliers. Because the infit measures are more sensitive to variability in the range of observations that are usually of most interest, these measures are the most often used in interpreting test data.

overfit

One type of poor **fit**, or failure of aspects of test **score** data to conform to the predictions of a data model (eg an **IRT** model). In analyses using **probabilistic models** (as in IRT) the model expects some variability from its expectations, within certain predicted limits. When this variability is significantly less than predicted, it is reported as overfit. In the case of an overfitting **item**, there is a deterministic rather than a probabilistic relationship between total score and chances of success on the particular item: all those scoring below a certain **level** get the item wrong, whereas all those scoring above that level get the item right. The item thus acts as an 'all or nothing' item: at a certain point along the **ability** continuum, one's chances of a correct **response** to this item change from 0 to 100%. In such cases, an explanation for the 'overfitting' is usually sought in terms of lack of independence of items in the test, so that you will only get item *x+1* correct if you have got item *x* correct, as answering item *x+1* depends in some way on having understood the answer to item *x*. This means that the overfitting item contributes no independent information on **candidate** ability, and is thus redundant.

Overfit can also be a characteristic of the ratings given by an individual **rater**, suggesting a lack of expected variability in **scores** given by the rater in question. In this case, overfit is often a sign that the rater is not using the full range of score points available, and thus not making the expected range of distinctions between candidates.

See also: **misfit, model data fit, implicational scaling**

Further reading: McNamara 1996; Pollitt & Hutchinson 1987

p

parallel forms

Forms of a test which aim to test the same **skills**, are constructed to the same specifications and are identical in the nature of their **sampling**, their length, **rubrics**, and so on. They should also demonstrate the same statistical characteristics fulfilling the requirements of **parallel forms reliability**. A less stringent form of **test equivalence, alternate forms**, does not always require this statistical support.

Further reading: Henning 1987

parallel forms reliability

An approach to estimating the **reliability** of a test where the **equivalence** of the **scores** derived from **parallel forms** of a test is examined. This approach is similar to the **test-retest** approach, both being used where **internal consistency measures** are not possible. When estimating reliability in this way, a counterbalanced design (with half the subjects taking form A first, and the other half taking form B first) is necessary to eliminate the **practice effect**.

According to **classical test theory**, the **mean** scores and score **distribution** must be equivalent. Score **correlations** can be interpreted as an indicator of the reliability of the tests in that they reflect low **measurement error**.

See also: **alternate forms**

parameter

In **item response theory**, one of three **item characteristics** which, according to the model being used, may or may not be taken into account when calculating the probability of a correct response. The three characteristics are **item difficulty, item discriminability** and the effect of **guessing**.

See also: **one-parameter model, two-parameter model, three-parameter model**

Further reading: Henning 1987

parametric

A type of statistical procedure which makes strong assumptions about the **distribution** of the data. Parametric tests assume that the **dependent variable** is measured on an **interval scale**, that the data are normally distributed, and that the observations are independent. Parametric tests are more 'powerful' than nonparametric tests because they use more of the information, that is, there is less likelihood of an **error** in accepting or rejecting the null **hypothesis**. While nonparametric tests can be used with data which conform to the requirements of parametric tests, parametric tests cannot be used where the assumptions are not met.

See also: **normal distribution**, **parameter**
Further reading: Hatch & Lazaraton 1991

partial credit

Refers to the scoring of test **items** or **tasks** where the simple (dichotomous) distinction between right and wrong does not apply and where partial credit is awarded for reaching an intermediate **level** of **performance** on a **test item**. Possible **scores** for partial credit items will range from 0–2 or more. So, for example, partial credit might be awarded for an answer to an **open-ended question** which contains some, but not all, of the relevant information.

Partial credit items cannot be dealt with in **classical test analysis**; however, one-parameter **item response theory** does allow for the use of both dichotomous and partial credit items within the one test.

pass mark

See **cut-score**

path analysis

A multiple **regression** procedure used to test the relationships between a set of independent **variables**. Path analysis differs from other regression analyses in that it allows us not only to predict **performance** on one **variable** from performance on another but also to establish whether the relationship between two or more variables is a causal one.

Like **factor analysis**, path analysis is generally used to validate an existing model rather than to generate an entirely new one. On the basis of previous research or logical analysis the researcher sets up a path diagram as in the following example.

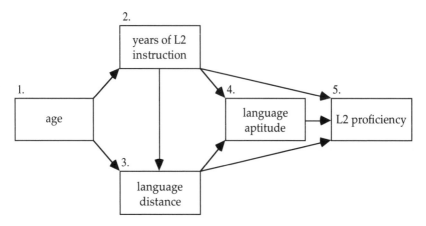

This model hypothesises a causal connection between success in second language (L2) learning as measured by an end-of-school **examination** (see Box 5) and a range of background variables: age (Box 1); years of L2 instruction (Box 2); language distance (Box 3); and language **aptitude** (Box 4). The model posits that years of instruction in a second language directly affects **proficiency** in that language but is also mediated in part by language aptitude and in part by language distance. Age has no direct effect on L2 achievement but is mediated by years of L2 instruction on the one hand and language distance on the other. The effect of language distance on second language performance is in turn partly mediated by language aptitude.

The **validity** of this path diagram is established by a procedure which regresses each variable on all the preceding variables and thus traces both direct and indirect effects (paths). The purpose of the analysis is to validate and, if necessary 'trim' the model in order to arrive at the most parsimonious explanation of the outcome variable.

Further reading: Hatch & Lazaraton 1991

Pearson product–moment correlation coefficient

Also **Pearson's *r***

The appropriate **correlation** to use when both **variables** under consideration are of the interval type. Because it takes account of more information than **Spearman's rho**, this product–moment coefficient is closer to the 'true' correlation.

See also: **scale**

Pearson's *r*
See **Pearson product–moment correlation**

percentile

A conversion of a **raw score** which provides a means of locating the **score** in relation to the distribution of all scores. Percentiles generally relate the score obtained by a particular **candidate** to the proportion of scores at or below it. Thus, if a score is said to be at the 68th percentile, this means that this candidate did as well as or better than 68% of the whole cohort (although in some cases the score may be related to established **norms** of **performance** based on previous administrations rather than on the particular cohort). The 50th percentile represents the **median** score.

In a **standardised test** percentiles or other **standardised scores** rather than scores are typically used to determine the **cut-score** for selection or placement purposes.

See also: **T score, stanine score, z score**
Further reading: Hatch and Lazaraton 1991

performance

1. The application of one's **competence** or **knowledge** of the rules of language to actual communication. The requirement of 'real life' or 'authentic' performance in a test reflects the prevailing view that knowing a language includes not only **knowledge** of the formal features of the language but also knowledge of how to use language appropriately for communicating in particular contexts. A test which requires **candidates** to perform **tasks** which replicate the sorts of things they are or will be required to do in particular contexts is termed a **performance test**. **LSP tests** are often of this type, requiring candidates to demonstrate both formal and sociolinguistic knowledge in performing the tasks.

2. The behaviour exhibited by a test candidate in completing a particular task, a ratable **sample** of language. While the **assessment** of **ability** is based on this observable behaviour, it is recognised that aspects of the testing situation may cause the candidate to perform in a way that does not allow an accurate measure of her ability to be obtained. These aspects may include features of the test itself (sometimes referred to as **test method facets**) or aspects relating to the individual candidates, such as **test anxiety**, fatigue, **test wiseness**, etc.

See also: **true score, measurement error**
Further reading: Bachman & Palmer 1996; McNamara 1996

performance test

A test in which the **ability** of **candidates** to perform particular **tasks**, usually associated with job or study requirements, is assessed. Performance tests (also known as **authentic** tests or **direct tests**) use 'real-life' performance as a criterion. They are attempts to characterise **measurement** procedures in such a way as to approximate non-test language performance. Performance tests are only possible where there is a relatively homogeneous clientele with known and relatively specific language use needs. The rationale is to replicate those aspects of context which can be shown to influence language **performance** in a systematic way and in so doing to establish greater **predictive validity**. A constructive distinction has been drawn between strong and weak performance tests, depending on the extent to which the **assessment** focuses on the quality of the language alone (a weak performance test) or on how well the candidate succeeds in the **task** (a strong performance test).

The extent to which performance tests can approximate to real life settings is disputed, some writers arguing for a continuum from direct to **indirect tests**, offering ways of approximating as closely to real life as possible in the test situation and introducing a category of **semi-direct tests.** Others have argued that the actual test encounter is authentic in itself and still others for the importance of **construct validity** in test construction and for a more precise analysis of the critical features of communicative language use. According to this view, performance testing becomes the testing not of authentic texts but of the authentic features which underlie such texts.

The **washback** of performance assessment onto the **curriculum** is seen as one of its main advantages, in that testing (and hence teaching) is tied to real world skills. Such tests generally also have higher **face validity**, an important factor in test uptake. A disadvantage of performance assessment, however, is the cost of **test administration**, given the individual administration typical of oral performance assessment, and the **subjective assessment** required for both oral and written skills.

Performance tests represent a marriage between **direct tests** and **LSP** tests. Like all direct tests they suffer from problems of coverage or generalisability and of **reliability**.

Further reading: McNamara 1996

person discriminability

See **discrimination**

phi correlation

A **correlation** statistic which is used to indicate the strength of association between two binary **variables** (ie each variable is a dichotomy such as male/female, correct/incorrect, pass/fail).

In language testing the phi correlation may be used, for example, to indicate the degree of interrelatedness of two dichotomous **test items** or pass/fail **grades** on two tests, or to investigate the relationship between success on a language test and success in an academic course (in terms of pass/fail).

Chi-square is normally first applied in order to determine whether a relationship exists (ie whether the **null hypothesis** can be rejected). Phi is then used to indicate how strong the relationship is. Tetrachoric correlation and **factor analysis** may also be used to measure inter-item correlation.

Further reading: Hatch & Lazaraton 1991

pilot test

See **pre-test**

placement test

A test intended to provide information which will help place students in appropriate classes. To be most effective, placement tests should reflect the features of the teaching context (such as the **proficiency level** of the classes, the methodology and the **syllabus** type). A **grammar** placement test, for example, may not be the most suitable placement test where the syllabus is **task**-oriented. Where large student intakes are the norm, efficiency in administration and marking is often a key consideration in the development of placement procedures. As it is relatively easy to rectify mistakes made on the basis of **test results**, eg students placed wrongly, issues of **reliability** and **validity** may be considered less crucial in the development or choosing of a placement test than in **high stakes** tests where outcomes are serious and irreversible (**selection** or **screening tests**, for example).

Placement tests often serve a double function of both placement and **diagnosis**. Where this is the case, teachers are able to use the information provided by the test on individual students to inform their course planning.

platokurtic distribution

See **kurtosis**

point–biserial correlation

A variation of the **Pearson product–moment correlation** used to relate two **variables**, one of which is continuous (such as **scores** on a test) and the other binary or dichotomous (such as pass/fail or male/female or native speaker/non-native speaker). In **classical test analysis** the point–biserial is used to measure **item discrimination** by relating (binary) item responses and total test scores.

Point–biserial correlation coefficients of 0.25 and above are considered to be acceptable, although magnitude will change according to the **sample** size and **ability** range.

See also: **biserial correlation**
Further reading: Henning 1987

polychotomous, polytomous

See **partial credit**

population

Also target population
The largest class of people to which the results of an investigation based on a **sample** can be generalised. The population will vary in type and breadth according to the characteristics to be studied. Thus, if we are interested in the **vocabulary** size of 11-year-old children in the UK, the population would be all children of this age within that country. Information on the **variable** of interest is gathered by testing a representative sample of this population, and the results (in this case the **mean** vocabulary size) can then be considered to be an estimate of the mean vocabulary size of the whole population, in other words it can be generalised to the whole population.

See also: **sampling, sampling error**
Further reading: Woods *et al.* 1986

portfolio

A collection of **texts** produced by a writer over a period of time. As well as final products, such as final versions of essays, it may include drafts and other process data such as comments from teachers and peers and working notes. Thus portfolios can show growth as well as **proficiency**.

In providing a range of **samples** obtained under different conditions and at different stages of completion, portfolios are intended to give the reader a more complex view of the writer than can be obtained from an **examination** result or a single final product of writing, and hence may be considered to be a more **valid** representation of the student's proficiency.

One drawback of **portfolio assessment** is that it is both subjective and time-consuming. **Assessment** which looks at the development of a piece of work, the end product and the writer's growth over time is necessarily complex. The lack of commonly accepted **criteria** and the training of assessors are two aspects of portfolio assessment which remain to be addressed.

A further problem is the difficulty of comparison across writers due to the variability of the **tasks**.

Further reading: Belanoff & Dickson 1990; Black & Daiker 1994

portfolio assessment

A technique for the collection and qualitative evaluation of student writing.
See also: **portfolio**
Further reading: Black & Daiker 1994; Hamp-Lyons & Condon 1998

positively skewed distribution

See **skewed distribution**

post-test

See **pre-test post-test design**

power test

One which is designed to measure levels of **ability**, in contrast to a **speed test** which is designed to measure rate of **performance**. In a power test sufficient time is allowed for all **candidates** to attempt all the **items**, but the items are so steeply graded in **difficulty** that no candidate will be able to answer all items correctly.

Ideally, both speed and power tests should be designed so that no candidate is able to answer all items correctly, as perfect **scores** are indeterminate (it is impossible to know how much higher a candidate's ability is than that of a candidate with an almost perfect score).

In practice the distinction between speeded and power tests is one of degree only, most tests having both power and speeded features. Even so, determining the proportion of each is important, as different statistical analyses are required to determine the **reliability** of speeded tests, procedures such as **split-half** and **Kuder-Richardson** being inappropriate.

Further reading: Anastasi 1990

practicality

Often quoted as the third consideration in test design, the first two being
validity and **reliability**, its inclusion as a major concern stems from the
recognition that however valid and reliable a test may be, if it is not practical
to administer it in a specific context then it will not be taken up in that context.
The term practicality covers a range of issues, such as the cost of development
and maintenance, **test length**, ease of marking, time required to administer the
test (individual or group **administration**), ease of administration (including
availability of suitable **interviewers** and **raters**, availability of appropriate
room or rooms) and equipment required (computers, language laboratory, etc.).
Further reading: Davies 1991; Alderson *et al.* 1995

practice effect

The fact that taking two tests with the same or similar content may result in a
higher **score** on the second test, despite there being no increase in **ability** in
the **skill** being measured. The practice effect reduces the **validity** of the test
by contributing to the **error of measurement**, and the more **speeded** the test,
the more serious the practice effect is likely to be.

The practice effect is potentially problematic in research studies with a
pre-test post-test design, and must be taken into account when interpreting
findings. It also poses a problem for **test-retest reliability** studies.

Where **parallel forms** of a test are available and where candidates are
likely to take the test more than once, the practice effect must be considered
in the writing of **test items**.
See also: **test method effect, test wiseness**

pragmatic competence

A component of **communicative language ability** which incorporates both
knowledge of the resources and conventions for performing acceptable
language functions and knowledge of the sociolinguistic conventions relevant
to those functions.
See also: **linguistic competence, sociolinguistic competence, strategic
competence, grammatical competence**
Further reading: Bachman 1990

pragmatic expectancy grammar

A theory developed by Oller in the 1970s to characterise the 'pragmatic
mapping' of **text** or discourse onto facts or experience known in some other

manner (the extralinguistic context). Such mapping is claimed by Oller to be a necessary and sufficient condition for language comprehension; in order to understand a text, the reader/listener must be able to map it onto her own personal experience.

A language test is **valid**, Oller argues, when it meets two naturalness constraints:

- the learner must be required to process sequences of language that conform to normal contextual constraints (linguistic and extralinguistic); and
- the learner must be required to understand the pragmatic interrelationship of linguistic and extralinguistic contexts.

Tests which demonstrate these features are termed **pragmatic tests**.

Further reading: Oller 1979

pragmatic test

A sub-set of **integrative tests**, pragmatic tests are defined by Oller as meeting two naturalness constraints:

- they must require the pragmatic mapping of sequences of elements of discourse onto the extralinguistic context; and
- they must press the **examinee** to do this under normal contextual constraints.

See also: **pragmatic expectancy grammar**
Further reading: Oller 1990

predictive validity

Measures how well a test predicts **performance** on an external **criterion.** Since the main purpose of a test is to provide information about likely behaviour in the **real world**, prediction of criterion performance is basic to test **validation**. For example, a test of **English for academic purposes** is said to have high predictive validity if performance on the test correlates highly with performance (eg as measured by **grades**) on a subsequent academic course which is taught through the language under test.

Predictive validity assumes particular importance in **proficiency** testing where the criterion may be so distant or vague that the test itself, by means of **construct validity**, may have to combine the roles of both **predictor** and criterion.

See also: **validity**
Further reading: Messick 1988

predictor

1. A test used to predict a **criterion** and therefore often a new test which has been designed in order to make more efficient decisions on likely outcomes in eg selection. Many **proficiency** tests are used as predictors of candidates' potential success in future employment, study, etc.

2. A measure (often a test) used in experiments as an **independent variable** which it is hypothesised will have an effect on the **dependent variable**, ie the criterion.

See also: **variable**

Preliminary English Test (PET)

PET was introduced by **UCLES** in 1981. It is based on the **Council of Europe**'s Threshold specification and was revised to bring it into line with *Threshold 1990*. PET tests the **skills** which are needed to survive in social and work situations in an English-speaking environment. PET is part of a coherent suite of UCLES examinations in English as a Foreign Language, which, in addition to the PET, include the **Key English Test**, the **First Certificate in English**, the **Certificate in Advanced English**, the **Certificate of Proficiency in English**, the Cambridge Examination in English for Language Teachers and several examinations in English for business. The present components of the PET are Reading, Writing and Listening papers, as well as a Speaking test. Each paper is equally weighted in order to determine the score, carrying 25% of the total marks.

pre-test

1. *Also* **pilot test**
Refers to various stages of piloting and **trialling** that occur during test development, before operational administrations of a test. Writers vary in their use of the term: some intend it to refer only to informal trialling on relatively small numbers of subjects, while for others, it embraces all forms and stages of trialling. Tests (especially those with serious consequences for **test takers**) tend to undergo various stages of trialling, moving generally from less formal (often in-house) review and trialling to more formal trials on subjects selected to represent the **target test population**.

The general purpose of pre-testing or pilot testing is to identify problems with **test content**, **test rubric**, rating procedures or other aspects of the testing procedure so that they may be removed. Analysis of **test content** by experts is also typically conducted during these stages, if considered desirable or necessary.

2. Refers to the first of two **test administrations** intended to measure change over time (**pre-test post-test design**).

See also: **operationalise, reliability, content analysis**
Further reading: Alderson *et al.* 1995

pre-test post-test design

1. Research in **Applied Linguistics** is often concerned with changes in language **proficiency** over time. In order to measure the extent of change, **parallel tests** are administered at the beginning and end of the research period (often a period of instruction). Ideally, half the students take form A and half form B as the **pre-test**, and this is reversed for the **post-test**. It is possible that a **practice effect** may influence outcomes on the post-test, especially where a short period of time between the two tests is involved, or that the content of the pre-test may alert students to the interests of the researcher and hence influence their learning.

2. Students are often pre-tested at the beginning of a course in order to obtain information about their language proficiency for the purposes of course design.

See also: **test-retest, Hawthorne effect**
Further reading: Hatch & Lazaraton 1991; Henning 1987

primary trait scoring

Involves the **scoring** of a piece of work (usually writing) in relation to one principal **trait** specific to that **task**. It is based on the view that a piece of work must be judged in relation to its specific purpose and context. The **criteria** used in primary trait scoring are limited to that particular task and **assessment** is not generalisable to other types of task. For example, where learners are required to write an academic essay, the trait to be assessed might be the extent to which they demonstrate the **ability** to incorporate specific prior reading into their writing. Given their lack of generalisability, and the detailed scoring guides that they require, such **assessments** are most common in relation to a course of teaching where information is sought on learners' **mastery** of specific writing **skills**.

See also: **holistic assessment, analytic scoring**
Further reading: Hamp-Lyons 1991, Ch. 14

probabilistic model

A **measurement** model in which change in one **variable** increases the probability of change in another variable. A probabilistic model may be contrasted with a deterministic one, in which behaviour is determined rather than predicted. In language testing, a deterministic model would be one in which a person's probability of success would be 0 or 1 depending whether their **ability** is greater or less than the **difficulty** of the **item**, in other words, there is a deterministic relationship. In a probabilistic model, on the other hand, **candidates'** chances of getting an item right will increase or decrease depending on how close they are in ability to the difficulty of the item. In terms of language testing, this is clearly a more reasonable assumption to make. **Item response theory** uses a probabilistic model as its basis.

See also: **stochastic**
Further reading: Vogt 1993; Wright & Masters 1982

probability theory

A theory which allows for the calculation of the probability of a particular event happening given particular circumstances.

See also: **significance test(ing)**

production test

A test of the **productive skills** of speaking and writing.

See also: **skills**

productive skills

The language **skills** of speaking and writing. The productive skills are directly observable in the test **performance**, in contrast with the **receptive skills** of reading and listening, and are normally assessed subjectively according to those **criteria** which are considered important for the purposes of the test.

It is often not possible to separate clearly the productive skills from the receptive in interpreting test performance; **writing tests** and **speaking tests** often depend upon the **candidates' comprehension** of spoken or written instruction or other **prompts**. This may be a source of **measurement error**.

Tests of the productive skills are sometimes referred to broadly as **performance tests**, although for some testers this term is limited to tests which relate to specific target language use contexts.

See also: **skills**

product–moment correlation

See **Pearson product–moment correlation**

proficiency

There are three main uses of the term **proficiency**.

1. A general type of **knowledge** of or **competence** in the use of a language, regardless of how, where or under what conditions it has been acquired;

2. Ability to do something specific in the language, for example proficiency in English to study in higher education in the UK, proficiency to work as a foreign language teacher of a particular language in the United States, proficiency in Japanese to act as a tour guide in Australia.

3. Performance as measured by a particular testing procedure. Some of these procedures are so widely used that **levels** of performance on them (eg 'superior', 'intermediate', 'novice' on the **FSI scales**) have become common currency in particular circles as indicators of language proficiency.

In its more portmanteau sense of general language ability, proficiency was widely used in the 1970s and early 1980s under the label **general language proficiency**, synonymously with **unitary competence hypothesis**. Proficiency has since come to be regarded as multifaceted, with recent models specifying the nature of its component parts and their relationship to one another. There is now considerable overlap between the notion of language proficiency and the term **communicative competence**.

Debates about the nature of language proficiency have influenced the design of language tests and language testing research has been used in the **validation** of various models of language proficiency.

See also: **proficiency scale, proficiency test, construct validity**

proficiency scale

Also **rating scale**

A **scale** for the description of language **proficiency** consisting of a series of constructed **levels** against which a language learner's **performance** is judged. Like a test, a proficiency (rating) scale provides an **operational definition** of a linguistic **construct** such as proficiency. Typically such scales range from zero mastery through to an end-point representing the well-educated native speaker. The levels or **bands** are commonly characterised in terms of what subjects can do with the language (**tasks** and functions which can be performed) and their mastery of linguistic features (such as **vocabulary**, syntax, **fluency** and **cohesion**). Proficiency scales typically consist of sub-scales for the **skills** of speaking, reading, writing and listening. Perhaps the most widely known of such scales is the **ACTFL/IFL** scale. Scales are descriptions of groups of typically occurring behaviours; they are not in themselves test instruments and need to be used in conjunction with tests appropriate to the test **population** and **test purpose**. **Raters** or judges are normally trained in the use of proficiency scales so as to ensure the measure's **reliability**.

See also: **profile, rate, production tests**
Further reading: Bachman 1990; Brindley 1998

proficiency test

A test which measures how much of a language someone has learned. Unlike an **achievement test**, a **proficiency** test is not based on a particular course of instruction. A proficiency test often measures what the **candidate** has learned relative to a specific **real world** purpose, for example, does he/she know enough of the **target language** to follow a lecture, train as an engineer or work as a ski instructor in that medium, or to translate to the requisite standard out of that language. Some proficiency tests have been **standardised** for worldwide use, such as the American **TOEFL** test which is used to measure the English language proficiency of foreign college students who wish to study in the USA; or the British–Australian **IELTS** test designed for those who wish to study in the UK or Australia. In spite of their worldwide standardisation, proficiency tests normally have a particular situation in mind. TOEFL is primarily relevant to those who wish to study in the USA and its use of American English is therefore justifiable.

Established proficiency tests such as the TOEFL or the **Cambridge examinations** tend to generate a **washback** effect on instruction (preparatory courses and textbooks which are oriented towards the test) and hence come more and more to be used as achievement tests. This achievement-proficiency dynamic rightly leads to new proficiency tests being designed.

Further reading: Davies 1991

profile

1. A means of recording the outcomes of education for a particular student. Profiles take the form of a comprehensive statement referring to the range of the pupil's educational experience, **competencies** and interests. Such schemes are becoming increasingly widely used in school contexts to supplement **examination** results and are seen as directing attention to those aspects of student development and learning which the **examination** system is not able to address (such as personal, social and intellectual qualities). The descriptive information which they offer may be seen as more 'user-friendly' than the **reporting** of **grades** or **scores**, providing prospective employers, for example, with information relevant to their selection procedures.

2. The information given about a language learner in terms of her **performance** across a range of **skills**. Most language learners have a marked profile, ie they perform better in some skills than in others, rather than a flat profile which indicates no noticeable strengths or weaknesses. Some tests, such as **IELTS**, and most **proficiency scales**, provide information on learners in terms of a **candidate** profile; scores for each skill or **sub-test** are reported separately. Such information may be useful for **diagnostic** purposes.

See also: **profiling**

Further reading: Kant & Orr 1990; Griffin & Nix 1991; Hamp-Lyons 1991b

profiling

A means of reporting educational outcomes in the form of comprehensive **level** statements. These statements describe the learners' **achievements**, attributes or **performance** in relation to specified **criteria** or **competencies**. In **reporting** language **proficiency**, profiles generally address the **macro-skills** of reading, writing, speaking and listening separately, and within each of these may focus on specific purposes or types of communication. Profiles may also include information other than that on proficiency, eg on learner background, attitudes, intellectual and cognitive qualities, personal qualities (such as diligence or creativity) and interests.

Such learner profiles serve a number of purposes, especially reporting to parents and informing other teachers. Profiles are not a method of **assessment** so much as a method of reporting, and are generally the result of systematic and continuous **criterion**-based monitoring of learners, rather than being based on **test results** (although test performance may be used as well). They may also form the basis for **curriculum** planning. Profiles may be formative or summative.

Further reading: Griffin & Nix 1991

program(me) evaluation

See **language programme evaluation**

progress test

A test intended to measure the progress that students are making towards defined goals. As such tests are commonly intended to measure progress during a course, their content is generally related to the course objectives, and are likely to be narrower or more detailed in focus than in an end-of-course **achievement test**. While such tests are generally teacher-made, many course books include progress tests to be administered on a regular basis.

prompt

Material provided to test **candidates** which is designed to stimulate a **response** (such as a piece of writing or oral production). A prompt may consist of a set of instructions and a **text**, a title, a picture or a set of pictures, diagram, table, chart or other data, and may be presented orally or in graphic form. The information provided on the purpose of the response or the intended audience may also be considered to be part of the prompt, although this is more properly termed test rubric.

See also: **stimulus, test rubric**

pronunciation

In language testing, a component of oral **language ability** which is commonly used as one of several **assessment criteria** in **oral proficiency interviews**. Pronunciation may also be one aspect of a broader **category** of production which also includes stress and intonation, or it may be subsumed within an even more general category of **intelligibility**. A problem inherent in the assessment of pronunciation is the choice of linguistic **norm** against which to **judge** the learners.

The **validity** of pronunciation as an **assessment** category is somewhat problematic. It has been claimed that pronunciation is a salient feature of language ability only when it impedes intelligibility. A **candidate's level** of **skill** in pronunciation is often found to be at odds with her demonstrated ability in other aspects of production.

See also: **holistic assessment**

protocol

A method of eliciting data from subjects for research purposes, which usually involves subjects talking or thinking aloud during or shortly after completing an activity, such as a test.

See also: **test-taker feedback**
Further reading: Ericsson & Simon 1993; Smagorinsky 1995; Weigle 1994

psychometrics

The **measurement** of psychological **traits** such as intelligence or language **ability**. In addition to deciding about **item types** and **test content**, the test developer needs to consider the psychometric or measurement properties of the **test items**, such as the **level** and range of **item difficulty** and **discrimination**. This information will typically be gathered during the **trialling** stage of test development, and decisions about the desired psychometric qualities of items will depend on the intended use of the test and interpretation of test **scores**.

Psychometrics provides a framework for the development and **evaluation** of tests. It is based on the assumptions of **normal distribution** and of maximising the distinction between **candidates**. Psychometric tests have properties such as **objective scoring**, and are evaluated according to an established set of methods. The **multiple-choice test** is probably the best known of such tests, although all **norm-referenced tests** are generally based on psychometric principles.

See also: **nominal scales**, **ordinal scales**, **interval scales**

Further reading: Cronbach 1964; Millman & Greene 1993

q

qualitative data

Data that are not in a numerical form, for example, open-ended questionnaire or **interview** data. It is often possible to transform qualitative data into numerical form.

See also: **test-taker feedback**

Further reading: Miles & Hubermann 1994

quantification

The assigning of numbers, as opposed to letter **grades**, rankings or descriptive statements, to subjects' **performances**. Only where numbers are used can they be considered to be measures rather than qualitative descriptions.

quantitative data

Data that are in numerical form, obtained through counting and **measurement**, for example test **scores** or data from fixed response questionnaires.

question

The term **question** is commonly used to refer to any **test item**, regardless of the form it takes (which may be in the form of instructions about what to do, a statement with which to agree or disagree, and so on).

r

random error

Also **unsystematic error**

An **error of measurement** or observation which is not clearly attributable to any specific cause and therefore cannot be controlled for.

While the purpose of any experiment is to determine what effect an **independent variable** has on the **dependent variable**, the dependent variable is always affected by other intervening **variables** which may be difficult to identify with any degree of certainty.

For example, if we are interested in determining the effect of different types of language instruction on test **performance** it will be possible to control for amount and type of language contact with native speakers outside the classroom. Differences in amount and quality of **target language** exposure outside the classroom could well affect growth in **proficiency** and such differences contribute random errors to the experiment. Other sources of random error might relate to the condition of **candidates** while taking the language test (eg fatigue, anxiety, illness) or factors in the test environment which may affect the performance of individual candidates (eg a leaking pen, an uncomfortable chair, a bumpy writing surface, bad lighting).

Random errors are generally considered to be normally distributed. They vary in direction (positive/negative) and magnitude from observation to observation and tend ultimately to average to zero. Unlike **systematic errors**, random errors are also assumed to be uncorrelated both with **true scores** and with each other.

Since random errors, by their nature, can never be completely eliminated it is common practice in **inferential statistics** to set a significance level high enough to absorb them. This avoids the possibility of changes in the dependent variable being mistakenly attributed to the independent variable (rather than to fluctuations caused by other random effects).

See also: **standard error of measurement, measurement error, error variance, reliability, bias, Type 1 error, Type 2 error**

Further reading: Robson 1973; Ferguson 1981; Cohen *et al.* 1992

random sampling

An orderly method of selection of members from a **population** in order to provide an unbiased cross section. A common procedure is to select every *n*th (eg tenth) member. The criteria are:

- every member of the population has an equal chance of being chosen in the **sample**;
- the choice of any one member does not influence the choice of any other.

Random sampling works best when all members of the population are available and listed in what is called a 'sampling frame', for example, drawing a hand from a deck of cards or drawing out of a hat slips with the names of say, six children from a class of 30. In larger populations such as those used in **language surveys**, random sampling can be difficult, especially when access to every member by the experimenter is not equal. Even so random sampling remains the most unbiased form of sampling.

See also: **sampling, sampling error**

Further reading: Butler 1985

Rasch analysis

Also Rasch measurement, Rasch modelling

A branch of **item response theory**, the one-parameter model, developed by the Danish psychometrician Georg Rasch and popularised by Ben Wright in Chicago. Rasch's Basic model was restricted to the analysis of **dichotomously scored** data, for example from **multiple-choice tests**. Further developments made possible the analysis of data from **rating scales** (the so-called Rating Scale model of Andrich and the **partial credit** model of Masters). Linacre's Extended model allows analysis of other **facets** of the **assessment** setting, for example, the impact of the characteristics of **raters**, in **multi-faceted Rasch measurement**. Rasch analysis has been controversial in its assumptions, although its flexibility in handling data from **performance** assessments has proved attractive.

See also: **one-parameter model**

Further reading: Wright & Stone 1979; Wright & Masters 1982; Linacre 1989; McNamara 1996

rate

Also **assess, score, judge**

To exercise judgement about a **performance**. Rating is a subjective activity, and particularly when there are serious consequences for the **test taker**, issues of **reliability** and **validity** need to be addressed.

See also: **subjective scoring, performance, assessment, rater, rating scale**

rater

Also **judge**, **marker**, **scorer**
The judge or observer who operates a **rating scale** in the **measurement** of **oral** and **written proficiency**. The **reliability** of raters depends in part on the quality of their training, the purpose of which is to ensure a high degree of comparability, both inter- and intra-rater. Since raters are human and are therefore subject to individual **biases**, close attention is paid not only to reliability, but also to analyses of rater bias.

Also used as a more general term for an **evaluation** of an individual on the basis of cumulative, uncontrolled observations of everyday life.

See also: **inter-rater reliability**, **intra-rater reliability**, **multi-faceted Rasch measurement**
Further reading: Anastasi 1990

rater training

The preparation of **raters** for their task of judging **performances**. The training often takes the form of a workshop in which raters are introduced to the **test format** and **test tasks** and the rating **criteria**, and exemplar performances at each defined **level** of performance are presented and discussed. Raters are then asked to evaluate a series of performances and to compare their ratings, discussing the grounds for any differences between them. Subsequent to the workshop raters may be asked to rate a further set of performances, and only those raters reaching a predetermined level of conformity with the generally agreed ratings of the performances in question (for example, where ratings deviate only by a single **score** level) are certified as raters. Studies of the effect of rater training show that training reduces extreme differences in **severity** between raters and makes raters more internally self-consistent, but that significant differences in severity between raters remain; further, that rater characteristics (relative severity, self-consistency) vary over time. Where important outcomes for the **candidate** depend on the test score (for example, admission to higher education, or to the workplace), differences between raters can be compensated for (for example, by double rating, or through statistical adjustment as in **multi-faceted Rasch measurement**).

See also: **inter-rater reliability**, **intra-rater reliability**
Further reading: Weigle 1994; McNamara 1996

rating scale

See **proficiency scale**

ratio scale

A scale or **level** of **measurement** in which adjoining values are the same distance apart, like the **interval scale**, but also with a true zero point. Used to measure physical characteristics (eg height) and therefore unlikely to be used in language testing where characteristics are typically constructed rather than given (eg **proficiency**).

See also: **nominal scale, ordinal scale, scale**
Further reading: Hatch & Lazaraton 1991

rational cloze

A type of **cloze** procedure whereby items for deletion are selected on some non-random basis such as membership of a linguistic category and then **candidates** invited to fill each gap with an appropriate word. For example, all the definite articles in a passage or all the modal verbs may be deleted. The difficulty of a rational cloze test is closely related to the linguistic category deleted. For example, deleted nouns are very hard to recover because noun choice is dependent on extra-textual factors. For this reason the acceptable word method of **scoring** is more appropriate than the verbatim (exact) word scoring method with rational cloze. Since the cloze procedure proper attempts to tap linguistic redundancy by the use of random deletion, rational cloze might more appropriately be called selective deletion gap filling. As such, rational cloze is probably more relevant to research in language testing than to the development of **language proficiency** and reading tests.

See also: **cloze test, c-test, clozentropy**
Further reading: Weir 1988

rational equivalence

A method of estimating test **reliability** which is based on the intercorrelations of the **items** in a test and their **correlations** with the test as a whole. **Kuder-Richardson formulae** use the method of rational equivalence which, like **split-half reliability**, provides an estimate of the **internal consistency** of the test. Rational equivalence and split-half techniques produce very similar results.

rational validity

See **content validity**

raw scores

Test data in their original format, not yet transformed statistically in any way (eg by conversion into percentages, or by adjusting for **level** of **difficulty** of **task** or any other contextual factor). **Scores** by **item** (such as right/wrong for that particular item) are the most 'raw' form of test data and are the appropriate object of most data handling because they contain information at a greater level of detail. For example, two **candidates** each of whom got 50 items right may have got different individual items correct. It is important not to lose access to this primary level of data if statistical analysis of data is to be attempted; analysis is more usually done of such data in test analysis than of total scores or scores transformed in other ways.

See also: **scale**, **logit**

readability

The degree to which a given group of people find certain reading matter comprehensible. Readability formulae are the most widely used method for predicting **text** difficulty. Most of those in current use are based on only two factors, **vocabulary** (frequency or length) and syntax (average sentence length). Attempts have been made to take account of important aspects of text **difficulty** such as interest, compellingness, legibility (including type face), conceptual load, organisation. These attempts have not been altogether successful, largely because of the problem of **valid measurement** of such factors. Among well-known readability formulas are the Dale-Chall, Bormuth, Fry and Gunning-Fog.

In spite of their limitations, readability formulas give a crude approximation to text difficulty and are reported to have **correlations** with one another. They are also fairly easy to compute.

However, in spite of their aim to assess comprehensibility (that is reader **comprehension**), what readability measures actually assess is relative difficulty among texts. It is to their failure to assess comprehensibility that we owe the development of the **cloze** procedure.

In language testing, readability formulas are useful in the selection of appropriate reading comprehension texts.

See also: **lexical density**, **type-token ratio**
Further reading: Cohen 1976; Gilliland 1972

reading comprehension test

A measure of understanding of **text**. Traditionally used in language testing (as in education generally), no doubt because of the social importance of literacy and because reading comprehension tests are considered more reliable (because objective) than are **speaking tests**. Traditional reading comprehension tests present a text as **stimulus** and a series of **multiple-choice test items** to measure understanding. The text in such a test is short, perhaps 300 words.

However, current thinking about language and reading raises two serious queries about reading comprehension tests of the traditional type. First, genre and language variety studies suggest that reading is always context based and that generalisation about reading ability from one type of text to another is improper. Second, post structuralism questions the naive assumption that there is one agreed understanding of a text. These influences have helped extend the range of reading comprehension tests into content specific texts, often using several related texts as stimuli. The methodology has also been broadened into an emphasis on open ended test items and **cloze tests**.

See also: **listening comprehension test, writing test**
Further reading: Clapham 1996

real life

An approach to describing language proficiency in which no definition of **language proficiency** is attempted. Instead, a **domain** of real-life language use which is considered to be characteristic of the performance of competent language users is identified. In language testing the major use of this 'real-life' approach has been in the **ILR Oral Proficiency Interview** and its derivatives. At each defined point of the interview **scale** a description is provided of what is considered real-life behaviour. Furthermore, because of the nature of the **interview**, the normal features of real-life encounters, such as the contextual features and the language features, are reckoned to be present.

See also: **direct test, indirect test**
Further reading: Bachman 1990

receptive skills

The language skills of listening and reading. The receptive skills, unlike the **productive skills** of writing and speaking, cannot be directly observed in test **performance**, since the processes of comprehending take place within the mind. For this reason, **test takers** are often required to produce some kind of written or spoken language to demonstrate **comprehension**.

See also: **skill**

receptive test

A test of the **receptive skills** of reading and listening.

See also: **productive skills**, **listening comprehension**, **reading comprehension**

reference group

Also **base group**

A term used in **DIF** or **bias** studies to describe the group of **test takers** (usually the majority) whose **performance** is used as a basis for comparison with a given **focal group** (usually a minority). The group that provides the most stable estimates of **ability** across the **score** range is generally the one selected as the reference group.

Further reading: Holland & Wainer 1993

register

A way of referring to an institutionalised language variety. Registers are linguistically distinct varieties in which the language is systematically determined by the context. A distinction has been suggested between variety determined by language use (that is register, for example military language) and variety determined by speaker, commonly referred to as dialect or accent (for example Tyneside English, Parisian French).

Attempts to describe discrete registers, such as the register of legal English or of radio sports announcers or of geography textbooks, have proved to be problematic because of the indeterminacy of the boundary between, for example, geography and geology textbooks and therefore the difficulty of making systematic linguistic distinctions.

Some authors use the terms **style** or genre instead of register, others use style for individual language use and genre for **text** type.

Register is relevant in language testing with regard to questions of testing **languages for specific purposes** (LSP).

See also: **domain**, **LSP testing**

Further reading: Halliday, McIntosh & Strevens 1964; Swales 1990; Ghadessy 1993

regression

Also **linear regression**

A statistical technique which calculates the relationship between two or more **variables** and hence allows predictions to be made about **performance** on one variable on the basis of information about performance on another.

Simple regression involves the use of a single variable to predict **scores** on an outcome measure (see example 1 below). Multiple regression (see example 2 below) is concerned with the contribution of a number of independent variables to **performance** on the dependent variable. The **coefficient** for any single variable against the outcome measure is an estimate of the effect of that variable while holding constant the effects of other predictor variables.

In language testing, regression analyses are typically used to answer questions such as the following:

- **Example 1: Simple regression**
  *What is the average university **grade** that can be expected of a **candidate** with an entry **score** of, say, 550 on the **TOEFL**?*
  This kind of information is useful in making **selection** decisions.

- **Example 2: Multiple regression**
  *2A – How important is **accuracy** relative to other **assessment criteria** in determining overall performance on a test of speaking **proficiency**?*

  or

  *2B – Which combination of the following **sub-tests** (metalinguistic awareness, auditory discrimination, short-term memory, inductive reasoning) in an **aptitude test** battery makes the most accurate prediction of success in foreign language learning?*

  Answers to 2A and 2B may be useful in deciding on the **weighting** of assessment criteria or test components in relation to one another and may also contribute to understanding about the nature of language proficiency.

The term regression was first used by Karl Pearson and the calculations needed to obtain the regression coefficient are in fact analagous to those required for the calculation of **Pearson's r**.

The regression technique draws on three separate pieces of information:
- the score **mean** and **standard deviation** on the independent variable (X);
- the score mean and standard deviation on the dependent variable (Y);
- an estimate of the slope of the **regression line**.

See also: **path analysis**
Further reading: Hatch & Lazaraton 1991

regression line

The line of best fit through the pattern of points on a scatterplot mapping the **score** distributions of two **variables**. The best fitting straight line is the one that results in the smallest **mean** of the sum of the squared **errors**.

Below is a scatterplot showing the relationship between candidates' **scores** on the **TOEFL** test (X axis) and the average **grade** achieved by the same **candidates** on their subsequent university course (Y axis).

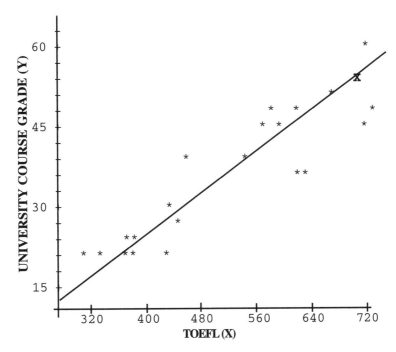

To estimate the most likely university grade of a candidate achieving a given score on the TOEFL we draw a vertical line from the relevant score point on the X axis to the regression line and from the point of intersection we draw a horizontal line across to the Y axis (as indicated in the above diagram). We thereby discover that a candidate with a score of, say, 640 is likely (give or take a certain amount of **error**) to achieve an average mark of 50 at the university. The distance between the point of best fit on the regression line (indicated in our example by a cross) and the candidate's actual score tells us the amount of error which can be expected in the estimate.

The simplest way of calculating the slope of the regression line is to multiply the **correlation coefficient** by the **standard deviation** of Y over the standard deviation of X as indicated in the following formula:

$$b = r_{xy} \times \frac{s_Y}{s_X}$$

where: b = estimate of slope
r = correlation coefficient
s = standard deviation

The estimate of the slope is essential for the calculation of the **regression** coefficient.

See also: **regression, residual**
Further reading: Hatch & Lazaraton 1991

reliability

Also **test reliability**

The actual level of agreement between the results of one test with itself or with another test. Such agreement, ideally, would be the same if there were no **measurement error**, which may arise from **bias** of **item** selection, from bias due to time of testing or from examiner bias.

These three major sources of bias may be addressed by corresponding methods of reliability estimate:

Source of Bias	Reliability Estimate
1. selection of specific items	a. **parallel forms**
	b. **split-half**
	c. **rational equivalence**
2. time of testing	**test-retest**
3. examiner bias	**inter-rater reliability** checks

Most reliability estimates of **objective tests** concern the first source, that of the selection of **test items** to test a more general **ability**. The three methods of estimating reliability associated with this source of measurement error are variations of the same method, which is to compare two versions of the same test. The split-half method assumes that one half of a test parallels the other half. To overcome logical problems of which halves to choose (which split to make) and at the same time to reduce testing time, it is usual to use the **rational equivalence** method which is reckoned to be an average of all possible split halves.

The second method of estimating reliability is not often used because of the difficulty of gaining access to the same group of subjects for repeat testing, in addition to the problem of interpreting the effect of learning on a repeat performance. The third method (using **correlations**) is relevant when nonobjective tests are being used (for example written compositions, spoken **interviews**).

The method used to estimate the effect of lengthening a test is known as the **Spearman-Brown Prophecy Formula**. This formula is also used to boost the split-half reliability index (which is for one half of the test) into an estimate for the full test (ie the two split halves together). Reliability for parallel forms, split-half and test-retest is normally quoted either as a **standard error of measurement** or as a **correlation coefficient**. For the rational equivalence method of establishing reliability, one of the **Kuder-Richardson formulas** or an **alpha coefficient** is used, and for inter-rater reliability (for subjective tests), it is usual to use correlations such as the alpha or the intra-class.

The discussion so far has been of estimating reliability according to **classical test theory.** Different methods are used in an **IRT** framework.

Three methods of improving reliability are available:

- standardising testing conditions; and
- lengthening the test;
- constructing better items since these are more likely to be responded to consistently.

It is common to say that reliability is a necessary but not a sufficient quality of a test. This third method of increasing reliability is an indication that reliability and **validity** are closely interlocked. While reliability focuses on the empirical aspects of the **measurement** process, validity focuses on the theoretical aspects and seeks to interweave these concepts with the empirical ones. For this reason it is easier to assess reliability than validity.

Further reading: Henning 1987

reported score

The score which is reported to test **candidates**. Reported scores may be **raw scores** or transformed scores. Raw scores may be transformed statistically in order that **performance** may be compared across different **test forms**, or they may be transformed to take account of other factors such as **task difficulty**, **rater harshness**, and so on.

See also: **standardised score**

reporting

The activity of informing **test users** (**candidates**, employers, admissions officers, etc.) about test results. The report may be in the form of **raw scores**, standardised scores, composite scores, **band** scores or scale descriptions.

See also: **reported score, scale**
Further reading: Alderson 1991

residual

The distance between the predicted value of a given **variable** as yielded by a **regression** analysis and the actual or observed value of that variable. For example when predicting university **grades** from a **candidate's TOEFL** entry **score** there is often a discrepancy (because of unforeseeable fluctuations in, say, the candidate's motivation or life circumstances) between what is predicted and what the candidate actually achieves.

The residual is thus an indication of the amount of **error** in an estimate. The sum of the squared residuals is used as an estimate of model fit. In a perfectly fitting (ie error free) model a **regression line** will pass exactly through the observed data points and all the residuals will have a value of zero. The larger the value of the residuals in a given data set, the greater will be the amount of **variance** in the model.

Regression analyses assume that the residuals have a **normal distribution** with a **mean** of zero and that the residual variance or **standard deviation** of the dependent variable about the regression line should be the same at all points of the line.

A few extreme residual values may sometimes have a disproportionate influence on the estimate of the slope of a regression line or on the value of a **sample correlation**. The possibility of such an effect can be investigated by plotting all the data points on a scattergram. It may be necessary to remove extreme **outliers** to improve the accuracy of prediction.

Analysis of residuals sometimes reveals sub-patterns within them that reduce the amount of unexplained variance in the data (in other words, what is assumed to be **random error** may be found to be systematic and its cause may therefore be identifiable). This approach is used by **generalisability theory** and by **bias** analysis in **Rasch analysis**.

Further reading: Woods *et al.* 1986

response

The answer produced by a **candidate** to the **input** from a **test item.** The candidate's expected response is usually characterised at the test design stage and elicited through instructions and some kind of **stimulus** and should be seen as one aspect of the **test method**.

A response on a language test may be the result of a choice between two or more alternatives which are provided on the test paper (as for example in **true/false** or **multiple-choice items**) or it may constructed by the candidates themselves (as in a **cloze** item where they are required to supply the appropriate word in a gapped text or an **essay** where they must produce an extended piece of writing).

Test responses differ from many other kinds of responses or reactions to stimuli in that they must be amenable to quantification or **scoring**. **Objectively**

scored responses are those for which there is a clear, undisputed answer; in other words, the responses are marked right or wrong according to a pre-specified answer **key**. **Subjectively scored** responses on the other hand rely on **judgements** from **raters** and their **reliability** must therefore be ascertained.

Analysis (whether quantitative or qualitative) of candidates' test responses is an important part of the test **validation** process, the purpose of which is to establish whether the actual behaviour matches what is expected, ie whether it gives adequate information about the **construct** of **ability** which the test purports to measure.

See also: **constructed response, forced-choice item**

response validity

The gathering of data regarding how test **candidates** tackle **test items**. Such data are typically gathered using introspective methodologies such as think-aloud protocols, and can provide useful **feedback** to test developers about what the test is actually testing and response patterns to particular items.

Further reading: Cohen 1984

results

See **test results**

retired test

Also retired form, retired version

A **test form** that is no longer live, or operational (and hence is no longer used for its original purpose); normally this implies that the test material was previously secure, and **test results** had important consequences for the **test taker**. For example, new forms of a test used to select university applicants might be developed every year. Once used, old forms of a test are sometimes put to other uses: a retired form of a **proficiency test** might then be published as practice material, or used for diagnostic or placement purposes, where **test security** is not a matter of concern; retired test forms are also sometimes used for research purposes.

See also: **consequential validity, operationalise**

role play

A task in a test of speaking **performance** in which the **test taker** adopts a specified role in an interaction with one or more additional speakers (for example, another test **candidate**, teacher or trained **interlocutor**). The roles and task are set out in instructions provided to the participants at or before the start of the test, and generally simulate **authentic** situations relevant to the communicative demands the test taker will face in **real life**. For example, in a test of English for doctors, the test taker might be required to assume the role of doctor, and the interlocutor the role of patient in discussing a management plan for the patient. The candidate's performance may be **rated** by one or more participants in the role play or may be recorded for subsequent rating.

Further reading: Weir 1993; Underhill 1987; McNamara 1996

Royal Society of Arts (RSA)
See **RSA**

RSA

The Royal Society of Arts, founded in London in 1754 as the Society for the encouragement of Arts, Manufactures and Commerce. Associated with the RSA is the RSA Examinations Board which has promoted general and vocational examinations since 1856. This body has been responsible for developments in language examinations such as the **Communicative Use of English as a Foreign Language Test**. RSA English language examinations are now jointly administered by RSA and the University of Cambridge Local Examinations Syndicate (**UCLES**).

rubric
See **test rubric**

rule

One of the three distinguishing features of **measurement**, the others being **quantification** and characteristics. By rule is meant the explicit nature of a measuring instrument such that the observation of an attribute (for example **proficiency**) and the consequent assignment of a numerical **score** must be replicable by other observers. There must be agreement among examiners on what is being measured and how to measure, in other words the measure (**test**, **rating scale**, **rank**) must be both **valid** and **reliable**.

See also: **inter-rater reliability**
Further reading: Bachman 1990

S

sample
See **sampling**

sampling

1. The process of choosing a subgroup to represent a larger group, or **population**, an important part of the process of **trialling** in the construction of **language tests**.

The reasons for working with a sample and not with the whole population are practical: the time and the resources are not available. In order to draw inferences through the use of **inferential statistics** of the extent to which sample results apply to the population as a whole, it is necessary to draw the sample carefully. If, for example we are interested in second language learners' communicative strategies, the population of all second language learners is so large and fluid that it is normal for the researcher to restrict the study to a smaller population (for example all first-year learners of English in the Singapore secondary school system).

The steps involved in sampling are:
- identifying the population;
- deciding how big the sample should be;
- choosing the sample.

In choosing the sample there are four major procedures to choose from:
- simple **random sampling**: every population member has an equal chance of being studied;
- stratified sampling (or cluster sampling): different types of randomisation within known population subgroups ensure coverage of all subgroups;
- incidental (also known as accidental sampling and purposive sampling): members of the target population who happen to be at hand are studied;
- systematic sampling: individuals are selected from a list (such as a list of voters) by writing down every *nth* name.

With regard to sample size, it is generally accepted that the **sampling error** decreases as the sample size increases. Since sampling error represents the difference between the sample **mean** and the population mean, the larger the sample the more it represents the population. Small samples require very clear results for any inference to the population to be drawn.

2. Choosing a selection of **tasks** from the **domain** of language under test. The test is then said to contain a sample of all the possible **items** and tasks that could be included. The adequacy of a sample may be assessed through **content validity**. But the inherent variability of language makes it difficult to ensure that the sample selected is adequate. Furthermore, our inadequate understanding of language needs, of language **skills** and of tasks and of their relative importance and frequency permits only an approximation to a representative sample. It is therefore important to support the results of content validity with other **validity** evidence eg from **predictive validity**.

Further reading: Woods *et al.* 1986; Bachman 1990

sampling error

Since any sample is designed to represent a **population**, it follows that if the sample is either insufficiently large or not well selected, there will be increased error in **inferences** made from that sample about the population.

There are two types of sampling error:

- Poor selection of sample subjects may lead to sampling **bias**, as in incidental or convenience **sampling** (relying on easily available subjects), instead of random, stratified or systematic sampling. For example, trial subjects for a test may not share important characteristics (such as language or educational background) with the **target test population**;
- **Random sampling** error results from chance differences (such as gender) in the members of the population included (or excluded) from the sample.

The main difference between these two types of sampling error is that random sampling error decreases as the sample size increases, whereas sampling **bias** may only be reduced if the sample selection procedures are improved.

See also: **trialling**
Further reading: Woods *et al.* 1986

scale(s)

1. A graded system of degrees. **Measurement** theory makes use of four kinds of scale. These are:

- **nominal**: different values are assigned to different categories (eg males=1; females=2);
- **ordinal**: individuals or objects are ranked on the basis of performance or possession of a trait;

- **interval**: an index (eg a test score) of that performance or **trait** is divided into intervals which are treated as being equal;
- **ratio**: a ratio scale (eg centimetres) starts at zero and has equal intervals.

There is a one-way relationship among these scales in that the more refined scales may be translated into the less refined: thus an interval scale may be translated into an ordinal scale; but not the other way round.

Language testing typically makes use of interval and ordinal scales.

2. The word also refers to a non-test approach to the **assessment** and **reporting** of language performance. Scales, also called **band** scales, **profile** bands, proficiency **levels** etc, use a series of increasing levels of language **ability** which may be from zero (or minimal) to educated native-speaker. The number of levels from lowest to highest varies and may be as few as 3 or as many as 11. It is common for there to be a description (or **descriptor**) of the ability expected at each level. Allocation to a level is made by a judge or **rater** in the case of written performance. In the rating of spoken performance the rater may be assisted by an **interlocutor**. The performance used for the judgement is normally elicited on a set **task** which may have been already calibrated for testing purposes.

Band scales do not represent an interval scale. It remains an open question as to whether they can be regarded as offering an ordinal or a nominal scale.

Scales are not in themselves strictly measuring devices but may be used (a) as a component of a testing procedure and (b) as a reporting method.

See also: **proficiency scale**

Further reading: Alderson 1991; Foreign Service Institute 1968; Ingram 1995

scaling

The act of putting measurements on a **scale** where **raw scores** are unavailable or unsatisfactory. Latent trait scaling is a particular and much used contemporary technique for the scaling of **abilities** of different kinds.

See also: **item response theory, Rasch analysis, stanine score, z score**

score

The numerical index indicating a **candidate**'s overall **performance** on some measure. The measure may be based on ratings, judgements, **grades**, number of **test items** correct, etc. However derived, all such measures may be converted into a score which is then assumed to form part of an equal **interval scale** and thus to be additive and divisible. Test scores are used for many types

of statistical test analysis, both **descriptive** and **inferential**.
    See also: **reporting**, **raw score**, **rate**

scorer
    See **rater**

scoring
The activity of awarding a **score** or **grade** to a language **performance**.

screening test
A test designed solely to screen out **candidates** who are to be rejected on a first-round selection (eg in a job application procedure) or those who may need special treatment (eg those with hearing disorders). Since the purpose of a screening test is to measure at the lower end of the group, it is usually very easy with a positively **skewed distribution**, tailing off to the left.
    See also: **gatekeeping test**

second language acquisition (SLA)
1. Refers in general to all types of learning of one or more languages additional to the first language or mother tongue. This sense of the term is all-encompassing, including both formal and informal types of language learning as well as foreign language learning.

2. In a more restricted sense, second language acquisition (SLA) refers to the academic field of research into the learning of second languages. While such academic studies range widely in scope it is increasingly the case that the term SLA research has become attached to a particular view of learning within one or other linguistic or psycholinguistic paradigm. Such studies are often closely associated with developmental studies of first language acquisition. Academic acceptance of the term is shown in journal titles, course labels and chair and department names.
    Attempts have been made to bring work in SLA and language testing together but so far without much success. This may be because of the different orientations to learning of the two fields: SLA being more concerned with suppliance (ie first occurrence of a linguistic feature), language testing more with **mastery** (ie consistent control over that feature).
    Further Reading: Ellis 1985; Bachman & Cohen 1998; *Studies in Second Language Acquisition* (4 x year)

selected response
See **forced-choice item**

selection test
See **gatekeeping test**

self-assessment

Also known as self-evaluation, self-rating, self-testing, and self-appraisal. An approach to **assessment** which involves learners in making judgements about their own **level** and/or progress. Moral reasons (eg the sharing of power between teacher and learner) as well as motivational ones (eg the excitement of self-discovery) are often used to justify self-assessment practices against the accusation of lack of **reliability**. There is well-documented research into ways of improving both **validity** and reliability in self-assessment. In language testing self-assessment has made less headway than elsewhere, no doubt because of the lack of authoritative **criteria** and because of the disagreement among expert native speakers as to what constitutes acceptable language behaviour. A wide range of self-assessment techniques is available, ranging from self-marked **standardised tests** to questionnaires and descriptive/reflective procedures probing affective gains in confidence and **motivation**. Self-assessment is part of the current movement towards the individualisation of language assessment.

Further Reading: Brindley 1989; de Jong & Stevenson 1990; Oskarsson 1984

semantic differential

A technique originally developed by Charles E. Osgood and colleagues as part of their qualitative study of meaning. It consists of an unspecified number of seven-point **rating scales** that are bipolar, with each extreme defined by an adjective: examples might be wise/foolish, strong/weak, excitable/calm, The **candidate** is given a set of such scales and the task is to rate each of a number of objects or concepts on every scale in turn. It is possible to submit sets of such ratings to **factor analysis**, in a search for the basic determinants of meaning.

In studies of language attitudes, both to language speakers and to languages themselves, the method of the semantic differential has been widely used, notably with the matched guise technique. In such studies, ratings on bipolar scales such as intelligent/unintelligent, competent/incompetent, kind/unkind are invited. While speakers of language varieties provide the

stimulus for the ratings, the purpose is of course to explore attitudes to the language varieties themselves.

A similar scale technique is widely used in subjective oral assessments.

See also: **Likert Scale**

Further reading: Fasold 1984; Osgood *et al.* 1957

semi-direct test

A test of the spoken language in which for practical and **reliability** reasons the **stimulus** is pre-recorded or **text** based, and the **response** by the **candidate** is recorded for distance **rating**. Hence also the terms 'tape-based' or 'tape-mediated' test. Research in the field of language testing is currently inconclusive on the degree of comparability between semi-direct and direct tests of the spoken language. The best known example of the semi-direct test is the **Simulated Oral Proficiency Interview** (SOPI) which is used as an alternative to the **Oral Proficiency Interview** (OPI).

See also: **direct test, indirect test**

Further Reading: Clark 1979; O'Loughlin 1997; Shohamy 1994

severity

Also **harshness**

A facet of **rater** behaviour: the attitude shown by a rater towards a **performance** by a **test taker**. Some raters may be consistently generous (lenient), always giving relatively high **scores** to test takers; others may be consistently harsh (severe), giving relatively low scores; alternatively, raters may show **bias** towards or against particular groups of test takers. Differences in severity between individual raters will increase the **error** associated with test scores and hence reduce their **reliability**. However, differences in severity may be masked in inter-rater reliability studies which only take account of score **correlations**.

Some statistical approaches to **test analysis** (eg **multi-faceted Rasch measurement**) can provide estimates of the level of severity in each **judge**, and include this in the calculation used to estimate test-taker **ability**.

See also: **performance test, inter-rater reliability**

short-answer question

A form of **test item** used in **comprehension** tests which requires **test takers** to formulate their own answers. One purpose for using such items is to avoid providing the correct answer (or interpretation) for the test taker, as in

multiple-choice items, in which case **guessing** may be a factor. Short-answer questions are also normally easier to write than multiple-choice items. Wrong answers to short-answer questions are sometimes used (eg at the piloting stage of test development) as the basis for **distractors** for multiple-choice items. Short-answer questions most commonly require written answers which vary in length between one word and one or two sentences, but spoken responses are sometimes required. The length of answer required may also be specified in the instructions.

A short-answer question may allow for only one possible answer (unique answer), eg:

Q: Which part of the tree is eaten by the beetle?
A: The bark.

Alternatively, a range of answers may be acceptable, eg:

Q: Give two reasons why the trees are dying.

Because short-answer responses may be **subjectively scored**, a comprehensive **marking scheme** (including acceptable alternative answers) is generally needed, to ensure adequate **reliability**. It may also be necessary to include instructions to **scorers** about how to **judge** answers with grammatical or spelling **errors**.

See also: **constructed-response item, open-ended question, forced-choice item**

Further reading: Weir 1993; Alderson *et al.* 1995; Hughes 1989

significance test(ing)

The use of statistics to make **inferences** about the strength of the effect of an **independent variable**(s) on a **dependent variable**, that is, whether the experimental treatment (eg extensive reading) has the hypothesised outcome (eg higher scores on a test of reading). What significance testing does is to estimate the probability of the obtained result occurring by chance; there are conventional tables of what counts as 'chance'. Well-known statistical tests which are used to test for significance are the z-test, **analysis of variance**, the *t*-test and **Chi-square**.

Further reading: Rowntree 1981; Hatch & Lazaraton 1991

Simulated Oral Proficiency Interview (SOPI)

A specific type of **semi-direct (tape-mediated) Oral Proficiency Interview**, developed by the Center for Applied Linguistics (CAL) in Washington. It is based on the OPI in that it follows as closely as possible the four phases of the

OPI (warm-up, probe, level check and wind down). Like the OPI, the SOPI is scored using the **ACTFL** Proficiency Guidelines or the US Government's language **skill level** descriptions (**FSI scales**). The SOPI was developed initially at CAL for use with the less-commonly used languages, such as Hausa and Portuguese, where it would not be possible to provide on-site assessors.

While this term was originally used to refer to the tests developed at CAL, it is now used generically to refer to any tape-based **language proficiency interview**.

Further reading: Stansfield 1989; Shohamy 1994

skewed distribution

Any deviation from the **normal curve** in a **distribution** of **scores** is said to be skewed. In the **normal distribution** the **mean**, the **median** and the **mode** all coincide and there is perfect balance between the right and left halves of the curve. A distribution is skewed when the mean and median fall at different points. A distribution is skewed negatively when the mean is located to the left of the high point of the curve, and it is positively skewed when the mean is located to the right of the high point of the curve. A large positive skew indicates that the test is difficult; a large negative skew that the test is easy. Even the best language test is likely to show modest skewedness.

skill

An aspect of **ability** underlying language use. **Language tests** are often characterised according to which of the four skills (also known as macro-skills) is involved in its **performance,** ie it is common to talk of tests of reading, writing, listening and speaking. The four skills are sometimes grouped as **receptive** (reading and listening) and **productive** (speaking and writing) skills. In early models of **language proficiency** skills were distinguished from components of language **knowledge** (grammar, **vocabulary**, phonology/graphology) while more recent models acknowledge the dynamic interaction between the two.

Skills can also be subdivided into sub-skills or micro-skills, such as discriminating sounds in a listening text, signalling relationships between different parts of an utterance in spoken or written discourse, identifying relevant information in a reading text. **Test items** may elicit one or more of these sub-skills.

A distinction is commonly made between lower order skills such as spelling, vocabulary recognition and the production of routinised speech or writing and higher order skills such as inferencing and argumentation which engage complex cognitive processes. This distinction between higher and lower order skills is often used as the basis for **reporting profiles** describing different **levels** of test performance.

While it is important for test developers to have some notion of what skills they are trying to elicit on any given **task**, the process of establishing exactly what is being tested may be problematic because of the range of **variables** involved in both the design and actual performance of test tasks (eg length and **lexical density** of the **stimulus**, familiarity of the topic, the way in which the **question** is formulated, the amount of time allowed, the learner's cognitive **style** and level of prior knowledge or **test wiseness**). The question of whether it is possible to characterise language performance according to the sub-skills involved is the subject of some debate.

See also: **test item, test type**
Further reading: Munby 1978; Alderson & Lukmani 1989

SLA
See **second language acquisition**

slope
See **regression line**

sociolinguistic competence
A component of one well-known language **competence** framework, the other components being **grammatical competence** and **strategic competence**. Sociolinguistic competence is taken to contain sociocultural rules and rules of discourse, although in later treatments these have been placed in separate components. Sociolinguistic competence has been an important theoretical **construct** in discussions of tests of **communicative competence**.

See also: **linguistic competence**
Further reading: Canale & Swain 1980; Bachman 1990

SOPI
See **Simulated Oral Proficiency Interview**

sound discrimination test
A test formerly much used by language testers influenced by structural linguistics, it consists of two or more one-word spoken stimuli distinguished

only by a single phoneme (eg 'bit' – 'bet'). The **testee** is required to demonstrate an **ability** to perceive phonemic contrasts, thereby indicating that the sounds of the **target language** can be discriminated. Various techniques for eliciting such discriminations have been used: a common one is to present three or four words, one or more of which may be different, and to ask the testee to indicate where (if anywhere) the difference lies. Such a technique lends itself readily to a multiple choice format. The move to more communicative types of language test have made the use of sound discrimination tests less popular.

Further reading: Lado 1961; Davies 1977

speaking test

An **assessment** of the **ability** to speak the **target language**. Speaking tests range from **indirect** (eg a paper-and-pencil test) to **direct** (eg observing the candidate's **performance** in some realistic interactive task such as explaining, complaining, reassuring). At the more direct end of the continuum is the distinction between tests of planned and unplanned speaking.

Most speaking tests involve an **interview** format of some kind with a single **candidate** or a pair of candidates. The **rater** commonly instructs on the **tasks**; there may also be a second rater present. In other cases the performance may be taped for later rating. Under another format, known as the **semi-direct** or **tape-mediated test**, the **stimuli** for the candidate may be on tape or in the test booklet. Semi-direct performances are always taped for later rating.

Much attention has been given in recent years to the **validity** of speaking test ratings and to the **rater training**. Rating of performance on speaking tests may be specific, eg of **traits** such as **fluency** and **comprehension** or of linguistic categories such as grammar and accent. Or it may be general, whereby raters are required to provide a **global assessment**.

The increased interest in the assessing of speaking (and of writing) may be the most important legacy of the communicative movement.

See also: **Oral Proficiency Interview, Simulated Oral Proficiency Interview**

Further reading: Weir 1990

Spearman-Brown Prophecy Formula

Also known as the Spearman-Brown correction formula

This equation is used to calculate how long (in terms of number of **items**) a test needs to be in order to achieve satisfactory **reliability**. One use of the formula is in calculating the reliability of the whole test from a **split-half reliability correlation coefficient**, which provides a result for only half the test.

Spearman's rho (written as ρ)

The Spearman rank **correlation coefficient**, named after Charles Spearman, a pioneer of **factor analysis.** This measure of relationship between two **variables** is appropriate when one **scale** constitutes **ordinal measurement** (ie ranks) and the other either ordinal or **interval**. This measure underestimates the 'true' relationship which a **Pearson product–moment correlation coefficient** approximates, but it is easier to calculate and can be used when interval data are unavailable.

See also: **scales**

specifications

See **test specifications**

specific objectivity

A property of the **Rasch model** whereby estimates of **item difficulty** remain invariant for subjects of differing ability **levels**, and estimates of person **ability** do not vary according to the **items** on which people perform. This allows for a single order of item difficulty to be estimated for **candidates** regardless of their ability, which enables important mapping and **test equating** functions to be carried out.

Further reading: McNamara 1996; Wright & Masters 1982

speed(ed) test

A test which provides too short a time limit for most **candidates**. A distinction is made between speed and **power tests**. Theoretically, the **items** in a speed test are intended to be of equal **difficulty** (or at least within the capacity of all candidates) and answer gaps will then appear at the end of the test, all early answered items being correct and the **discrimination** among candidates produced by finishing or not finishing. Again theoretically, items in a power test all discriminate and answer gaps (or errors) therefore appear at all points in the test and not only (or perhaps not mainly) at the end. In practice, all language tests are likely to contain a speed element: this is necessarily the case in a listening test. A caveat is also required with regard to the power test; because of grading (presenting items in order of difficulty), it is likely that more gaps (or **errors**) will in practice appear towards the end of a power test, thus removing, at least in part, its major formal difference from a speed test. Whether or not tests should be speeded (other than those concerned with skills which are intrinsically speed **skills**, such as reading rate or reading speed), is of theoretical dispute. The weight of psychological opinion appears to be that speed is irrelevant to cognitive tasks and that therefore all tests should be power tests.

Further reading: Davies 1989

split-half reliability

Split-half reliability belongs to the category of internal consistency reliability, where **reliability** is established by comparing **scores** on the component parts of the test rather than by relating the test scores to those derived from some other external measure. It provides a measure of adequacy of item **sampling**. This method of determining reliability is possible with a single **test administration** but is only suitable if the test is long. By basing the estimate on the results of one test administration rather than on repeated measures, the possibility of **errors** arising from differences in testing conditions is avoided.

To calculate this type of reliability, subjects' scores on the two halves of the test are correlated. It is important that the test be split in such a way that the two halves are more or less comparable. The procedures for assigning **items** to one or other half will differ according to whether the items are homogeneous or not. If the test is homogeneous, the items can be separated using the **odd–even method**. If it is not, **item difficulty** estimates should be calculated for each of the items before assigning them to the two halves on the basis of equivalent difficulty and similarity of content. The **correlation coefficient** indicates reliability for the half-test only and should be corrected with the **Spearman-Brown Prophecy Formula** to arrive at a reliability estimate for the whole test.

See also: **alternate forms**, **reliability**, **test-retest reliability**, **internal consistency**, **Kuder-Richardson formulae**.

Further reading: Anastasi 1990; Hatch & Lazaraton 1991

stakeholders

All those who have a legitimate interest in the use or effect of a particular test, such as the **candidates**, their teachers and parents/families, the test constructors and their clients who have comissioned the test, the receiving institutions (including government bodies, eg, Ministries of Education and of Immigration) in the case of a **selection test**.

See also: **test user**

stakes

The extent to which the outcomes of a test can affect the **candidates'** futures. The term high stakes is generally used to refer to a test upon which candidates' career or study plans hinge. Examples of such tests are **TOEFL** and **IELTS** when used as **selection tests** for tertiary study, or a language test required of migrants in order to pursue their profession in the new country. A low stakes test is one where the outcomes are less likely to affect the candidates' future lives substantially, for example **placement** or classroom **achievement tests**.

Further reading: Bachman & Palmer 1996

standard(s)

1. Standard refers to a **level** of **performance** required or experienced ('the standard required for entry to the university is an A in English'; 'English standards are rising').

See also: **cut-score**, **standard setting**

2. A second sense refers to a set of principles which can be used as a basis for evaluating what **language testers** do. Standards in this second sense may lead to codification in an agreed set of guidelines or Code of Practice. Such codification indicates a concern to establish professional **ethics**.

See also: **International Language Testing Association**, **impact**
Further reading: Alderson *et al.* 1995; Stansfield 1993; Joint Committee on Testing Practices 1988; Davies, 1997b

standard deviation

The standard deviation is a property of the normal curve. Mathematically, it is the square root of the **variance** of a test. Along with the **mean**, it is one of the more widely used statistics in language testing. The standard deviation (often referred to as SD or σ, the Greek letter for sigma) provides an informative summary of the variation or **distribution** of a set of **scores** around the mean. In principle, for **norm-referenced** tests, the larger the standard deviation the better, on the grounds that what such a test aims to describe is the range of **abilities** in the group under test. It follows that in norm-referenced tests a small standard deviation indicates that the true variation of the ability in the **population** has not been captured by the test. And since the standard deviation is an indicator of **reliability**, the larger the standard deviation the more reliable the test.

See also: **normal distribution**
Further Reading: Hatch & Lazaraton 1991

standard error of measurement

Also SEM, standard error of a score

A way of expressing test **reliability**, but concerned with the interpretation of individual **scores**, unlike the **reliability coefficient**, which is more appropriate for considering or comparing the reliability of tests. The standard error of measurement (s_e) is calculated statistically on the basis of test trials, and gives an indication of how accurate the test score of an individual is likely to be, by defining the probable limits (or **confidence intervals**) surrounding this score. These limits define the space within which a person's **true score** has a given probability of occurring (the most common levels of probability considered are 68%, for scores falling within one standard error of **measurement**, and 95%, for scores falling within two standard errors of measurement).

For example, if two **test takers** both obtain a score of 75% in a test of reading comprehension, with a standard error of measurement (s_e) of 3% (0.03), then there is a 68% chance that the true score for each of them lies between 72% ($-1\ s_e$) and 78% ($+1\ s_e$), or a 95% chance that the true score lies between 69% and 81%.

See also: **normal distribution, sample, sampling error, error variance**
Further reading: Feldt and Brennan 1993; Anastasi 1990

standard setting

The process of determining **cut-scores** for a test. There may be a single **pass mark**, or **performance** may be reported on a **scale**, with each **level** representing a specified standard. Standards may be described by number or letter **grades**, by single words such as pass/fail, or by longer **descriptors**.

The methods for setting standards all ultimately rely on the subjectivity of human judgement. This judgement is typically exercised by experts in relation to **test content** (the test **tasks** or **items**: a test-centred approach), performance of **test takers** (an examinee-centred approach), or a combination of the two. A variety of statistical methods is used for dealing with the results of these judgements; the drawback faced by attempts to set reliable standards is that the different methods do not necessarily agree.

See also: **criterion, proficiency scale, criterion-referenced test**
Further reading: Angoff 1971; Berk 1986; Jaeger 1993

standardised score

A transformation of **raw scores** which provides a measure of relative standing in a group and allows comparison of raw scores from different **distributions**, eg from tests of different lengths. It does this by converting a raw score into a standard frame of reference which is expressed in terms of its relative position in the distribution of scores. The z score is the most commonly used standardised score.

See also: **percentile**, *T* **score**, **stanine score**, **z score**
Further reading: Hatch & Lazaraton 1991

standardised test

A test which ideally has the following characteristics, not all of which are always fully met in language tests referred to as standardised:

- A rigorous development, **trialling** and revision process, determining the **measurement** properties of the test. This process includes principled **sampling** from the **population** of interest; defining the measurement **scale**; establishing adequate **reliability** and **validity** for the test's intended purpose; creating **norms** for the population on the basis of the score **distribution** of the sample under test; and statistical equating of all forms of the test, so that reported **scores** always represent the same level of **ability**. Standardised language tests make the assumption of normality;

- Standard procedures for **administration** and **scoring** of the test. **Raw scores** obtained on the test are often transformed into **percentiles** or **z scores** for reporting;

- Standard **test content** in all versions. This content is based on a set of **test specifications** which may reflect a theory of **language proficiency** or a view of **candidates**' anticipated needs. **Alternative forms** of the test are examined for content **equivalence**.

Standardised tests place heavy emphasis on reliability. This reliability is seen as making the test suitable for the purposes of comparability across large groups of **test takers**. Because their **measurement** properties have been established (but sometimes simply because they have obtained wide acceptance as commonly used measures of language ability), standardised tests are often used for investigating the **concurrent validity** of other measures of language. They may also be used as a control for conducting research into the effects of other **variables**. For example, a researcher trying to determine the relative value of two methods of language instruction might use a suitable standardised test as a means of comparing learner **performance** before and after the course of instruction.

However, the attention to reliability may not be matched by a similar consideration of issues of validity. For example, a) the emphasis on reliability in standardised tests often leads to a reliance on **objectively scored test items**, which may not represent a valid method of judging communicative ability; b) the validity of test content may not be properly established for the entire test population, since it is extremely hard to generate material which is suitable for large populations which may have very disparate learning backgrounds and experiences.

Examples of language tests which are generally considered to be standardised include the Test of English as a Foreign Language (**TOEFL**), the **Michigan Test of English Language Proficiency**, the English Proficiency Test Battery (**EPTB**) and the International English Language Testing System (**IELTS**).

See also: **standardised score, test equivalence, objective scoring, test fairness, norm-referenced test**

Further reading: Cohen *et al.* 1992

stanine score

Also standard nine

A **standardised score** where scores comprise a nine-point equal **interval scale** and the **distribution** has a **mean** of 5 and a **standard deviation** of 1.96. Stanine scores are often used for reporting test **performance**.

See also: **percentile, z score, *T* score**

Further reading: Henning 1987; Hatch & Lazaraton 1991

stem

The first part of a **multiple-choice item**, which takes the form of either an incomplete sentence or a **question**. The stem is followed by the correct or best option (the **key**) and several **distractors**, as in the example below, where the key is *(b)*.

Example:

Stem:	*Wine is a kind of:*
Options:	*a) meat*
	b) drink
	c) animal
	d) fruit

step

The amount of improvement required to move one **band**-width on a **rating scale** or interval between two **scores**. The assumption is generally made in language testing that all bands/intervals are of equal width, thus the difference between the Eurocentres Global Scale Band 5 ('Can understand extensive simple information encountered in everyday situations') and Band 6 ('Can understand information on topics of interest in unsimplified but straightforward language') is the same as the difference between Band 6 and Band 7 ('Can express ideas and opinions clearly on a wide range of topics'). The issue is similar to the **interval scale** problem in **test items**.

See also: **scale**, **proficiency scale**

Further reading: North 1996a, 1996b; McNamara 1996

stepwise regression

A technique for performing a multiple **regression** analysis whereby **variables** are entered one by one, or step by step into the equation until the best model (ie the one in which the greatest proportion of **variance** is explained) is arrived at. Variables may be entered one at a time until the addition of further variables does not cause a significant improvement in model fit (forwards stepwise). Alternatively all possible **independent variables** can be included in the model and then removed one at a time until the best solution is achieved (backwards stepwise).

Stepwise regression is often used to determine what **weighting** to give to particular test components in selecting **candidates** for a particular course of study. It may be found, for example, that, of the various components of an **aptitude test** battery, grammatical sensitivity is the best predictor of subsequent success on an end-of-course foreign language **examination**. It will therefore make sense to give greater weighting to this component with respect to the others in any future **selection** process. Components which are found to contribute relatively little to examination **scores** may accordingly, for the sake of **efficiency**, be excluded from the **test battery**.

Further reading: Woods *et al.* 1986

stimulus

Material provided as part of a **test item** or **task**, to which the **test taker** has to respond. Stimulus material generally includes input **text** (presented orally, visually or in writing) and **questions**.

See also: **test rubric**

stochastic

Refers to a **probabilistic model** of describing data, which includes random (unexplained) elements; it may be contrasted with a deterministic model, which contains no such elements. Probabilistic models are the basis of **item response theory**, which is commonly used in analysing data from language tests.

strategic competence

The capacity that relates language competence to the user's contextualised **performance** ability. It is considered to be a general cognitive **ability**, akin to intelligence. Strategic competence, **sociolinguistic competence** and **grammatical competence** (with the later addition of **pragmatic competence**) were proposed by Canale and Swain as necessary components of a model of communicative language ability. In their model strategic competence was intended as a compensating mechanism for inadequacies in performance variables or in grammatical or sociolinguistic competence.

In later models of **communicative competence**, strategic competence has a more substantial role. For example in tests of reading comprehension, the ability (and willingness) to go beyond the text in answering the questions may be regarded as a type of strategic competence.

Further reading: Canale & Swain 1980; Bachman 1990

structural equation modelling

Also causal modelling, **structural modelling, linear structural equation modelling**

A multivariate **hypothesis-testing** technique allowing exploration of the cause–effect relationship between factors included in the specification of a complex theoretical **construct**. This technique has been used, for example, to plot the relationship between unobserved **test-taker** characteristics such as first language and instructional background (elicited via questionnaire) and second language **performance** (as measured by a language test). Attempts are made by the researcher to fit the data to a number of theoretically plausible models (or provisional constructs) which postulate in advance the cause–effect relationships between **variables**. The most parsimonious solution is then selected as the best explanation of these relationships. The technique is essentially a combination of factor analysis and path analysis, because it includes factors, as well as tests, in the structural equations.

See also: **path analysis, factor analysis, LISREL, EQS**
Further reading: Kunnan 1995

structural modelling

See **structural equation modelling**

style

Variation of speaking and writing in terms of social and contextual factors.

A **candidate**'s style will be judged as effective if the writing or speaking is appropriate to the given **task**. For example, a test may require a candidate to write a formal letter or to engage in informal conversation. Language tests are unlikely to require command over literary style except in advanced translation exercises.

See also: **register, appropriateness**
Further reading: Lado 1961

subjective item

A **test item** that is **subjectively scored**.
See also: **objective item, objective test**

subjective scoring, subjectively scored

Any scoring procedure which involves the exercise of judgement by the **scorer**, ie where all possible answers are not specified. Subjectively scored **test items** may range from **short-answer questions** (where the margin for judgement on the part of the scorer is limited) to **tasks** involving extended complex **performance** (where the potential for disagreement between **raters** is large). In tests where the results hold serious consequences for the **test taker**, multiple ratings by trained raters contribute to improved **reliability**.

See also: **objective scoring, inter-rater reliability, intra-rater reliability**

sub-skill

See **skill**

sub-test

A discrete section of a **test battery** which is dedicated to the **assessment** of a particular **skill**, such as grammar, speaking or reading. Separate **scores** are sometimes reported for individual sub-tests, in addition or as an alternative to scores reporting overall test **performance**.

summary

A type of **test task**, commonly used to assess reading or listening comprehension in combination with writing (or sometimes speaking) **ability**. The **test taker** listens to or reads a **text**, and is then required to produce a written or spoken summary of the content of the text, generally of a specified length. In such integrated test tasks, it is impossible to report receptive ability separately from productive ability, as it cannot be clear which is responsible for strengths and weaknesses in the **performance**. Since summary writing requires an integration of many **skills** it is necessary in such a task to specify the scoring **criteria** clearly in order to reduce the element of subjectivity. Because of the difficulties of producing satisfactory **marking schemes** for this kind of task, a **summary cloze** is sometimes used as an alternative.

See also: **reliability, assessment, receptive skills, productive skills**
Further reading: Alderson *et al.* 1995

summary cloze

A method of testing in which the **test taker** has to read or listen to an extended **text**, and to fill a series of gaps in a version of the same text which has normally been summarised and paraphrased from the original. Either the test taker is required to produce the word(s) to fill the gap (**constructed-response item**), or a list of alternative expressions is supplied, from which the test taker must select the best one for each gap (**forced-choice item**). If the test includes constructed responses then it is important to provide a comprehensive **marking scheme**, to ensure adequate **reliability**. If the test taker has to supply more than one or two words for each gap, then the test involves also an assessment of writing **ability**. There is dispute about exactly what is tested by this form of test.

See also: **receptive skills, summary, gap filling, reading comprehension test, listening comprehension test**
Further reading: Weir 1993

summative assessment

A term brought into language testing from **programme evaluation**. Summative **evaluation**, in contrast to formative evaluation, was intended to suggest a concern with the outcome of a programme for accountability purposes in order to provide a report to external **stakeholders**. Summative assessment, normally by a test or **examination** procedure, provides a public outcome statement on **performance** at the end of a period of language instruction for the benefit of all interested stakeholders.

See also: **formative assessment**
Further reading: Scriven 1991; Bachman 1990; Brindley 1995

syllabus

The timetabled content of instruction for one class in a subject area within the school system. A syllabus may be part of a larger plan of goals, materials and intended learning outcomes which is referred to as the curriculum.

Language teaching syllabuses reflect different philosophies of language learning, for example the structural syllabus, the notional syllabus, the communicative syllabus. An issue of interest to language testers is that of test **washback** to the syllabus.

Further reading: Johnson 1989

systematic error

See **bias**

systemic validity

The **impact** of a test upon an educational or other institutional system.

See also: **washback**, **consequential validity**

t

T score

A transformation of a **z score**, equivalent to it but with the advantage of avoiding negative values, and hence often used for **reporting** purposes.

Further reading: Hatch & Lazaraton 1991

t-test

A **parametric** statistic for comparing sets of **scores**. There are two types of measure:

- Between-groups design. This kind of *t*-test is referred to as an independent *t*-test, and compares differences between groups. For example, an independent *t*-test would be appropriate to determine whether the **TOEFL** scores of a group of male students were significantly different from scores of a group of female students;
- Repeated-measures or matched-pairs design. This kind of *t*-test is referred to as a dependent *t*-test, and compares the differences between two sets of scores provided by a single group or by matched pairs of subjects. For example, a dependent *t*-test would be appropriate for testing whether the difference between the TOEFL scores obtained by a group of 100 students and the scores obtained by the same group of students on a 50-point **vocabulary test** is significant.

t-tests may be **one-tailed** or **two-tailed**, depending on whether or not the direction of any difference between the measures is predicted in the **hypothesis**. In the first example above, if it was expected that the females would obtain higher TOEFL scores (on the grounds that they generally do better on tests of language **ability**), then the test would be one-tailed, or directional. On the other hand, if there were no reason for expecting either group to perform better than the other (since females have also been shown to perform less well on tests made up of **multiple-choice items**), the test would be two-tailed, or non-directional.

The statistic is reported as a *t* value, and the significance of the differences observed between the sets of scores is determined by reference to a table of *t* values, taking into account the degrees of freedom.

The non-parametric alternative to a *t*-test is **Mann Whitney U**.

Further reading: Hatch & Lazaraton 1991

T-unit

A measure of syntactic complexity, consisting of one independent clause. So, for example, the sentence 'I bought the tickets with the money she gave me' consists of one T-unit, whereas the sentence 'She gave me some money so I bought the tickets' consists of two T-units.

tailored test

See **adaptive test**

tape-mediated test

A **speaking test** in which the **test taker** is required to respond to pre-recorded **questions** or **input** by speaking into a microphone. The **responses** are audiotaped and normally assessed later from the audiotape. This type of test is commonly administered in a language laboratory.

It has been argued that this kind of test has the advantage of standardising the conditions of **administration** (assuming the equipment functions properly) by eliminating any **interlocutor effect**. On the other hand, questions have been raised about the **validity** of a procedure which does not involve live **interaction**; these questions focus on the nature of the discourse produced as well as the effect of such a procedure upon test takers who are unfamiliar or uncomfortable with such a **test method**.

See also: **test anxiety, test method effect, Simulated Oral Proficiency Interview, semi-direct test**

Further reading: Shohamy 1994; O'Loughlin 1997

target language

The language that is being tested in a particular test. Whilst the **test rubric** and **item** instructions are often in the target language, particularly where test **candidates** are likely to be of various language backgrounds, this is not always the case. It may be preferable to use the candidates' first language for tests with a candidature from one language background (for example, in foreign language tests in schools), particularly where candidates are likely to be of a low **proficiency** level.

target test population

That group for whom a test is designed and on whose known or estimated **ability/proficiency** the test **construct** is based. Since whole **populations** are not usually available for test trials, it is common practice for test **norms** to be based on a **sample** of the target test population.

task

1. What a **test taker** is required to do during a test or part of a test, such as note-taking from a spoken text, participating in an **interview** or **role play**, reading a text and answering comprehension questions. This general sense of the term thus includes the **input** and the instructions as well the task itself.

2. More specifically, the term task is used to refer to a type of **test item** involving complex **performance** in a test of **productive skills**. Examples of **writing test** tasks are: writing an essay, drafting a business letter, and completing a **summary** of a text. Examples of **speaking test** tasks are: adopting a specified role in a role play, describing a photograph, and presenting an argument to a small group of peers. However, it should be noted that tasks of this type, which often attempt to replicate **real-life** tasks, often involve more than one **skill**; presenting an argument, for example, may involve reading and even writing, as well as speaking.

In this more specific sense the task (for example, writing a letter to a friend) is generally distinguished from the input material (for example, information to be included in the letter). The requirements of the task are normally clearly specified to the test taker in the instructions, and include information about what is expected of them (eg purpose of the task, audience for the language produced, time allotted, length of text required) as well as an indication of the **criteria** on which it will be judged.

There is some overlap between the terms **item** and task. Where a distinction is made between them, there is usually an implication that an item is smaller and less complex, while a task is larger and more complex. A test would typically include either a large number of relatively short items or a small number of relatively complex tasks.

See also: **performance**, **assessment**
Further reading: Bachman & Palmer 1996; McNamara 1996

test administration

See **administration**

test analysis

Data from test **trials** are analysed during the test development process to evaluate individual items (their **difficulty** and **discrimination**, for example) as well as the **reliability** and **validity** of the test as a whole. Test analysis is also carried out following test **administrations** in order to allow the **reporting** of results. Test analysis may also be conducted for research purposes.

There are a number of different methods of or approaches to statistical test analysis. Among the most important are classical true score theory, **item response theory** and **generalizability theory**.

Analysis may be not only statistical, but also qualitative; for example, the content of a test may be analysed and reviewed as part of the process of establishing **content validity**.

See also: **item analysis, content analysis**
Further reading: Henning 1987; Alderson *et al.* 1995; McNamara 1996

test anxiety

An emotional reaction of a **test taker** to a test, one of a number of factors other than **language ability** which may affect **performance** and hence contribute to **measurement error**.

The level of test anxiety varies amongst individuals and can be influenced by, for example, the test taker's personality, the extent to which the **test results** will affect the test taker's future, the test taker's **level** of **motivation**, familiarity with the **test format**, the topics occurring in the test, the time available to complete the test and the item **ordering**.

Anxiety may have a beneficial or detrimental effect on test performance, although research findings commonly suggest that test anxiety interferes with the **ability** of individuals to concentrate on the test. Any of the **variables** mentioned may combine to influence test taker performance: for example, high anxiety and low motivation is likely to lead to a poorer performance than a situation of low anxiety and high motivation.

Test-taker feedback is one method commonly used in the growing body of research investigating the **affective reactions** by test takers to various types of test.

Further reading: Wolf & Smith 1995

test battery

In clinical psychology a test battery refers to a selected assortment of tests and **assessment** procedures (such as an **interview**) used for **diagnosis** and **evaluation**. Such an assortment need not be homogeneous. In language testing the term test battery more usually refers to a set of purpose related tests or **sub-tests**, which make sufficiently independent contributions, but are considered homogeneous enough to produce a total **score**. Many of the widely used language **proficiency tests** consist of test batteries, for example **TOEFL** and **IELTS**.

test bias

See **bias**

test content

The **skills** and components of **language ability** which are measured in a test, and the manner in which they are measured. The test content may be based on a theory of **language proficiency**, as in a **proficiency test**, or on a specified **syllabus**, as in an **achievement test**. In either case, the content of the test should be a representative **sample** of the **domain** to be tested; it may be derived from some form of **needs analysis** or job analysis, or from analysis of the syllabus. In a language **aptitude test** the test content will be based on a sampling of the abilities deemed to be associated with successful language acquisition.

The content is normally defined in the **test specifications** in terms of a range of features of the test. These features may include: macro-skills, **vocabulary**, structures, and language functions tested; topics, type and length of **texts**, **task** or **item** types and format used; and form of **responses** required.

See also: **content validity, validation**

Further reading: Bachman & Palmer 1996; Davies 1990; Alderson *et al.* 1995

test equating

The process of comparing the difficulty of two or more **forms** of a test, in order to establish their equivalence. This is important when **parallel forms** of a **standardised test** are to be administered on different occasions.

See also: **test equivalence, equate, item response theory**

test equivalence

1. The relationship between two or more **forms** of the same test. **Test forms** may be equated or equivalent.

Equivalent forms of tests are constructed from the same **test specifications** in order to measure the same **skills**. **Scores** on the two test forms will be expected to be equivalent; the **mean** and **variance** will be equal.

In equated tests, on the other hand, the aim is not to produce parallel versions of a test with equivalent score **distribution**, but to transform scores from both tests onto a common **scale** which allows for comparison across the tests.

One method of establishing the equivalence of two test forms is to administer both to the same group of **trial** subjects or **test takers**; alternatively, if **IRT** analysis is used, different composite forms containing some common **items** or **tasks** may be administered to different groups of test takers. The final forms will include items testing the same skills and resulting in overall test score equivalence. It is also becoming increasingly common to use IRT analysis to develop **item banks** containing a large number of items of known characteristics, from which equivalent test forms may be constructed.

2. The relationship between two different tests. Strictly speaking, this concept is unjustifiable, since each test is designed for a different purpose and a different **population**, and may view and assess language **traits** in different ways as well as describing test-taker **performance** differently. However, in reality, **test users** may demand statements of equivalence between different tests (for example, admissions officers at educational institutions).

One approach to this issue is to conduct **concurrent validity** studies, comparing performance by the same group of test takers on two tests. For practical reasons this is seldom done, however, and decisions are generally on less sure ground. When the issue cannot be avoided, it is surely one of the roles of **language testers** to apply their expertise in providing practical advice.

See also: **alternate forms, equating, regression**
Further reading: Petersen *et al.* 1993; Bachman, Davidson *et al.* 1995

test fairness

Fairness is concerned with the consequences of testing for individuals, groups or society as a whole. It relates to both the **validity** of a given test as an index of **ability** and to the whole testing process insofar as it reflects or contributes to social equity.

Issues of fairness may arise at the **test construction** stage in relation to who has **input** into the **test specifications** and, subsequently, which **tasks** or **items** are chosen as representative of the target **domain**. It might be considered unfair for example to include only **multiple-choice items** to test reading when it has been shown that boys generally do better than girls on such items. Test development committees usually include representatives of relevant minority groups to ensure that the test content is sensitive to their interests and experience, and **bias** analyses are often undertaken to ensure that

test items function uniformly across groups.

To ensure fairness at the **test administration** stage it is important to ensure that the conditions under which the test is administered are constant across **candidates** and testing occasions. If candidates' chances of success on the test are liable to increase or diminish according to when or where they are tested or who happens to be assessing them, then the test is unfair. For this reason tests with **objectively-scored** items are generally considered fairer to candidates than those which are **subjectively-scored.** Fairness in this sense is synonymous with **reliability**.

Test fairness also depends on the provision of adequate information about **test content** so that candidates have adequate opportunity to prepare themselves and so that test users are able to interpret the **test results**. A candidate's rating on an oral proficiency interview, for example, might be mistakenly interpreted as evidence of suitability for entry to an academic institution if selection officers are not acquainted with the nature of the tasks from which **scores** are derived.

Determination of test fairness is ultimately a philosophical matter and, in spite of general agreement about its importance, there are different views as to what the **criteria** for fairness ought to be or indeed whether fairness is possible given the nature of the testing enterprise.

See also: **bias**, **ethics**, **culture-fair test**, **consequential validity**
Further reading: Davies 1997a/b

test form

A specific version of a test, which assumes that other forms of the same test exist or will exist. For example, a test used to select students for university entrance, administered annually, would typically require a new form every year, for reasons of **test security**.

See also: **test equivalence**, **alternate forms**

test format

Refers to the overall design of a test. This includes characteristics such as the **test length**, the number and type of sections, the **skills** or sub-skills tested, the **item** and **task** types used and their number, the ways in which **stimulus** material is presented and the kinds of **responses** required of **test takers**. Information about test format is often presented in a **test handbook**. The format is likely to remain broadly the same from one **test form** to another.

See also: **test type**, **test method**, **test purpose**

test handbook

A handbook for **test takers**, teachers or **test users** which contains information about the content and format of a test. The general purpose of providing a handbook is to ensure that all **candidates** have clear expectations about the test before they take it, hence handbooks are typically available for tests with important consequences for test takers. A test handbook normally contains information about the **test purpose**, **test format** (including length, sections, physical appearance), **test item** and **task** types, **test administrations** (including dates, places, fees and administration officers), **assessment criteria** and **reporting** procedures (including interpretations of results). Information about test development procedures may also be included. Practice material is often included in the handbook, although for large-scale **standardised tests**, this may be provided in separate publications.

See also: **test wiseness, washback, test manual, test fairness**

test item

Those parts of a test which require a specified form of **response** from the **test taker**. On the basis of this response or set of responses a decision is made about the test taker's **knowledge** or **ability**.

The items in a test can be of widely varying kinds, according to the **test type** and **test purpose**.

An item includes a **prompt** or **stimulus** of some kind, which may take a form such as:

- a **question** ('How many tourists visited Indonesia in 1986?');
- a **stem** which requires completion (as in some **multiple-choice** or **short-answer** responses);
- a quotation to be discussed; or
- an instruction (eg 'write a summary of …'; 'adopt the role of …').

Each stimulus will require a response of some kind from the test taker. Item responses fall into two general categories:

- **selected response** (eg binary- or multiple-choice) and
- **constructed response** (eg **cloze**, short-answer and extended response).

Test items can also be regarded as being on a continuum from **discrete-point** (analytical, testing individual or finite components of language) to **integrative** (requiring the ability to manipulate a range of features of language). Discrete-point items tend to produce greater **reliability**, but may for certain purposes be considered to lack **validity**, while integrative items may offer greater validity but at the expense of reduced reliability.

Test items may be further categorised as either **objectively** or **subjectively scored**, and different items may use different scoring procedures: **dichotomously-scored**; **partial credit**; **rating scale**; **analytic** or **holistic**.

Test items yield results which are quantifiable in some way. Item **scores** may be aggregated and/or transformed in different ways to produce a final score or **grade** on one or more parts of the whole test.

Further reading: Hughes 1989; Weir 1993; Alderson *et al.*1995; Bachman & Palmer 1996

test length

An important consideration in test design, related to the central concerns of **practicality**, **validity** and **reliability**.

Practical concerns demand a short test, since this will minimise the cost and time involved for both **test takers** and administrators. This is set against the reality that generally, the longer a test is, the more valid and reliable it is likely to be. It is likely to be more reliable because it contains more **score** points, and it is likely to be more valid because it will allow a broader (and hence more valid) **sampling** of test takers' **knowledge** and/or **ability**.

Generally, the aim of test developers and administrators is to produce and use the shortest test that will provide valid and reliable information about test takers for the intended purpose; another way of looking at this is that the test should provide the best representation of **ability** possible within the practical constraints that apply.

During the test development process, a longer test is generally produced than will be used operationally, so that the best **items** may be retained following **item analysis**.

See also: **split-half reliability**, **Spearman-Brown prophecy formula**

test maintenance

All matters related to the management of operational tests.

One aspect of test maintenance involves producing alternate versions of a test. Another involves control of a range of general test **administration** matters such as the setting up and management of test centres, the organisation of the **scoring** and reporting of **test-taker** performance (including the maintenance of an adequate supply of trained **interviewers** and **raters** where necessary), publicity and information about the test, management of **test security** (including secure transport of test materials).

Those concerned with test maintenance may also involve themselves or outside bodies in research issues related to **test validation**, and the modification or revision of tests in the light of research findings.

See also: **test security**

Further reading: Alderson *et al.*1995; Bachman & Palmer 1996

test manual

A booklet giving technical information about a test, including **test specifications**, evidence of its **validity** and **reliability**, and guidance on the interpretation of **scores**. Public tests, upon the results of which important decisions are made, should provide such information for researchers and those seriously interested in investigating a test's claims to **fairness** and **appropriateness** for a particular purpose. Test manuals are just one of many forms of information about tests designed for those involved in the testing process; other booklets (normally termed **test handbooks**) with less technical information (for example, illustrating **question** formats or test **reporting** formats) may be available for **test takers** or administrators interested in test preparation or practical procedures for the interpretation of test scores.

test method

The way in which language or **knowledge** of language is elicited from a **test taker**. Test methods may be characterised as varying along a continuum from **direct** to **semi-direct** to **indirect**, according to the relationship between the test **task** and **authentic** language use. In testing speaking, for example, an oral proficiency interview (direct) involves face-to-face **interaction** of the test taker with one or more other persons; a **tape-based test** (semi-direct) may require the test taker to produce spoken **responses** to spoken or written **stimuli**; whereas an indirect test may require the test taker to identify **samples** of language that would be contextually appropriate or grammatically correct in speech, without actually producing any spoken language.

Different test methods produce different information about test takers. Within a particular test, a number of **facets** or aspects of a test method (such as **item** type or response mode) may affect a test taker's **performance**.

See also: **test method effect, multi-trait multi-method**
Further reading: Bachman 1990; Bachman & Palmer 1996

test method effect

Any aspect of the method used to obtain evidence of language **ability** which may have a significant impact on the picture of that ability emerging from the test. For example, speaking **skills** may be assessed in a one-to-one **interview** or in group **interaction**; writing may be assessed by an essay, or by a **cloze test**. **Task** characteristics normally replicate where possible the actual use of the **target language** in the relevant target language use situation; they thus cover the area traditionally dealt with under **content validity**. However, artificial methods of **response** (for example, multiple-choice format) may be required because of test administrative constraints, and it is then important to consider the **impact** of the method on **scores**. Research on the impact of methods is sometimes done using **multi-trait multi-method** designs.

The effect of the **test method** may account more substantially for differences in test-taker **performance** than do real differences in **ability**. For instance, scores derived from two **multiple-choice tests**, designed to test grammatical **knowledge** and reading ability, respectively, may be more highly correlated than scores for the same individuals on a multiple-choice test of grammar and a writing **sample** judged for grammatical **accuracy**; it would be reasonable to conclude that the multiple-choice method used was principally assessing ability to answer that kind of **item**. These kinds of differences in test method generate systematic **measurement error**.

Additional characteristics of the test method used may also influence test-taker performance. These include aspects of the testing situation (eg physical conditions, time of **administration**, equipment used), the **test rubric** (eg organisation of the test, time allowed, the nature of the instructions given), the **input** given to the **test taker** (eg channel of presentation, design, nature of language used), the nature of the expected **response** by the test taker (eg format, nature of language, constraints on response, **background knowledge** requirements), and the test taker's level of familiarity with the test method. Differences associated with these kinds of test characteristics lead to random measurement error.

Further reading: Bachman 1990

Test Of English as a Foreign Language (TOEFL)
See **TOEFL**

Test Of English for International Communication (TOEIC)
See **TOEIC**

Test of Written English (TWE)

Included as an obligatory component at some administrations of the **TOEFL**, it was developed by **ETS** in order to provide a **direct test** of the writing **ability** of **test takers**. Following development and **trialling** of a prototype in the mid-1980s the test was formally administered for the first time in July 1986. A **score** on the TWE is now required by many institutions which use TOEFL scores as part of their admissions policy.

Candidates are required to write a single short essay in English. This is assessed by multiple **raters** using a **holistic** scale which includes **criteria** such as organisation, development and support of ideas, and use of syntax and vocabulary. A very strong emphasis is placed by the test developers on the **reliability** of the raters. Scores are reported separately from the TOEFL, on a **scale** of 1 to 6, at intervals of 0.5.

See also: **essay test**
Further reading: Spolsky 1995; Stansfield 1986

test purpose

The intended or stated purpose of a test. This can be defined in a number of ways, with perhaps the broadest characterisation being a **proficiency**, **achievement** or **aptitude test**.

Within these categories, there are further distinctions. A proficiency test, for example, may have a **selection**, **placement** or **diagnostic** purpose as well as offering a means of **certification** of **language proficiency**. Alternatively, an achievement test may, in addition to indicating **progress**, be used for certification or form part of a process of **programme evaluation**. An achievement test may also have a diagnostic function, which in turn may assist in selection or placement decisions, or it may simply be intended as a means of motivating students to learn. An aptitude test is likely to be used to assist in decisions about selection of participants for a course of instruction. A test may also be designed expressly to influence the **curriculum** of a course leading up to it.

The purpose determines the **test content**, which is related to the kinds of language proficiency, **ability** or **knowledge** that a test is designed to **assess**, so that a test may have a general or specific purpose, and may focus on one or more language **skills** or components of language ability.

See also: **test type**, **ethics**, **consequential validity**
Further reading: Davies 1990; Henning 1987; Bachman 1990

test reliability

See **reliability**

test results

The information, based on test **performance**, reported to **test takers** or other **test users**. This can take the form of a numerical **score** (eg 550), a percentage (eg 70%), a letter (eg B) a descriptive **level** on a **scale** (eg minimum professional **competence**), or a simple categorisation (eg pass/fail). A reported result may take the form of a **raw score**, or this may be transformed in some way, following analysis.

If the test includes a number of sections (eg, reading, writing, speaking), then performance on these sections is sometimes aggregated or combined in some way, and a single overall score is reported. This is likely to depend on the **test purpose**: in a **diagnostic test**, for example, where maximum information about test-taker performance is required, scores are unlikely to be combined; in a test used purely for selection purposes, they are more likely to be combined.

See also: **reported score, cut-score**

test-retest

The simplest method of computing test **reliability**, it involves administering the same test to the same group of subjects on two occasions. The time between **administrations** is normally limited to no more than two weeks, in order to minimise the effect of learning (or unlearning) upon subjects' **true scores**. A **product–moment correlation** between the two sets of **scores** obtained provides a measure of the stability or consistency of the test scores over time. To save time, and because of a possible **practice effect**, other ways of computing reliability which involve only one administration of the test, are often used, such as **parallel forms** or **split-half reliability** (both of which are in fact surrogate test-retest methods).

See also: **Kuder Richardson formulae, internal consistency**

test rubric

The instructions appearing on the test paper which explain how a test should be taken. The rubric consists principally of information about test organisation (including format and relative importance of the various parts of the test) and time allocation, as well as instructions for **tasks** and how **test takers** should respond to them. It may include descriptions of what each part of the test is aiming to **assess** (eg 'This is a test of your **ability** to write a coherent and grammatically correct paragraph'), or it may simply name the **skill** being tested (eg 'writing'). The level of detail provided to the test taker, both before the test in a **test handbook** or **manual,** as well as in the test rubric during the test itself, may influence the test taker's **performance**.

The test rubric, or parts thereof, may be in the **candidates'** first language or in the **target language**.

Where detailed information is to be passed on to the test taker, for example explicit detail on the **assessment** criteria, relative **weighting** of test sections or **criteria**, or information on how the test is marked, then this is often provided in the test handbook.

Further reading: Bachman 1990; Hamp-Lyons 1991a

test security

An issue of major concern for most public tests. It is important that **candidates** are not advantaged by prior **knowledge** of a **test's content**. Such knowledge may allow candidates to memorise answers for **selected response** or **short-answer questions**, or to prepare for topics or **items** requiring an **extended response**. Maintaining adequate test security may entail elaborate and costly procedures.

Measures taken by test administrators and developers to ensure test security include:

- developing new versions of a test for each **administration** or developing **item banks**;
- during test **trialling**, selecting trial subjects who are not potential members of the final test **population**, nor likely to reveal the content to potential **test takers**;
- ensuring that there is no opportunity for test materials to be viewed by unauthorised people, or for candidates' test papers to be modified in any way after the test administration.

See also: **alternate forms, test maintenance**

test specifications

A document which sets out what a test is designed to measure and how it will be tested. Whilst the primary audience for the test specifications is test developers/**item** writers, specifications (or a modified version thereof) may also be referred to by test evaluators and **test users**. Specifications in their most detailed form are often confidential.

As well as providing a blueprint for item writers, specifications are important in the establishment of the test's **construct validity**. They should include information about the **test purpose**, the **target population**, **test content**, **test format**, and other relevant details such as the language of the **rubric**, time allowances, method of **scoring**, etc.

Further reading: Bachman & Palmer 1996; Davidson & Lynch 1993; Alderson *et al.* 1995

test taker

A term used to refer to any person undertaking a test or **examination**. Other terms commonly used in language testing are **candidate, examinee, testee**.

See also: **test-taker feedback**

test-taker characteristics

A wide range of **variables**, any of which may significantly influence test **performance**, hence producing **measurement error** and affecting the **validity** of an **assessment**. These may include language background, age, sex, educational background, **background knowledge, affective reactions** to test taking, **level** of **proficiency** in the **target language** and familiarity with the **test method**.

During test **trialling** or test **validation** studies it is generally important to identify trial subjects who are representative of the **target test population**, rather than simply locating a convenient group of non-native (or native) speakers of the target language.

Further reading: Kunnan 1995

test-taker feedback

Reactions to a test, produced by **test takers** and normally recorded by test developers in order to establish **face** or **content validity** during or after the test development process or to investigate the test-taking process. To establish face validity, test takers may be asked about, for instance, their general attitude to the test, including its **difficulty**, or how well it related to the instruction they have received, or their perceptions of how well it measured test takers' **ability**. If test takers include those with relevant specialist **knowledge** they may contribute to the content validation of an **LSP test** by giving **feedback** about its relevance to or coverage of the linguistic demands of a particular field or profession. A significant body of research is developing in which test takers are asked to use introspective techniques to record the processes they used in responding to individual **test items**. Formats for recording information commonly used are **Likert**-type **scales, open-ended questions** and **protocols**.

test type

Perhaps the most common ways of distinguishing types of language test are **test purpose** or use, and test components. Additional features of test type include **test method, assessment** method and **scoring** procedures.

Considerations of test type are very important in all areas of test use, including test design and in making choices about which test is appropriate for any given situation.

An example of some of the different ways in which a test of English for university selection might be categorised (in answer to the question, 'What type of test is this?') is as follows:

- purpose/use – **proficiency test**; test of **English for Academic Purposes** for prospective students of non-English-speaking background; assists in selection decisions made by universities;
- components – four-**skills** test (reading, writing, speaking, listening);
- test method (eg for the speaking **sub-test**) – **direct**; oral **interview**;
- **assessment** method/**scoring** procedures – (for the speaking sub-test) **subjective scoring** by two **raters**, using **analytic scoring scales** with five **steps** each for four assessment categories.

See also: **criterion-referenced test, test item, test purpose**
Further reading: Henning 1987; Alderson *et al.* 1995; Weir 1993

test user

Any individual or system which makes use of a particular test. Test users are likely to require information about the suitability of the test for their particular purpose as well as about how to interpret test **scores**. It is the responsibility of the test developer to make such information available.

The most common groups of test users are:

- teachers and administrators who use the scores of a test for diagnostic or placement purposes (eg in language teaching programmes);
- employers, admissions officers and others, for example in educational or other institutional systems (such as businesses or government departments), who use test scores to assist in selection decisions;
- teachers, institutions providing language courses and parents of students, who use test scores for monitoring progress, for giving **feedback**, and/or for advising students;
- students who need to take a test for any purpose; they also need to know how best to prepare for the test;
- researchers who use tests to help them to investigate particular issues (such as evaluating language teaching programmes).

See also: **test type, test purpose, consequential validity, stakeholders**
Further reading: Alderson *et al.* 1995

test version

See **test form**

test wiseness

This refers to the amount and type of preparation or prior experience that a **test taker** has. Familiarity, or lack of it, with the **item** or **task** types, the kinds of **text** used, or appropriate techniques (such as reading the **questions** relating to a text before reading the text itself, or apportioning a suitable time to each section of the test), are likely to affect a test taker's **score**. Practice at taking the same **version** of a test more than once, or a highly developed **ability** in a **candidate** to answer certain types of question (for example in ruling out **distractors** in **multiple-choice items**) may reduce **validity** by overestimating a candidate's **true score**. Alternatively, other candidates' lack of previous exposure to a **test's format** may lead to an underestimation of their true score. A student seeking a certificate of **proficiency** in English after undertaking a course of study in preparation for the **TOEFL** test (with its multiple-choice format), for example, may be disoriented if confronted with the task demands of the **IELTS** test, as the tests differ substantially in format and in the expectations they have of the test taker. Tests administered on a large scale (such as the **IELTS** or the **TOEFL**) often publish low-cost **sample** materials to allow test takers to familiarise themselves with the form of the test.

See also: **practice effect, test handbook**

testee

A term used to refer to any person undertaking a test or **examination**. Other terms commonly used in language testing are **candidate, examinee** and **test taker**.

See also: **test-taker feedback**

text

Any piece of written or spoken language, of variable length. It may be as short as a single word (eg 'Help!'), but is more often considered to consist of two or more utterances or sentences joined together according to rules of **cohesion** and rhetorical organisation, and may include an extended piece of spoken discourse or any number of pages of writing.

In language testing, a text commonly forms the reference point or **stimulus** for one or more **test items** (eg a series of listening or reading comprehension **questions**). Any text may pose a variety of processing problems for a **test taker**, depending on many contextual factors including the nature of the language used, the way it is presented, the test taker's **background knowledge**, the **tasks** relating to it and the time allowed.

In other tests, the **candidate's response** may take the form of a text,

produced according to the test instructions and assessed according to specific **criteria**.
Further reading: Halliday & Hasan 1976

The British Council

An independent but part publicly financed body (cf the BBC) established in 1934 to promote **knowledge** of British culture internationally. A large component of the British Council's work has always been the encouragement of the learning and teaching of English (as a Foreign and Second Language), including the testing of English language **proficiency**.
See also: **EPTB, ELTS, IELTS**.

theta

Greek letter (θ) used to symbolise **ability estimates** in some **IRT** and other statistical models. The Greek letter beta (β) or the symbol B is used to symbolise **ability** in **Rasch analysis**.

three-parameter model

The most complex of three **item response theory (IRT)** or **latent trait theory** models used for the analysis and interpretation of test data. Less widely used in language testing than the **one-parameter model**, the three-parameter model adds to estimates of **item difficulty** and **candidate ability** the **parameters** of **discriminability** and **guessing**, and is the model used in the development and analysis of the **Test of English as a Foreign Language**.
See also: **two-parameter model**
Further reading: Henning 1987

Threshold Level

See **Council of Europe**

Thurstone Scale

A type of **attitude scale**, divided into equal intervals, showing relative agreement or disagreement with a stated attitude, it is named after L. L. Thurstone, who developed a method for constructing such a scale. Its particular relevance to language testing is in investigating attitudes to language tests. Because constructing a Thurstone scale requires an elaborate procedure, either a **Guttman scale** or, more commonly, a **Likert scale** is generally used for measuring attitude.

Further reading: Thurstone 1959; Anastasi 1990

TOEFL

A widely administered **standardised test** of **proficiency** in English, developed and administered by the **Educational Testing Service** (ETS) in the USA.

The test uses a multiple-choice format to measure the **ability** to understand North American English, and consists of three sections, listening comprehension, structure and written expression, and reading comprehension.

The multiple-choice format of the test allows computer marking of papers, thus keeping the costs of **test administration** as low as possible as well as ensuring maximum **reliability**. With **test security** being a major concern, new **versions** of the test are developed for each **administration**.

The test is most commonly used by students intending to study at North American universities, but is also accepted as a measure of English proficiency by educational institutions in other countries where English is the medium of instruction, as well as by a range of government and other agencies.

TOEFL is a standardised **norm-referenced** test. **Raw scores** on each section of the test are converted to **scaled scores** by a process known as score **equating**, using **item response theory** analysis, to provide a test **score**. This process is designed to ensure that equal test scores represent equal **levels** of proficiency, regardless of the level of **difficulty** of the particular test version, or of the raw score obtained by the **candidate**. Section scores can range from 20 to 68, while total scores in the TOEFL can range from 200 to 677. Institutions determine individually what constitutes an acceptable score, depending on such things as type of course to be undertaken and level of ESL support available, with scores above 600 generally regarded as excellent, and those below 400 as weak.

Because the test is taken by such large numbers of candidates (in 1996–97, 953,000 people registered to take the test worldwide), there is an enormous bank of data available for investigation of issues related to language testing. ETS has published regular research reports based on TOEFL score data since 1977, investigating issues such as **test-taker** behaviour, effects of variation in **item** type, content and level of contextualisation, and **performance** of native and non-native speakers of English on the test. As a result of this research base, and the wide use of the test, it is often used by test developers as a basis for establishing **concurrent validity**.

A major revision process for the test, called TOEFL 2000, is currently underway. The first phase of this effort will be a computer-based TOEFL (**CBT**) scheduled for implementation in July 1998.

See also: **Test of Written English (TWE)**
Further reading: TOEFL Bulletin, annual

TOEIC

The Test of English for International Communication (TOEIC), intended for students of business and administration, and largely taken up in the Pacific Region, was first administered in 1979 and became fully operational in 1982. TOEIC provides a combination of **norm** and **criterion referencing**, in that the **proficiency scale** on which **candidates** are placed is universal while the **achievement level** needed/required in an organisation, company, etc. is locally determined. It is no doubt partly this flexibility that explains the geometric rise in **candidate** numbers, now over a million annually.

TOEIC, like TOEFL before it, has so far operated only in the receptive modalities of reading and listening. Investigations are currently in train to investigate the feasibility of developing a **speaking test**. TOEIC was developed at **ETS** but is now operated by a separate company, the Chancery Group International (CGI).

trait

An enduring feature or characteristic of a person, which underlies and explains their behaviour. In language testing, we make **inferences** about people's **ability** on particular traits through **assessment** of their **performance** in a language test, and make inferences from these behaviours about their traits.

See also: **validity**, **construct validity**
Further reading: Bachman 1990

trial(ling)

Also test trial(ling)

A stage of the test development process, conducted in order to ensure the quality of the **test items** and the suitability of the test for its designated purpose or **population**. Trialling involves administering **tasks** or sets of test **items** to a representative **sample** of the test population, and is normally essential for any test which will have significant implications for **test takers**.

Analysis of data produced in the trials provides information about the characteristics of each test item, such as **difficulty**, **discriminability** and **fit**, as well as about the **internal consistency** of the test as a whole, and its **appropriateness** in terms of difficulty for the test population. This kind of analysis facilitates such test revisions as the elimination or rewriting of items or their **distractors**, alterations to the **test rubric** (where instructions prove to be ambiguous or unclear, for example), and revision of the **marking scheme** or **assessment criteria**. Analysis of trial results may also provide information about the characteristics of **raters**, including **inter-rater reliability**, internal consistency and level of **harshness**.

Trialling may pose a number of practical difficulties for the test developer, including the identification of adequate numbers of suitable trial subjects who are not potential test **candidates** or who pose no other threat to **test security**. Essentially, test developers should aim to trial **objectively scored** tests on as many subjects as possible, in order to increase the confidence that the results are not due to chance, and to identify as many ambiguities in distractors or wording of items as possible. For **multiple-choice** tests designed for public use, some people suggest that 1000 trial subjects should be used, but this is often an entirely unrealistic goal for language test developers. For **subjectively scored** test items, a much smaller number of trial subjects is commonly regarded as sufficient. However, adequate numbers are still needed both to allow identification of unintended **responses** to tasks and to provide information about rater characteristics. Most important in the selection of trial subjects is that they be representative of the target population, with a similar range of **abilities** and backgrounds, since tests may work very differently with different populations.

A second problem faced by test developers is that of ensuring that trial subjects take the test seriously, thus providing a true indication of their ability; otherwise, trial results may be of little value. Problems of trialling are sometimes solved by including a group of new, untrialled test items in a live version of a test, which is then taken by a true sample of the target population under operational test conditions. Then either the old items, whose characteristics are known, are used for **reporting** results, or else all items, including the new ones, are used, except those which are shown to be unreliable.

See also: **test analysis**, **pilot testing**, **sampling**

Further reading: Alderson *et al.* 1995; Bachman & Palmer 1996, McNamara 1996

true score

Estimated from the **observed score** (actual test score), this is a hypothetical score reflecting a **candidate**'s true **ability**, once an adjustment has been made within the range of + / – one **standard error of measurement** (that portion of the observed score that is due to **sampling error**). However, because it cannot be known whether this adjustment should increase or lower the observed score, nor exactly by how much, the true score is in fact impossible to calculate.

For example, if two **test takers** both obtain a score of 75% in a test of reading comprehension, with a standard error of measurement (s_e) of 3%, then the true score for each of them may be anywhere between 72% (-1 s_e) and 78% ($+1$ s_e); it is impossible, on the basis of the observed score, to state with confidence whether or not they share the same true score and therefore the same ability. Estimates of the true score may be used in reporting **test results** and in determining the **cut-score**.

Further reading: Bachman 1990; Henning 1987; Cronbach 1964

true/false item

A **dichotomously scored test item**, where only two options about a statement (ie that it is 'true' or 'false') are offered to the **test taker**. Although **objectively marked**, it has the disadvantage that a guess gives the **candidate** a 50% chance of answering the item correctly, which may lead to reduced test **reliability** and **validity**. An attempt may be made to discourage **guessing**, by deducting a mark for each wrong answer rather than simply adding the number of correct (true) answers.

Because of the difficulty of estimating whether wrong answers are due to guesswork or other **ability** factors, in certain public tests true/false items have been deemed unacceptable. **Multiple-choice items** tend to be favoured over true/false items because they reduce the probability of candidates' guessing the right answer.

See also: **three-parameter model**

truncated sample

A **sample** from which the extreme scores of the **distribution** are missing (from either or both ends). This happens when either low-scoring or high-scoring **test takers** are excluded from consideration. In language testing, where certain **candidates** may be excluded on the basis of their **scores**, the existence of only a truncated sample can be problematic in the determination of the test's **predictive validity**. For example, for a **gatekeeping test** used to select university entrants, one might wish to follow the success of test takers in completing university courses, to determine the **validity** of the **cut-score**. However, those candidates who score below the cut-score are not permitted to undertake these courses and it is thus impossible to know whether they would have succeeded at university, and hence to establish with certainty whether the cut-score is valid.

two-parameter model

An **item response theory (IRT)** or **latent trait theory** model for the analysis and interpretation of test data. This model is more complex than that most commonly used in language testing, the **one-parameter model** (which considers **item difficulty** and candidate **ability**) in that it adds the **parameter** of **discriminability**, but it omits the estimates for **guessing** included in the **three-parameter model**.

Further reading: Henning 1987

two-tail(ed) test

See **one-tailed test**

Type 1 error

In **hypothesis testing**, the false rejection of a null **hypothesis**, that is, the conclusion that there is a relationship between **variables** (such as test **performance** and gender) when no such relationship in fact exists. Such an **error** is considered to be serious (more serious than a **Type 2 error**) and procedures are established to estimate the chance of such an error having been made; the probability of such an error is estimated precisely and reported as a *p*-value. Only in the case that the probability of such an error is less than 5% ($p<0.05$) (or more stringently, 1% ($p<0.01$), 0.1% ($p<0.001$), etc.) are we conventionally permitted to reject the null hypothesis (that there is no relationship between the variables) as the most appropriate explanation of our data. Hypothesis testing thus takes a conservative approach to the acceptance of evidence as appearing to confirm the existence of hypothesised relationships.

See also: **significance test**

Type 2 error

In **hypothesis testing**, the false acceptance of a null **hypothesis**, that is, the conclusion that there is no relationship between **variables** when such a relationship in fact exists; for example, the conclusion on the basis of data analysis that there is no relationship between test **performance** and gender where such a relationship does in fact exist; see **Type 1 error**. Although such an **error** is considered to be less serious than a Type 1 error (that is, the preference is to err on the side of caution in accepting evidence for the existence of a relationship between two variables), in practical terms (for example, when information is urgently needed about the benefit or the disadvantage of a particular procedure) a failure to recognise a relationship may also be harmful. The establishment of what confidence interval we should set in rejecting the null hypothesis is a matter of convention, and this convention may need to be evaluated for its **appropriateness** in particular contexts. The likelihood of making a Type 2 error is related to **sample** size; our power to identify relationships in data where they exist is improved with larger sample sizes.

See also: **significance tests**

type/token ratio

A measure of **vocabulary** flexibility, very commonly used in **Applied Linguistics** research. It expresses the ratio or proportion of unique (different) words (type) to the total number (tokens) of words used in a **text**. For example, consider the sentence: 'In casual conversation we generally use a narrower range of words than we use in formal written language.' Here, the total number of words (tokens) is 18; the words *in*, *we* and *use* all occur twice, but are only counted as one type each, so the type/token ratio is 15:18.

See also: **readability**, **lexical density**

u

UCLES

See **University of Cambridge Local Examinations Syndicate**

underfit

See **misfit**

unidimensionality

See **dimensionality**

unitary competence hypothesis

Also UCH, unitary trait hypothesis

The proposition that a single factor, or an internalised expectancy grammar, underlies **language proficiency**. It sprang from the idea that it was not considered possible to measure accurately individual aspects of a person's language **ability**, and that a single factor underlying language ability was analogous to the single **trait** of general intelligence (or indeed that intelligence and language ability were possibly not distinct traits). The unitary trait hypothesis was espoused in the late 1970s along with the concomitant belief that certain types of test, integrating numerous aspects of language use, such as **cloze** or **dictation**, were able to test this general **proficiency**. However, with the rise in popularity of communicative language teaching, this type of testing has now been superseded by multiple trait and **performance** testing.

See also: **general proficiency test, g factor**.

Further reading: Oller 1979, 1983

unit-credit scheme

See **Council of Europe**

University of Cambridge Local Examinations Syndicate (UCLES)

A major university-based examining body concerned with school-based **exams** in both the UK and internationally. It is also one of the major agencies involved in producing tests of English as a Foreign Language. Established in 1857 at the University of Cambridge, it introduced its first EFL test, the **Certificate of Proficiency in English (CPE)** in 1913, originally designed to **assess** the **proficiency** of foreign teachers of English. Since then, UCLES has developed a wide range of EFL/ESL tests at different **levels** for general and specific purposes, accompanied by a research programme which leads to regular revision of the design and content of these tests. UCLES EFL tests are administered in 1500 centres in 150 countries with 650,000 candidates taking the tests in 1997.

Other internationally recognised EFL tests developed by UCLES (with the date of introduction) include the **FCE (First Certificate in English** – 1939), the **PET (Preliminary English Test** – 1980), the **IELTS (International English Language Testing System** – 1989), the **CCSE (Certificates in Communicative Skills in English** – 1990), the **CAE (Certificate in Advanced English** – 1991), the **KET (Key English Test** – 1994), the **BEC (Business English Certificates** – 1993–96) and the **YLE (Cambridge Young Learners English Test** – 1997).

unsystematic error

See **random error**

V

validation

The process of establishing the **validity** of a test, which is one of the basic concerns of language testing. It is generally considered desirable to establish validity in as many ways as possible. Confidence in a test is directly proportional to the amount of evidence that is gathered in support of its validity.

Validation involves gathering and evaluating the evidence for the **reliability** and validity of a test when used for a given purpose. If the test is described as appropriate for a particular context or group of learners, for example, this claim should be evaluated on the basis of evidence derived from test **scores**, which should be produced by a representative **sample** of this **population**. If the test is to be used for a different population or purpose from that for which it was originally developed, or in a modified form, it may be appropriate for a further 'local' validation study to be carried out.

Validation is either internal (relating to the content of the test, the characteristics of the **test items**, and the kinds of **responses** elicited) or external (concerning the **construct** being tested, or the **criterion** to which test **performances** are related).

One approach to internal validity involves scrutiny (by relevant 'experts': normally professional testers, or linguistic or subject experts) of the test content (**content validity**). This process investigates systematically how relevant, representative (and, if necessary, how comprehensive) the **test content** is in its coverage of the language **knowledge**, **skills** and **ability** it should test: these are normally described in the **test specifications**, in a language **domain** specification, or in a teaching course or **syllabus**. **Test-taker feedback** may also contribute to the process of establishing content validity.

The other main approach to establishing internal validity is by gathering evidence about the **measurement** properties of the test items or **tasks** and the responses produced by test takers. This permits statements about the **difficulty** of the test as well as the extent to which the components of the test measure the same or different things, discriminate between test takers, and elicit responses of the kinds expected.

In evaluating claims to external validity, scores obtained on the test may be used to investigate **criterion-related validity**, for example by relating them to other test scores or measures such as teachers' **assessments** (**concurrent validity**) or future **achievement** (**predictive validity**).

Perhaps the most important question, however, to be considered in validation of a test is that of its **construct validity**. This involves analysing how test scores may be understood in relation to the theoretical framework underlying the construct the test is designed to measure. It thus aims to answer the fundamental (and fundamentally difficult) **questions**: 'What exactly does the test claim to measure?' 'What **inferences** may be made about **test takers**?' 'On what basis may these inferences be made?' Complex statistical procedures involving **correlations** of various kinds, such as **factor analysis**, are sometimes used in construct validation studies. **Multi-trait multi-method** designs are a standard approach to construct validation. Construct validity can, indeed, be seen as embracing all other kinds of validity.

Other issues to be considered in test validation relate to how test takers perform, including examination of possible **test bias**, and ethical questions of how tests are used, including **consequential validity**.

See also: **test purpose**, **convergent validity**, **face validity**

Further reading: Bachman 1990; Alderson *et al.* 1995; Davies 1984, 1990; Messick 1993; Cohen *et al.* 1992

validity (valid)

The quality which most affects the value of a test, prior to, though dependent on, **reliability.** A measure is valid if it does what it is intended to do, which is typically to act as an indicator of an abstract concept (for example height, weight, time, etc.) which it claims to measure. The validity of a language test therefore is established by the extent to which it succeeds in providing an accurate concrete representation of an abstract concept (for example **proficiency**, **achievement**, **aptitude**).

The most commonly referred to types of validity are:
- **content**;
- **construct**;
- **concurrent**;
- **predictive**.

Content and construct validity are conceptual; concurrent and predictive validity are statistical.

A fifth type of validity, **face** validity, refers to the degree to which a test appears to measure the **knowledge** or **abilities** it claims to measure, as judged by an untrained observer (such as the **candidate** taking the test or the institution which plans to administer it).

Other terms that occur in relation to validity are: consequential, systemic, discriminant, divergent and **ethicality**.

Content validity is established by specifying the **domain** to be **sampled** for testing and then selecting **test items** to represent that domain. For example, a test of **LSP** has content validity if it contains key indicators of the **LSP** domain, as determined by professional judgement, which may include **needs analysis**.

Construct validity refers to the quality of a test in terms of the theoretical model on which the test is based. **Factor analysis** or **IRT analysis** is often used to determine statistically to what extent the test provides empirical backing for such claims.

Criterion-related validity (which incorporates concurrent and predictive validities) of a new test is established statistically in terms of the closeness of a test to its criterion. This may be an existing test or some other measure within the same domain (concurrent validity) or a future test or other measure (predictive validity). In both cases validity is judged in terms of how closely the new test correlates with the criterion measure. The relation of two parallel tests with one another, which is a special case of the relation of a new test to a criterion test, is a matter of both reliability and validity, reminding us of the close link between the two.

See also: **consequencial validity**, **systemic validity**, **discriminant validity**, **convergent validity**

Further reading: Bachman 1990; Cronbach 1964; Davies 1990

Vantage Level
See **Council of Europe**

variable
An attribute or **trait** of people or things which can take on different values. Variables may be very broad in scope (eg educational background) or more narrow (eg age). Variables can be measured or quantified in different ways, and different kinds of **scale** are used accordingly – **nominal scale**, **ordinal scale** or **interval scale**.

Variables may be dependent or independent. The dependent variable is the principle attribute that is being investigated, such as the writing **proficiency** of a group of **test takers**, or the level of agreement among a group of **raters**. An independent variable is one which is thought to influence the dependent variable – the **test method** or the rater's background, for example.

Further classifications of variable include moderator variable, control variable, contaminating variable and intervening variable. These refer to additional variables, either anticipated at the outset of a study or recognised later, which influence the dependent variable.

Further reading: Hatch & Lazaraton 1991

variance

A descriptive statistic, derived by calculating the square of the **standard deviation** of a set of **scores**, and often symbolised by s^2. It is used in two ways:

- to describe the degree of variation within one **variable**: the variance is a measure of the **dispersion** from the **mean**, or how far scores on a single test (one variable) are spread;
- to describe the degree of **correlation** between two variables: the shared variance is a comparison of the dispersion of two sets of test scores (two variables), calculated by squaring the correlation between them. For example, if scores obtained by a group of students on a test of English for academic purposes taken before a course of instruction were correlated 0.3 with scores obtained by the same students after one semester of the course, the shared variance would be 0.09 or 9%. The remaining 91% of the variance (the non-shared variance, ie the variance unaccounted for by factors common to the two tests), could be explained by non-linguistic factors such as **motivation**, learning style and intelligence.

version

See **alternative forms, test form**

vertical equating

The process of establishing the relationship in terms of **level** of **difficulty** of one test to another, and used where tests to be compared might share a number of characteristics such as general purpose or **skills** tested, but be designed for use with groups of language learners who differ in age or level of **language proficiency**.

Various statistical techniques are used in the process of determining the relationship in difficulty between tests. A group of **items** with known psychometric properties, common to adjacent levels of a test, may be used to provide a link between the tests: on the basis of **performance** on these items, the relative difficulty of the complete versions of the two tests is calculated. Alternatively, a group of learners whose **ability** has been established on the basis of performance on one level of a test may be required to attempt items from a different level, thus acting as a link between the two tests, allowing calculation of the difficulty of the second test.

See also: **equating, item bank**

vocabulary

Refers to the total number of lexical items (single words, compound words or idioms) of a language, or (as a measure of **ability**) to the total number of lexical items of a **target language** that a user or learner knows. It may also refer more specifically to the technical vocabulary of a particular **domain** in **LSP** (eg the vocabulary of civil engineers, the vocabulary of speech pathologists).

Evidence of **knowledge** of vocabulary may be obtained by testing it explicitly, using **discrete-point test items**, each testing individual lexical **items**, or implicitly, such as in an **integrative test**, where knowledge of a set of vocabulary items is required to complete the test **task**. Discrete-point vocabulary tests most commonly test a learner's breadth of vocabulary (the number of words known) but may also test depth (how well words are known: the variety of contexts in which a word may be used, or the shades of meaning that may attach to it). In an integrative test, the vocabulary items tested may be specified exactly (as, for example, in a **dictation** test), may be specified, but less exactly (as in a **cloze test** using a semantically acceptable **scoring** method), or may be unspecified (as in a **performance test** of speaking). In this last case, judgements of vocabulary knowledge may be based on such factors as ability to use precise or technical terms, to choose words of an appropriate **register**, or to use circumlocution.

See also: **readability**

vocabulary test

A test of word knowledge. Vocabulary testing is a traditional type of language test which lost popularity during the heyday of the communicative movement because **vocabulary** test **items** were largely decontextualised. But vocabulary tests are now returning to favour, supported by the more central role of vocabulary in current linguistic and cognitive theories.

Further reading: Laufer & Nation 1995

W

washback

Also **backwash**

The effect of testing on instruction. Language test washback is said to be either positive or negative.

Negative washback is said to occur when **test items** are based on an outdated view of language which bears little relationship to the teaching **curriculum**. If, for example, the **skill** of writing is tested only by **multiple-choice items**, then there is great pressure to practise such **items** rather than to practise the skill of writing itself. Any important test which remains very structure based may be said to have negative washback if its influence prevents desired changes in **proficiency** teaching towards a more communicative methodology.

Positive washback is said to result when a testing procedure which encourages 'good' teaching practice is introduced. For example, the use of an **oral interview** in a final **examination** may encourage teachers to practise conversational language use with their students. However, when the testing procedure is too much in advance of the teaching method it is unlikely that positive washback will occur because teachers and learners may not understand what the test items require of them.

It has been pointed out that there is little empirical evidence for many of the claims which are made about the positive or negative impact of language testing.

Further reading: Alderson & Wall 1993

Waystage Level

See **Council of Europe**

weighting

The awarding of extra value to certain **items**, **assessment criteria**, **tasks** or **sub-tests**. While the simplest approach is to give each test component equal weighting, the test developer may choose to give certain components more weight in the overall **score**, reflecting a perception of the relative importance of the different test components. The differential weighting may reflect:

- the fact that certain **skills** (eg speaking or reading) are considered more crucial than others (in the assessment of **proficiency**);
- the nature of the **assessment criteria** (overarching or general criteria such as overall **intelligibility** sometimes being weighted more heavily than specific criteria such as **pronunciation** or **fluency**);
- the time the test developer wishes candidates to spend on each task; or
- the importance the teacher wishes to place on particular skills in a pedagogic context.

Where sub-tests are of different lengths and the test developer wishes to give them equal weighting, then the **raw scores** will need to be transformed before adding or averaging them. Such weighting can be seen as internal to the test.

It may be the case with certain tests used for selection purposes that users of the **test results** are encouraged to determine their own weighting. This is the case, for example, with the **IELTS**, where receiving institutions are recommended to set entry **levels** for the four sub-tests according to the demands of the particular course. Thus a second type of weighting is undertaken by the **test users**.

A third type of weighting is that associated with the **raters** themselves and their inherent (and often unconscious) orientation to particular features of language. Where **holistic scoring** is used, particular raters or groups of raters may focus on particular aspects of the **performance** to the neglect of others. Where **analytic scoring** is employed, this may lead to a **halo effect** of the judgement made on one feature affecting the judgements made on other unrelated features. It is commonly reported that language teachers place more emphasis on grammar than on other aspects of language use.

Statistical procedures such as **stepwise regression** may be used to investigate this third type of weighting of assessment criteria.

word frequency count

A count of the total number of different **vocabulary** items occurring in a **text** or corpus. Such counts have led to the creation of word lists (eg the 20 most frequently occurring words, the 1,000 most frequent, etc.) which can be used, for example, to select appropriate vocabulary for language teaching or **assessment** or to compare the **difficulty** of different texts.

Further reading: Kucera & Francis 1967

writing test

A test of the **ability** to write in a language. There are two broad approaches to the **assessment** of writing. The first is indirect, and relies on **objectively scored** item types in which the **test taker** is required to recognise, produce or correct a variety of carefully specified written forms. The focus is thus on formal elements of the language at the word or sentence level, such as grammar, **vocabulary**, spelling and punctuation.

The second approach is direct, requiring the test taker to produce (typically) between one and three written **texts**. This latter approach, because it requires test takers to demonstrate ability to write longer texts, is often considered to have greater **validity** than **indirect tests**. **Task** types used depend upon the **test purpose**, and vary widely in specification (including topic, text type, length, audience, and the **input** provided for the test taker). The writing is subjectively scored, using a **scale** which is (normally) constructed during the test development process. A variety of approaches to scoring may be used, again depending on the test purpose: **holistic, analytic, primary-trait** or **multiple-trait scoring** procedures. Features represented in **scales** used for writing assessment include grammatical control, **coherence, cohesion**, organisation of ideas, **fluency** of expression, conventions of presentation (eg spelling, handwriting, paragraphing, layout), awareness of audience and use of vocabulary.

An extension of the **performance**-based approach to writing assessment is **portfolio assessment**, in which the **candidate** is required to produce a **portfolio** containing a range of texts, generally over a period of weeks or months.

In addition to the above, tests of the **receptive skills** of reading and listening sometimes require the test taker to produce written **responses** to **items**. In this way, writing ability is (however indirectly or implicitly) inevitably included in the assessment.

See also: **objective scoring, subjective scoring**
Further reading: Weir 1993; Hamp-Lyons 1991a

xyz

χ-Square
See **Chi-square**

yes/no question
See **forced-choice item**

YLE
see **Cambridge Young Learners English Test**

z score
A way of placing an individual **score** in the whole **distribution** of scores on a test; it expresses how many **standard deviation** units lie above or below the **mean**. Scores above the mean are positive; those below the mean are negative.

An advantage of z scores is that they allow scores from different tests to be compared, where the mean and standard deviation differ, and where score points may not be equal.

See also: **standardised score**, ***T* score**, **stanine score**, **percentile**
Further reading: Hatch & Lazaraton 1991

References

Alderson, J. C. (1979) The cloze procedure and proficiency in English as a foreign language. *TESOL Quarterly* 13: 219–27.

Alderson, J. C. (1981) Report of the discussion on General Language Proficiency. In Alderson, J. C.& Hughes, A. (Eds.) *ELT Documents 111: Issues in Language Testing*. London: The British Council: 187–94

Alderson, J. C. (1991) Bands and Scores. In Alderson & North (Eds.) *Language Testing in the 1990s: the Communicative Legacy*. London: Macmillan: 71–86.

Alderson, J. C. & Clapham, C. M. (1992) Applied linguistics and language testing: A case study of the ELTS test. *Applied Linguistics* 13: 149–67.

Alderson, J. C., Clapham, C. M. & Wall, D. (1995) *Language Test Construction and Evaluation*. Cambridge: Cambridge University Press.

Alderson, J. C., Krahnke, K. J. & Stansfield, C. W. (1987) *Reviews of English Language Proficiency Tests*. Washington, DC: TESOL.

Alderson, J. C. & Lukmani, Y. (1989) Cognition and reading: Cognitive levels as embodied in test questions. *Reading in a Foreign Language* 5 (2): 253–70.

Alderson J. C. & North, B. (1991) *Language Testing in the 1990s: The Communicative Legacy*. London: Macmillan.

Alderson, J. C. & Wall, D. (1993) Does Washback exist? *Applied Linguistics* 14 (2): 115–29.

Allen J. P. B. & Davies, A. (1977) *Testing and experimental methods: The Edinburgh Course in Applied Linguistics*, vol. 4. Oxford: Oxford University Press.

ALTE (1998) *ALTE Handbook*. Cambridge: EFL Division, The University of Cambridge Local Examinations Syndicate.

ALTE Newsletter. Twice a year. University of Cambridge Local Examinations Syndicate.

American Council on the Teaching of Foreign Languages (ACTFL) (1986) *ACTFL Proficiency Guidelines*. Hasting-on-Hudson, New York, NY: ACTFL.

American Education Research Association, American Psychological Association, and National Council on Measurement in Education. (1985) *Standards for Educational and Psychological Testing*. Washington, DC: American Psychological Association, Inc.

Anastasi, A. (1990) *Psychological Testing* (6th ed.). New York: Macmillan.

Anderson, L. W. (1981) *Assessing Affective Characteristics in the Schools.* Boston, MA: Allyn & Bacon.

Angoff, W. H. (1971) Scales, norms and equivalent scores. In R. L. Thorndike (Ed.) *Educational Measurement.* Washington, DC: American Council on Education: 508–600.

Anstey, E. (1966) *Psychological Tests.* London: Nelson.

Bachman, L. F. (1988) Problems in examining the validity of the ACTFL Oral Proficiency Interview. *Studies in Second Language Acquisition* 10: 149–64.

Bachman L. F. (1990) *Fundamental Considerations in Language Testing.* Oxford: Oxford University Press.

Bachman, L. F. & Cohen, A. D. (Eds.) (1998) *Interfaces Between SLA and Language Testing Research.* Cambridge: Cambridge University Press.

Bachman, L. F., Davidson, F., Ryan, K. & Choi, I.-C. (1995) *An Investigation into the Comparability of Two Tests of English as a Foreign Language: The Cambridge-TOEFL Comparability Study.* Cambridge: Cambridge University Press.

Bachman, L. F. & Palmer, A. (1996) *Language Testing in Practice.* Oxford: Oxford University Press.

Baker, F. B. (1993) Computer technology in test construction and processing. In Linn (Ed.) *Educational Measurement.* Phoenix, AZ: ACE/Oryx.

Bartsch, R. (1987) *Norms of Language.* London: Longman.

Beech, J. R., Harding, L. & Hilton-Jones, D. (1993) *Assessment in Speech and Language Therapy.* London: Routledge-NFER Assessment Library.

Belanoff, P. & Dickson, M. (1990) *Portfolios: Process and Product.* Portsmouth, NH: Heinemann Boynton/Cook.

Berk, R. A. (Ed.) (1980) *Criterion-Referenced Measurement: State of the Art.* Baltimore, MD: The John Hopkins University Press.

Berk, R. A. (1984) *A Guide to Criterion-referenced Test Construction.* Baltimore, MD: The Johns Hopkins University Press.

Berk, R. A. (1986) A consumer's guide to setting performance standards on criterion-referenced tests. *Review of Educational Research* 56: 137–72.

Berwick, R. & Ross, S. (1996) Cross-cultural pragmatics in oral proficiency interview strategies. In Milanovic, M. & Saville, N. (Eds.) *Performance Testing, Cognition and Assessment: Selected Papers from the 15th Language Testing Research Colloquium, Cambridge and Arnhem.* Cambridge: Cambridge University Press: 34–54.

Black, L. & Daiker, D. (1994) *New Directions in Portfolio Assessment.* Portsmouth, NH: Heinemann Boynton/Cook.

Brindley, G. (1989) *Assessing Achievement in the Learner-Centred*

Curriculum. Sydney, Australia: National Center for English Language Teaching and Research, Macquarie University.

Brindley G. (Ed.) (1995) *Language Assessment in Action*. Sydney, Australia: National Center for English Language Teaching and Research, Macquarie University.

Brindley, G. (1998) Describing language development. Rating scales and second language acquisition. In Bachmann, L. F. & Cohen, A. D. (Eds.) *Interfaces Between SLA and Language Testing Research*. Cambridge: Cambridge University Press.

Buck, G. (1994) The Appropriacy of Psychometric Measurement Models for Testing Second Language Listening Comprehension. *Language Testing* 11(2): 145–70.

Buros, O. K. (Ed.) (1975) *Foreign Language Tests and Reviews*. Highland Park, NJ: The Gryphon Press.

Burt, M. K., Dulay, H. & Hernandez-Chavez, E. (1975) *Bilingual Syntax Measure 1*. New York, NY: Harcourt Brace Jovanovich.

Butler, C. (1985) *Statistics in Linguistics*. Oxford/New York: Blackwell.

Byrnes, H. & Canale, M. (Eds.) (1987) *Defining and Developing Proficiency: Guidelines, Implementations and Concepts*. Lincolnwood, IL: National Textbook Company.

Campbell, D. T. & Fiske, D. W. (1959) Convergent and dicscriminant validity in the multitrait-multimethod matrix. *Psychological Bulletin* 56: 81–105.

Canale, M. (1983) On some dimensions of language proficiency. In Oller, J. W. Jr. (Ed.) *Issues in Language Testing Research*. Rowley, MA: Newbury House: 333–42.

Canale M. & Swain M. (1980) Theoretical bases of communicative approaches to second language teaching and testing. *Applied Linguistics* 1(1): 1–47.

Cangelosi, J. S. (1982) *Measurement and Evaluation: An Inductive Approach for Teachers*. Dubuque, IA: W. C. Brown.

Carroll, J. B. & Sapon., S. M. (1958) *Modern Language Aptitude Test*. New York, NY: The Psychological Corporation.

Cattell, R. B. (1940) A culture free intelligence test, Part 1. *Journal of Educational Psychology* 1(31): 161–79.

Charney, D. (1984) The validity of using holistic scoring to evaluate writing: A critical overview. *Research in the Teaching of English* 18: 65–81.

Choppin, B. H. (1990) Correction for guessing. In Walberg & Haertel (Eds.) *The International Encyclopedia of Educational Evaluation*. Oxford: Pergamon, 345–8.

Clapham, C. (1996) *The Development of IELTS: A Study of the Effect of Background Knowledge on Reading Comprehension*. Cambridge: University of Cambridge Local Examination Syndicate/Cambridge University Press.

Clark, J. L. D. (1979) Direct versus semi-direct tests of speaking ability. In Brière, E. J. & Hinofotis, F. B. (Eds.) *Concepts in Language Testing: Some Recent Studies*, Washington, DC: TESOL: 35–49.

Clark, J. L. D. (1987) *Curriculum Renewal in Foreign Language Learning*. Oxford: Oxford University Press.

Clark, J. L. D. & Gifford, R. T. (1988) The FSI/ILR/ACTFL proficency scales and testing techniques: Development, current status and needed research. *Studies in Second Language Acquisition* 10: 129–47.

Cohen, A. D. (1984) On taking tests: What the students report. *Language Testing* (1)1: 70–81.

Cohen, L. (1976) *Educational Research in Classroooms and Schools: A Manual of Materials and Methods*. London: Harper & Row.

Cohen, R. J., Swerdlik, M. E. & Smith, D. K. (1992) *Psychological Testing and Assessment: An Introduction to Test and Measurement*. California: Mayfield Publishing Company.

Cole, N. S. & Moss, P. A. (1993) Bias in test use. In Linn (Ed.) *Educational Measurement* (3rd ed.). New York, NY: American Council on Education/Macmillan: 210–19.

Cooper, J. (1979) *Think and Link: an advanced course in reading and writing skills*. London: Edward & Arnold

Criper, C. & Davies, A. (Eds.) (1988) ELTS Validation Project Report. *ELTS Research Report Vol 1(i)*. Cambridge: University of Cambridge Local Examinations Syndicate.

Cronbach, L. C. (1964) *Essentials of Psychological Testing*. Tokyo: Harper & Row.

Darnell, D. K. (1970) Clozentropy: A procedure for testing English language proficiency of foreign students. *Speech Monographs* 37(1): 36–46.

Davidson, F. & Lynch, B. (1993) Criterion-referenced language test development. A prologomenon. In Huhta, A., Sajavaara, K. & Takala, S. (Eds.) *Language Testing: New Openings*. Jyvaskyla, Finland: University of Jyvaskala.

Davies, A. (1977) The construction of language tests. Chapter 3. In Allen and Davies (Eds.) *Testing and Experimental Methods*, vol. 4 in *Edinburgh Course in Applied Linguistics*, Oxford, Oxford University Press: 38–104.

Davies, A. (1978a) Language Testing. Survey Article Part I. *Language Teaching and Linguistics Abstracts* 2: 145–59.

Davies, A. (1978b) Language Testing. Survey Article Part II. *Language Teaching and Linguistics Abstracts* 3/4: 215–31.

Davies, A. (1984) Validating three tests of English language proficiency. *Language Testing* 1(1): 50–69.

Davies, A. (1989) Testing reading speed through text retrieval. In Candlin, C. N.

& McNamara, T. F. (Eds.) *Language Learning and Community.* Sydney: NCELTR, Macquarie University: 115–24.

Davies, A. (1990) *Principles of Language Testing.* Oxford: Blackwell.

Davies, A. (1991) *The Native Speaker in Applied Linguistics.* Edinburgh: Edinburgh University Press.

Davies, A. (1997a) Introduction: The limits of ethics in language testing. In Davies, A. (Ed.) *Language Testing* 14/3 (Special Issue on Ethics in Language Testing): 225–41.

Davies, A. (1997b) Demands of being professional in language testing. In Davies, A. (Ed.) *Language Testing* 14/3 (Special Issue on Ethics in Language Testing): 329–39.

de Jong, H. A. L. & Stevenson, D. (1990) *Individualizing the Assessment of Language Abilities.* Clevedon, Avon: Multilingual Matters.

Douglas, D. (forthcoming) *Testing language for specific purposes: theory and practice.* Cambridge University Press.

Eells, K. W., Davies, A., Havighurst, R. J., Herrick, V. E. & Tyler, R. W. (1951) *Intelligence and Cultural Differences: A Study of Cultural Learning and Problem-Solving.* Chicago, IL: University of Chicago Press.

Ellis, R. (1985) *Understanding Second Language Acquisition.* Oxford: Oxford University Press.

Ericsson, K. A. & Simon, H. A. (1993) *Protocol Analysis: Verbal reports as data.* Cambridge, MA: MIT Press.

Fasold, R. (1984) *The Sociolinguistics of Society.* Oxford: Oxford University Press.

Feldt, L. S. & Brennan, R. L. (1993) Reliability. In Linn (Ed.) *Educational Measurement.* Phoenix, AZ: ACE/Oryx: 105–46.

Foreign Service Institute (1968) *Absolute Language Proficiency Ratings.* Washington, DC: Foreign Service Institute.

Fulcher, G. (1996) Does thick description lead to smart tests? A data-based approach to rating scale construction. *Language Testing* 13(2): 208–38.

Ghadessy, M. (Ed.) (1993) *Register Analysis: Theory and Practice.* London: Pinter Publishers Ltd.

Gilliland, J. (1972) *Readability.* London: London University Press.

Glaser, G. R. (1963) Instructional technology and the measurement of learning outcomes. *American Psychologist* 18: 519–21.

Griffin P., Adams, R. J., Martin, L. & Tomlinson, B. (1986) *The Development of an Interview Test for Adult Migrants.* Melbourne Ministry of Education (Schools Division).

Griffin, P. & Nix, P. (1991) *Educational Assessment and Reporting: A New Approach.* Sydney: Harcourt Brace Jovanovich.

Halliday, M. A. K. & Hasan, R. (1976) *Cohesion in English.* London: Longman.

Halliday, M. A. K., McIntosh, A. & Strevens, P. D. (1964) *The Linguistic*

Sciences and Language Teaching. London: Longman.

Hambleton, R. K., Swaminathan, H. & Rogers, H. J. (1991) *Fundamentals of Item Response Theory.* Newbury Park, CA: Sage.

Hamilton, J., Lopes, M., McNamara, T. F. & Sheridan, E. (1993) Rating scales and native speaker performance on a communicatively oriented EAP test. *Language Testing* 10(3): 337–54.

Hamp-Lyons, L. (Ed.) (1991a) *Assessing Second Language Writing in Academic Contexts.* Norwood, NJ: Ablex Publishing Corporation.

Hamp-Lyons, L. (1991b) Scoring procedures for ESL contexts. In Hamp-Lyons (Ed.) *Assessing second-language writing in academic contexts.* Norwood, NJ: Ablex Publishing Corporation.

Hamp-Lyons, L. & Condon, W. (1998) *Assessing College Writing Portfolios: Theory, Practice, Research.* New Jersey: Hampton Press.

Harley B., Allen, P,. Cummins, J. & Swain, M. (Eds.) (1987) *The Development of Bilingual Proficiency: Final Report Vol 111: Social Context and Age.* Toronto: Modern Language Centre, OISE.

Hatch, E. & Lazaraton, A. (1991) *The Research Manual – Design & Statistics for Applied Linguistics.* Los Angeles, CA: Newbury House.

Heaton, J. B. (1975/1987) *Writing English Language Tests.* London: Longman.

Henning, G. (1987) *A Guide to Language Testing.* Cambridge, MA: Newbury House.

Holland, P. W. & Thayer, D. T. (1988) Differential Item Functioning and the Mantel-Hainszel Procedure. In Wainer, H. & Braun, H. I. (Eds.) *Test Validity.* Hillsdale, NJ: Lawrence Erlbaum: 129–45.

Holland, P. W. & Wainer, H. I. (1993) *Differential Item Functioning.* Hillsdale, NJ: Lawrence Erlbaum.

Hudson, T. (1989) Mastery decisions in program evaluation. In Johnson, R. K. (Ed.) *The Second Language Curriculum.* Cambridge: Cambridge University Press.

Hudson, T. & Lynch, B. (1984) A criterion-referenced measurement approach to ESL achievement. *Language Testing* 1: 171–201.

Hughes, A. (1987) Review of English Proficiency Test Battery. In Alderson, J. C., Krahnke, K. J. & Stansfield, C. W. (Eds.) New York: TESOL: 31–2.

Hughes, A. (1989) *Testing for Language Teachers.* Cambridge: Cambridge University Press.

Hughes, A., Porter, D. & Weir, C. (Eds.) (1988) ELTS Validation Project: Proceedings of a Conference Held to Consider the ELTS Validation Project Report. *ELTS Research Report* 1(ii). London and Cambridge: British Council and University of Cambridge Local Examinations Syndicate.

Hymes, D. H. (1972) On communicative competence. In Pride, J. B. & Holmes, J. (Eds.) *Sociolinguistics*. Harmondsworth: Penguin: 269–93.

Ingram, D. E. (1984) *Australian Second Language Proficiency Ratings*. Canberra: Australian Government Publishing Services.

Ingram, D. E. (1995) Scales. *Melbourne Papers in Language Testing* 4(2): 12–29.

Jacobs, L. C. & Chase, C. I. (1992) *Developing and Using Tests Effectively: A Guide for Faculty*. San Francisco, CA: Jossey-Bass.

Jaeger, R. M. (1993) Certification of student competence. In Linn (1993): 485-514

Jafarpur, A. (1995) Is C-testing superior to cloze? *Language Testing* 12(2): 194–215.

Jenks, F. (1987) Review of Michigan Test of English Proficiency. In Alderson *et al.* (1987): 58–60.

Jensen, A. R. (1980) *Bias in Mental Testing*. New York, NY: Free Press.

Johnson R. K. (Ed.) (1989) *The Second Language Curriculum*. Cambridge: Cambridge University Press.

Joint Committee on Testing Practices. (1988) *Code of Fair Testing Practices in Education*. Washington, DC: National Council of Measurement in Education.

Kant, L. & Orr, L. (1990) Educational Profiles. In Walberg & Haertel (1990): 420–24.

Klein-Braley, C. (1997) C-Tests in the context of reduced redundancy testing: An appraisal. *Language Testing* 14(1): 47–84.

Kucera, H. & Francis, W. (1967) *Computational Analysis of Present-day American English*. Providence, RI: Brown University Press.

Kunnan, A. J. (1995) *Test Taker Characteristics and Test Performance*. Cambridge: Cambridge University Press.

Lado, R. (1961) *Language Testing*. London: Longman.

Language Testing Update (1996) *ILTA Official Newsletter* (no. 20). Lancaster, Centre for Research in Language Education, University of Lancaster.

Laufer, B. & Nation, P. (1995) Vocabulary size and use: Lexical richness in L2 written production. *Applied Linguistics* 16(3): 307–22.

Linacre, J. M. (1989) *Many-faceted Rasch Measurement*. Chicago, IL: MESA Press.

Linn, R. L (Ed.) (1993) *Educational Measurement* (3rd ed.). Phoenix, AZ: ACE/Oryx.

Livingston, S. A. & Zieky, M. J. (1982) *Passing Scores: A Manual for Setting Standards of Performance on Educational and Occupational Tests*. Princeton, NJ: Educational Testing Service.

Ludlow, L. (1995) Rasch Model Logits: Interpretation, use, and transformation. *Educational & Psychological Measurement* 6: 967–75.

Lumley, T. (1993). The notion of reading comprehension sub-skills: an EAP example. *Language Testing* 10(3): 211–34.

Lumley, T. & Brown, A. (1996) Specific-purpose language performance tests: task and interaction. In Wigglesworth, G. & Elder, C. (Eds.) The Testing Cycle: From Inception to Washback. *Australian Review of Applied Linguistics Series* S(13): 105–36.

Lynch, B. J. (1996) *Language Program Evaluation: Theory and Practice.* Cambridge: Cambridge University Press.

McNamara, T. (1996) *Measuring Second Language Performance.* London: Longman.

Messick, S. (1988) The once and future issues of validity: Assessing the meaning and consequences of measurement. In Wainer & Braun (1988): 32–45.

Messick, S. (1993) Validity. In Linn (1993): 13–103.

Miles, M. B. & Huberman, A. M. (1994) *Qualitative Data Analysis: An Expanded Sourcebook.* Thousand Oaks, CA: Sage Publications.

Millman, J. & Greene, J. (1993) The specification and development of tests of achievement and ability. In Linn (1993).

Milroy, J. & Milroy, L. (1985) *Authority in Language: Investigating Language Prescription and Standardisation.* London: Routledge & Kegan Paul.

Morrow, K. (1977) *Techniques of Evaluation for a Notional Syllabus.* London: Royal Society of Arts.

Munby, J. (1978) *Communicative Syllabus Design.* Cambridge: Cambridge University Press.

North, B. (1996a) *The Development of a Common Framework Scale of Language Proficiency Based on a Theory of Measurement.* Unpublished PhD thesis, Thames Valley University.

North, B. (1996b) Scales of language proficiency. *Melbourne Papers in Language Testing* 4(2): 60–111.

O'Loughlin, K. (1995) Lexical density in candidate output on direct and semi-direct versions of an oral proficiency test. *Language Testing* 12(2): 217–37.

O'Loughlin, K. (1997) *Direct and Semi-direct Tests of Spoken Language.* Unpublished PhD thesis. The University of Melbourne, Australia.

Oller, J. W. (1979) *Language Tests at School.* London: Longman.

Oller, J. W.(1983). *Issues in Language Testing Research.* Rowley, MA: Newbury House.

Osgood, C. E., Suci, G. J. & Tannenbaum, P. H. (1957) *The Measurement of Meaning.* Urbana, IL: University of Illinois Press.

Oskarsson, M. (1984) *Self-assessment of Foreign Language Skills: A Survey of Research and Development Work.* Strasbourg: Council for Cultural Co-operation.

Petersen, N. S., Kolen, M. J. & Hoover, H. D. (1993) Scaling, norming and equating. In Linn (1983).

Pienemann, M. (1985) Learnability and syllabus construction. In Hyltenstam & Pienemann, M. (Eds.) *Modelling and Assessing Second Language Acquisition.* Clevedon, Avon: Multilingual Matters, 23–75.

Pollitt, A. (1984) Item banking. *Issues in Educational Assessment Occasional Papers.* Edinburgh UK: Her Majesty's Stationery Office.

Pollitt, A. (1991) In Alderson, J. C. & North, B. (Eds.) *Language Testing in the 1990s.* Modern English Publications and the British Council: 87–94.

Pollitt, A. & Hutchinson, C. (1987) Calibrated graded assessments: Rasch partial credit analysis of performance in writing. *Language Testing* 4 (1): 72–92.

Popham, W. J. (1975) *Educational Evaluation.* Englewood Cliffs, NJ: Prentice Hall.

Popham, W. J. (1978) *Criterion-Referenced Measurement.* Englewood Cliffs, NJ: Prentice Hall.

Popham, W. J. (1990) *Modern Educational Measurement: A Practitioner's Perspective* (2nd ed.). Boston, MA: Allyn and Bacon.

Porter, D. (1991) Affective factors in language testing. In Alderson & North (1991): 32–40.

Quellmalz, E. S. (1990) Essay Examinations. In Walberg & Haertel (1990): 510–5.

Reilly, R. (1971) A note on 'clozentropy'. *Speech Monographs* 38(2): 350–3.

Ross, S. (1992) Accommodative questions in oral proficiency interviews. *Language Testing* 9(2): 173–86.

Rowntree, D. (1981) *Statistics without Tears.* Harmondsworth: Penguin.

Scriven, M. (1991) *Evaluation Thesaurus* (4th ed.) Newbury Park, CA: Sage.

Shavelson, R. J. & Webb, N. M. (1991) *Generalizability Theory: A Primer.* Newbury Park, CA: Sage.

Shohamy, E. (1994) The validity of direct versus semi-direct oral tests. *Language Testing,* 11: 99–123.

Skehan, P. (1989) *Individual Differences in Second and Foreign Language Learning.* London: Edward Arnold.

Smagorinsky, P. (1995) *Speaking about Writing: Reflections on Research Methodology.* Thousand Oaks, CA: Sage.

Spearman, C. (1904) 'General intelligence': Objectively Determined and Measured. *American Journal of Psychology* 15: 202–9.

Spolsky, B. (1995) *Measured Words.* Oxford: Oxford University Press.

Stansfield, C. W. (1986) A history of the Test of Written English: The developmental year. *Language Testing* 3(2): 224–34.

Stansfield, C. W. (1989) *Simulated Oral Proficiency Interviews.* Washington,

DC: ERIC Clearinghouse on Languages and Linguistics.

Stansfield, C. W. (1993) Ethics, standards and professionalism in language testing. *Issues in Applied Linguistics* 4(2): 189–205.

Studies in Second Language Acquisition (4 per year), Cambridge: Cambridge University Press.

Swales, J. (1990) *Genre analysis : English in academic and research settings*. Cambridge: Cambridge University Press.

Thurstone, L. L. (1959) *The Measurement of Values*. Chicago, IL: University of Chicago Press.

TOEFL Bulletin (annual) Princeton, N.J: Educational Testing Service.

Underhill, N. (1987) *Testing Spoken Interaction*. Cambridge: Cambridge University Press.

University of Cambridge Local Examinations Syndicate, The British Council, IDP Education Australia (1996) *The IELTS Handbook*. Cambridge: Author.

Ure, J. (1971) Lexical density and register differentiation. In Perren, G. E. & Trim, J. L. M. (Eds.) *Applications of Linguistics: Selected Papers of the Second International Congress of Applied Linguistics, Cambridge* (1969). Cambridge: Cambridge University Press.

Valette, R. M. (1967) *Modern Language Testing*. New York, NY: Harcourt, Brace & World.

van Ek, J. A. & Trim, J. L. M. (1991) *Threshold Level 1990*. Strasbourg: Council of Europe Press.

Van Lier, L. (1989) Reeling, writhing, drawling, stretching and fainting in coils: Oral proficiency interviews as conversation. *TESOL Quarterly*, 23(3): 489–508.

Vogt, W. P. (1993) *Dictionary of Statistics and Methodology*. Newbury Park, CA: Sage.

Wainer, H. & Braun, H. I. (Eds.) (1988) *Test Validity*. Hillsdale, NJ: Lawrence Erlbaum.

Walberg, H. J. & Haertel, G. D. (Eds.) (1990) *The International Encyclopedia of Educational Evaluation*. Oxford: Pergamon.

Weigle, S. C. (1994) Effects of training on raters of ESL compositions. *Language Testing* 11(2): 197–223.

Weir, C. (1988) The specification, realization and validation of an English language proficiency test. In Hughes, A. (Ed.) *Testing English for University Study: ELT Document 127*. London: Modern English Publications/The British Council.

Weir, C. (1990) *Communicative Language Testing*. Hemel Hempstead, Herts: Prentice-Hall International.

Weir, C. (1993) *Understanding and Developing Language Test*. Trowbridge, Wiltshire: Prentice-Hall.

Weiss, D. J. (1990) Adaptive testing. In Walberg & Haertel (1990):454–8.

Wilds, C. P. (1975) The Oral Interview Test. In Jones, R. L. & Spolsky, B. (Eds.) *Testing Language Proficiency.* Washington, DC: Center for Applied Linguistics: 29–38.

Williamson, M. M. & Huot, B. A. (Eds.) (1993) *Validating Holistic Scoring for Writing Assessment: Theoretical and Empirical Foundations.* Cresskill, NJ: Hampton Press.

Wolf, L. F. & Smith, J. K. (1995) The consequences of consequence: motivation, anxiety and test performance. *Applied Measurement in Education* 8(3): 227–42.

Woods, A., Fletcher, P. & Hughes, A. (1986) *Statistics in Language Studies.* Cambridge: Cambridge University Press.

Wright, B. D. & Masters, G. N. (1982) *Rating Scale Analysis.* Chicago, IL: MESA Press.

Wright, B. D. & Stone, M. H. (1979) *Best Test Design: Rasch Measurement.* Chicago, IL: MESA Press.

Appendices

Appendix 1
The role of the segmental dictionary in professional validation: constructing a dictionary of language testing

ALAN DAVIES:

> *He that undertakes to compile a Dictionary undertakes that*
> *which, if it comprehends the full extent of his design, he knows*
> *himself unable to perform.*
> *(Johnson, 1773)*

The argument of this chapter is that professionalisation in the field of language testing is an important aspect of validation by virtue of its attempt to help establish the 'values, ideologies and broader theories related to the conceptual framework guiding the program of construct validation' (Messick 1988). The chapter proposes that the writing of a specialist dictionary, also called a segmental dictionary (Opitz 1983), can foster agreement among a profession of language testers on goals, procedures, methods of evaluating innovations, and terminology and norms, fulfilling a similar role to dictionaries in language standardisation.

Professionalisation

Two of the stages in the formation of a new profession are, according to Elliott (1972), the establishment of training and selection procedures and the formation of a professional association. It is our contention that the preparation of a specific purpose glossary or dictionary of language testing is a necessary part of the continuing process of setting the standards and norms which a new profession requires. But it is not only public agreement on standards and norms that is required; it is also the need in a profession to make available to everyday use among new entrants and trainees the accepted and understood vocabularies of expertise (Atkinson, 1981: 20–1).

It is not so much that a profession needs a terminological dictionary, providing both the vocabulary and the concepts in use in the profession, as that the consensus allowing one to be constructed must be in place. As an institutional icon of value implications, a dictionary of language testing meets Messick's construct validity demands by marrying test consequences to test interpretation.

Means of Professional Education

The present discussion of writing a dictionary of language testing must first be viewed within the context of the educational role of an organisation such as the National Languages and Literacy Institute of Australia (NLLIA) of which the Language Testing Research Centre (LTRC) at the University of Melbourne forms part. Very properly the NLLIA sees its task as wider than the improvement of language teaching throughout Australia. Or to put that another way, the improvement of language teaching requires work at many levels, theoretical and practical. One aspect of that work is educational, making skills, techniques, methodologies, and knowledge about language and about languages widely known. A serious commitment to this educational responsibility means that the various Research and Development Centres of the NLLIA within their own areas of expertise need to concern themselves with the provision of information both for practitioners and for the public at large.

Such provision includes (in the case of the LTRC) training courses in methods of test construction and in assessment techniques (at the narrowest in the operating of a particular test instrument or procedure). The Language Testing and Curriculum Centre (LTACC) at Griffith University and the LTRC have discussed the setting up of the first type of training, perhaps a modular certificate course; and the LTACC itself is involved in training of the second kind.

Other types of educational activity range from the essential (and internal) training of research assistants to reading papers at conferences and to lecturing for outside groups. There is textbook writing, one aspect of which, for example, is represented by a series of videos on language testing for use by postgraduate students in Applied Linguistics, currently being prepared by the LTRC[*]. There is writing about the work of the Centre, this time not so much for the profession as for a more public audience.

What a professional dictionary does in this context is to bring together the functions of training and of establishing norms and standards. What I will show in this description of our first attempts to compile a specialist dictionary of standard terminology used in language testing is what logical steps are necessary to prepare definitions for key terms. Further, I will argue that a transparent consensus on such terms is necessary to achieve a broad construct validation for language testing practices among co-operating professionals. Indeed I would maintain that unless it is possible to reach such consensus (and make it explicit in a dictionary), then it becomes supererogatory to speak of

---

[*] Now available from LTRC, University of Melbourne: MARK MY WORDS: 6 videos on second language assessment.

there being a profession of language testing. This argument raises such questions as: how does one determine what count as fundamental concepts informing constructs of language testing? What does the training of language testers involve? How are the specialised techniques and practices of language testing best conveyed to other professionals in language education?

The Role of a Dictionary

The idea for a dictionary was an attempt to provide a solution to such questions. Centre members need one, a kind of in-house set of glosses so that they all know what is being talked about, their own register; then, as with textbooks, there is a possible compromise between the profession (in this case, those working in Applied Linguistics and language testing) and the public. Typically this targets those with general rather than specialist knowledge, such as MA students of the relevant disciplines. Very much, in fact, like the audience targeted by Richards, Platt & Weber in their *Longman Dictionary of Applied Linguistics* (1985). Centre staff have found that working together on this dictionary is a felicitous way of sharing and educating one another, precisely because it helps define, explore and create the very register they need for their work. Those working on the dictionary, all very much on a part-time basis, are aware that this is a long-term task for a small team. (This group includes Annie Brown, Chris Corbel, Alan Davies, Cathie Elder, Tom Lumley, Tim McNamara and Yap Soon Hock, all of the NLLIA Language Testing Centre, University of Melbourne.)

In the task of writing a dictionary, care must obviously be taken that the definitions or explanations can be understood by the reader, attributing to the dictionary a pedagogic role. This raises the questions of just what a dictionary is and in particular what sort of word-book is needed for a professional-academic audience. Some views by dictionary makers will be of interest.

Abercrombie, Hill & Turner, authors of a Dictionary of Sociology (1984) claim that 'A dictionary of sociology is not just a collection of definitions, but inevitably a statement of what the discipline is. It is also prescriptive in suggesting lines of development and consolidation (p. vii) '... a statement of what the discipline is': a tall order indeed but nevertheless inevitably what all dictionary making assumes in its normative role.

Angeles (1981: ix) states that his dictionary (of philosophy) 'is intended as an at-hand reference for students, laypersons, and teachers. It can be used as a supplement to texts and philosophy readings; it can also be consulted for philosophy's own enjoyment and enlightenment'. Even the 'laypersons' Angeles referred to must surely be informed, interested, educated and so on. Audience is critical and when it includes students necessarily demands some measure of simplification; if not of language, certainly of substance.

Terms listed in a professional dictionary are typically (Illingworth *et al.*, 1985) those of use to students, and teachers of [the subject] and [sometimes] of all related subjects. It should also be of some use to the interested layman. A professional dictionary needs to be distinguished from an ideological one, for example, *A Feminist Dictionary* (Kramarae & Treichler, 1985), which asserts itself as a feminist dictionary, not a dictionary of feminism.

The problems encountered in preparing the dictionary have to do with audience and definition; equally important are selection and coverage, scope and format of entry. In attempting to reach agreement themselves over these matters LTRC staff have been helped by the realisation that such concerns are not at all new in lexicography.

Types of Dictionary

Kipfer (1984:1), writing for trainee lexicographers, notes that a dictionary may he more than a reference book about words: *it can contain biographical and geographical knowledge as well as information on pronunciations, meanings, grammar and usage and even the kind of information an encyclopedia gives about the thing the word names.* In other words, the term dictionary has many interpretations.

There are indeed many terms for the LTRC's dictionary ambition: but is it for a dictionary, an encyclopedia, a word list, a glossary, a reference list? Opitz writes of a 'segmental dictionary', but is that what it is or is it a glossary, that is, a list of technical terms rather than an attempt 'to isolate a distinct register', which is what Opitz meant by a segmental dictionary (1983: 58)?

A glossary is defined by Hartmann (1983: 223) as a *word-list with explanation of meanings.* Moulin (1983: 146) describes a glossary as a list of glosses appended to text, often specialised, and details two techniques of ordering by areas of interest and by alphabet: *most authors* [of specialist dictionaries] *are neither linguists nor professional lexicographers, but specialists in the particular discipline ... [T]hese glossaries are commissioned ... to try and introduce a measure of normalisation in the use of specialist terms and thus facilitate the exchange of information.* I shall return to that concern for a 'measure of normalisation'.

Is it an encyclopedia? Hartmann tells us that encyclopedic information has to do with 'practical knowledge of things versus lexical information' (1983: 223). A more elaborate distinction is made by Read (1976: 713ff), quoted in McArthur (1986): *The distinction between a dictionary and an encyclopedia is easy to state but difficult to carry out in a practical way: a dictionary explains words, whereas an encyclopedia explains things.* He points out that because words achieve their usefulness by referring to things, a dictionary cannot be constructed without considerable attention to the objects and abstractions designated.

McArthur reminds us that the Encyclopedia Britannica had as its original title: The Encyclopedia Britannica or a Dictionary of Arts and Sciences compiled upon a New Plan (Edinburgh, 1768–71, sponsored by the Society of Gentlemen in Scotland). The Britannica was a very obvious product (no doubt influenced by the French philosophers) of the Scottish Enlightenment, that high point in Scottish history. From that high point we are brought down to earth by the comment of William Smellie, one of the original Britannica authors: 'with pastepot and scissors I composed it' (W. Smellie in Kogan, 1956: 14, quoted in McArthur, 1986: 106–7).

McArthur (1986: 104) suggests as a way of resolving the overlap in the uses of the terms dictionary and encyclopedia that it is probably best not to bother proposing a continuum between the two. At one end of McArthur's continuum is the dictionary, at the other the encyclopedia and in between the encyclopedic dictionary. Malkiel (1962: 15) refers to this as a 'hybrid genre' which has been tolerated by publishing centres 'in definace of commonsense'.

Undismayed, McArthur suggests as a way of relating dictionaries and encyclopedias (which in the USA and France have always been linked): the terms micro- and macro-lexicography. The first deals with words, producing in most instances an alphabetic dictionary. The second (macro-lexicography) shades out into the world of things and subjects, and centres on compendia of knowledge. In most instances this leads to an encyclopedia, which nowadays is usually also alphabetic (McArthur 1986: 109).

When we look at attempts within the field of Applied Linguistics two well-known products are the Longman Dictionary of Applied Linguistics and the First Dictionary of Linguistics and Phonetics. In the Introduction to their Longman Dictionary of Applied Linguistics, Richards, Platt & Weber asked who their dictionary was intended for and concluded that it was intended for students of Applied Linguistics and General Linguistics and for language teachers both in training and in the field. Richards *et al.* (1985: v) explain that their aim was to produce clear and simple definitions which communicate the basic and essential meanings of a term in nontechnical language. As far as possible their definitions were self-contained, but cross-referencing was used where necessary.

Crystal, on the other hand, finds it necessary in the First Dictionary of Linguistics and Phonetics (1980: 5) to introduce a discursive approach to the definitions: *Most entries accordingly contain encyclopedic information about such matters as the historical context in which a term was used, or the relationship between a term and others from associated fields.* (Crystal uses no obligatory cross-referencing in his dictionary, each entry being self-contained.) He points out that this leads to some repetition. *This repetition,* he says, *would be a weakness, if the book were read from cover to cover; but a dictionary should not be used as a text-book, and while the result has been a*

*somewhat longer volume than would have been the case if the See ...
convention had been used, I remain convinced of the greater benefits of look-
up convenience and entry coherence.* (Crystal 1980: 5)

The LTRC Language Testing Dictionary Project

After some preliminary trials, pilot entry writing and a small-scale survey of
the entries among teachers and MA students, we agreed upon the following
guidelines:

- the entries should be on the encyclopedia side of McArthur's
  continuum, explaining where appropriate;
- they should where possible (and appropriate) give examples so as to
  situate the explanations;
- they should accept overlap, in Crystal's sense, so that referring to other
  entries for necessary explanation would be avoided, except where
  necessary for informative purposes;
- citations would be minimised except in the sense of the informative
  purpose above;
- where possible one clear definition should be attempted, in other
  words coming down on the side of being normative rather than
  descriptive. The view has been taken that unlike a truly descriptive
  dictionary (such as the OED) it is this dictionary's role to contain and
  confine, to 'try and introduce a measure of normalisation in the use of
  specialist terms and thus facilitate the exchange of information'.
  (Moulin, 1983: 146)

These guidelines have recently received support by a further small-scale
probe. A small group of Masters' students attending a Language Testing
course were invited to consider four graded versions of a definition of 'face
validity': A B C D. (See Appendix 2.) D is the full version (contributed by
Cathie Elder); C removes the Further Reading and Citations from the D
version; B removes the alternative definitions from version C; and A removes
the remaining examples from version B. A question was also asked about
cross-referencing, following Crystal (1980) quoted above. The results
suggested that while some simplification of the D version was preferred, there
was a clear distinction between two types of simplification. The inclusion of
the features: Further Reading, Citations and Examples is more desirable than
provision for cross-referencing and offering one single clear definition. This
suggests that the view taken by users of such a dictionary is more that of a
text-book than of a word list.

Whether this project therefore should be called a dictionary or an
encyclopedia is really beside the point. However, while it does veer towards
the encyclopedia side of the McArthur continuum it retains important aspects

of dictionary-ness. It does attempt definitions, it avoids essays (so it is not strictly a glossary: 'I have retained the procedure of organizing the Glossary as a series of essays' [Abrams, 1981: v]) but unlike many dictionaries it has no information of a pronunciation kind (though obviously it would not eschew this where it seemed relevant) nor does it systematically contain historical material about derivations. So it probably is what McArthur calls an encyclopedic dictionary.

The distinction made by Landau (1974) between extracted and imposed meanings relates directly to the value-bearing and norm-imposing characteristics of a professional dictionary and therefore reinforces our claim that the construction of a segmental dictionary is an act of construct validation. At the same time Landau's distinction between extracted and imposed meanings is relevant:

General words are defined on the basis of citations illustrating actual usage: the meanings are EXTRACTED from a body of evidence ... The meanings of scientific entries, on the other hand, are IMPOSED on the basis of expert advice. The experts may have sources apart from their own knowledge and experience, but their sources are informative and encyclopedic rather than lexical, that is they are likely to consist of authoritative definitions composed by other experts whose concern is maintaining the internal coherence of their discipline rather than faithfully recording how terms are used. Their goal is ease and accuracy of communication between those versed in the language of science. (Landau, 1974: 242)

Survey

The plan for the *Dictionary of language testing* is to establish a uniform style of entry and at the same time to ensure adequate coverage. To illustrate these questions and through them the importance of being more encyclopedic than dictionary-like, I turn now to a comparison of alternative entries.

The LTRC *Dictionary of language testing* team of writers (TW) anticipate that the final version will contain somewhere between 500 and 1,000 entries. Given the choice between the B versions and the A versions (Appendix 2) below, TW's present view is very much in favour of the B versions, even though use of the A versions would permit a larger number of entries. In each case the A version is much shorter than the B version, in some sense therefore the B version is more encyclopedia-like and the A version more dictionary-like.

In making the comparisons reported below TW's hypothesis was that because of their perceived nature of this dictionary the B versions were more likely to be readable than the A versions. A class of MA students (N = 21) was asked to read three sets of alternative dictionary entries (see Appendix 2) and comment on their length – were they too long, too short or about right; and on their difficulty – were they too difficult, too easy or about right. With hindsight it is apparent that these were unsatisfactory choices to have to make. What after all does 'too easy' mean? Nevertheless the responses do provide some indication of the readability of the contrasting versions TW had provided.

Next a comparison was made between the A and B versions on the basis of their lexical density (Halliday 1985). Lexical density is an indication of the ratio of lexical to grammatical loading clause by clause. Halliday reports that in informal spoken English lexical density is about two; in adult written language it is typically more dense, say about six per clause. In scientific writing it can be as high as 10–13 per clause. That is one reason why scientific writing is often so difficult except to the expert. (It is also an explanation of why newspaper headlines can be almost uninterpretable, unless the reader knows the context in which they were written.)

Here are the summed responses of the Masters' students alongside the lexical density finding for each entry.

Table A1.1

Draft entries: Responses and lexical density

	IA	1B	2A	2B	3A1	3A2	3B
Too long	0	9	0	7	0	0	16
Too short	14	0	17	0	19	8	0
About right	7	12	3	14	2	13	4
No response	0	0	1	0	0	0	1
Difficult	5	10	6	3	6	2	9
Easy	7	1	9	0	13	4	1
About right	9	10	4	18	2	14	9
No response	0	0	2	0	0	1	2
Lexical density	7	7	12	5.8	11	6.5	6.8

Note: N = 21; see Appendix 3 for draft entries.

As a rule of thumb I suggest that 50+% approval for an entry indicates acceptability (with an N of 21, to reach 50% requires a raw score of at least 11 on both 'about right' entries, ie for Length and for Difficulty). On that basis, two entries, 2B and 3A2, may be labelled acceptable. That judgement is supported by the lexical density comparison for these two entries. Note that 2B has a much lower lexical density than 2A (less than half) and that 3A2, while much lower on lexical density than 3A1, is also marginally lower than 3B. The problem with 3B, which TW had predicted would be rated as more acceptable by the class, seems to be sheer length. It is interesting that (see Table A1.1) there is substantial agreement (16/21) that this entry is too long and yet at the same time as many as 9/21 accorded it 'about right' for difficulty. A similar result emerges for Entry 1 where there is no separation between the A and the B versions in terms of lexical density (= 7). At the same time (and here is the similarity with entry 3B), there were nine responses in the 'about right' response for 1A and 10 for 1B. It might therefore be suggested that acceptability as indicated by being accorded 'about right' for difficulty is in part a function of lexical density. Where lexical density does not discriminate (as in the 1A and 1B entries), neither choice is regarded as being more acceptable. Where there may be little to choose in terms of lexical density (as between Entries 3A2 and 3B), length of an entry may militate against the choice of an entry (as with Entry 3B).

Concluding Remarks

Of course it may be queried whether a response of 'about right' is appropriate, whether indeed (as with the figure quoted above for scientific writing, a lexical density of between 10 and 13) specialists – as opposed to lay people – tolerate a high density, a 'more difficult' entry. But that is after all a comment on the sampling of the Survey's responses and it is indeed TW's contention that the class whose responses are reported here is the appropriate audience for this *Dictionary of language testing*, students on Masters' programmes who are in the process of being introduced to courses in Applied Linguistics, including Language Testing. Specialists in the field (pace Abercrombie *et al.* 1984) are not TW's concern in this task. We distinguish the consensus of the specialists as to what the key terms are and how they are commonly used and the learning needs of the trainees (MA students for example). Both groups are needed to validate our dictionary since agreement on norms of a profession (or indeed of a society) is achieved both by consensus and by learnability. Consensus and learnability together are recognised signs of the value implications of construct validity. In my view dictionaries (and here I would agree with Abercrombie *et al.* 1984) are always normative in the sense that they are drawing boundaries with a pedagogic intent. No dictionary, certainly not a segmental dictionary, can ever satisfy the specialist! And that is what TW have decided to term their effusion, a segmental dictionary: as such it retains its professional/vocational/registral association and at the same time its normative/pedagogical purpose.

References

Abercrombie, N., Hill, S. & Turner, B. S. (Eds.) (1984) *The Penguin Dictionary of Sociology*. London: Penguin.

Abrams, M. H. (1981) *A Glossary of Literary Terms* (4th ed.) Japan: Holt-Saunder.

Angeles, P. A. (1981) *Dictionary of Philosophy*. New York, NY: Barnes & Noble/Harper & Row.

Atkinson, P. (1981) *The Clinical Experience: The Construction and Reconstruction of Medical Reality*. Farnborough: Gower.

Crystal, D. (1980) *A First Dictionary of Linguistics and Phonetics*. London: André Deutsch.

Elliott, P. (1972) *The Sociology of the Professions*. London: Macmillan.

Halliday, M. A. K. (1985) *Spoken and Written Language*. Deakin University, Australia: Deakin University Press.

Hartmann, R. R. K. (Ed.) (1983) *Lexicography: Principles and Practice*. London: Academic Press.

Illingworth, V., Glaser, E. L. & Pyle, I. C. (1985) *Dictionary of Computing*. Oxford: Oxford University Press.

Johnson, S. (1773/1955) *The Dictionary, with a Grammar and History of the English Language* (Preface to 4th ed., 1773) London.

Kipfer, B. (1984) *Workbook of Lexicography*. Exeter: University of Exeter Linguistics Department.

Kramarae, C. & Treichler, P. (1985) *A Feminist Dictionary*. London: Pandora (Routledge & Kegan Paul).

Landau, S. I. (1974) Of matters lexicographical: Scientific and technical entries in American dictionaries. *American Speech* 49: 242.

Malkiel, Y. (1962) A typological classification of dictionaries on the basis of distinctive features. In Householder, F. and Saporta, S. (Eds.) *Problems in Lexicography*. Bloomington, in *Folklore and Linguistics*. Indiana University Research Center in Anthropology: 3–24.

McArthur, T. (1986) *Worlds of Reference: Lexicography Learning and Language from the Clay Tablet to the Computer*. Cambridge: Cambridge University Press.

Messick, S. (1988) The once and future uses of validity: Assessing the meaning and consequences of measurement. In Wainer, H. & Braun, H. (Eds.) *Test Validity*. Hillsdale, NJ: Lawrence Erlbaum: 33–45.

Moulin, A. (1983) L.S.P. dictionaries for E.F.L. Learners. In Hartmann (1983): 14–52.

Opitz, K. (1983) On dictionaries for special registers. In Hartmann (1983): 53–74.

Read, A. W. (1976/1991) Dictionaries. *Encyclopedia Britannica* (15th ed.). New York.

Richards, J., Platt, J. & Weber, H. (1985) *Longman Dictionary of Applied Linguistics*. London: Longman.

Appendix 2
Four graded versions of a definition of 'face validity'

FACE VALIDITY (A)

A type of VALIDITY referring to the degree to which a test appears to measure the knowledge or abilities it claims to measure, as judged by an untrained observer (such as the candidate taking the test, or the institution which plans to administer it).

FACE VALIDITY (B)

A type of VALIDITY referring to the degree to which a test appears to measure the knowledge or abilities it claims to measure, as judged by an untrained observer (such as the candidate taking the test, or the institution which plans to administer it).

For example, a gate-keeping test administered prior to entry to a particular profession (eg dentistry) which simulates actual work-place conditions can be said to have high face validity (even though the skills measured may not in fact be reliable predictors of future performance).

FACE VALIDITY (C)

A type of VALIDITY referring to the degree to which a test appears to measure the knowledge or abilities it claims to measure, as judged by an untrained observer (such as the candidate taking the test, or the institution which plans to administer it).

For example, a gate-keeping test administered prior to entry to a particular profession (eg dentistry) which simulates actual work-place conditions can be said to have high face validity (even though the skills measured may not in fact be reliable predictors of future performance).

Conversely, if a test of listening comprehension uses a speaker with a strong regional accent which is unfamiliar to the majority of candidates, the test may be judged as lacking face validity. A more obvious example of poor face validity is the use of a dictation activity to measure an apparently unrelated skill such as speaking ability (although there may be empirical evidence of a high correlation between the two skills). The term is often used in a pejorative sense.

However, failure to take issues of face validity into account may jeopardise the public credibility of a test (and indeed the curriculum on which the test may be based) and the notion of 'test appeal' insofar as it is achievable is a practical consideration which test designers cannot afford to overlook. DIRECT TESTS are in fact often produced out of a concern for face validity.

See also CONTENT VALIDITY (a clear distinction is not always made between the two terms).

FACE VALIDITY (D)

A type of VALIDITY referring to the degree to which a test appears to measure the knowledge or abilities it claims to measure, as judged by an untrained observer (such as the candidate taking the test, or the institution which plans to administer it).

For example, a gate-keeping test administered prior to entry to a particular profession (eg dentistry) which simulates actual work-place conditions can be said to have high face validity (even though the skills measured may not in fact be reliable predictors of future performance).

Conversely, if a test of listening comprehension uses a speaker with a strong regional accent which is unfamiliar to the majority of candidates, the test may be judged as lacking face validity. A more obvious example of poor face validity is the use of a dictation activity to measure an apparently unrelated skill such as speaking ability (although there may be empirical evidence of a high correlation between the two skills).

The term is often used in a pejorative sense:
- 'in some trivial sense face or faith validity perhaps still has a role, but in diplomacy rather than psychology'. (Cattell 1964: 8)
- 'the term face validity is ... used to imply that the appearance of a relationship between the test and the external criterion is sufficient evidence of pragmatic validity'. (Mosier 1947)
- 'validity of interpretations should not be compromised for the sake of face validity'. (Cronbach 1984: 182–3)

However, Davies (1977) and Alderson (1981) argue that failure to take issues of face validity into account may jeopardise the public credibility of a test (and indeed the curriculum on which the test may be based) and that the notion of 'test appeal' insofar as it is achievable is a practical consideration which test designers cannot afford to overlook. DIRECT TESTS are in fact often produced out of a concern for face validity.

See also: CONTENT VALIDITY (a clear distinction is not always made between the two terms).

Further reading: Bachman (1990: 285-9)

Appendix 3
Draft entries for table A1.1

Entry 1A

Variance: (in testing and statistics) a measure of the DISPERSION of a SAMPLE. The variance of a set of scores, on a test for example, would be based on how much the scores obtained differ from the MEAN, and is itself the square of the STANDARD DEVIATION.

Entry 1B

Variance: a statistical measure of the DISPERSION of a SAMPLE which can be expressed in a standardised square root form as a STANDARD DEVIATION, that is to say that the variance of a sample is the standard deviation squared.

The dispersion of a sample on one measure (or test) may be compared with its dispersion on another; this comparison is referred to as the shared variance. Such a comparison is achieved by means of a CORRELATION and further comparisons of dispersion on other measures are carried out by means of ANALYSIS OF VARIANCE. The square of the correlation indicates in percentage terms the shared variance between two measures. Two tests which correlate 0.7 would have a shared variance of 49%, while a higher correlation of 0.9 would still indicate a shared variance of only 81%, leaving 19% of the variance unexplained by the overlap between the two tests.

Entry 2A

Analysis of variance: a statistical procedure used for estimating the relative effects of different sources of variance on test scores (ANOVA). (Bachman 1990: 193)

Entry 2B

Analysis of variance: a statistical procedure which combines correlations of several variables with one another and against a common criterion, with the intention of determining the influence (if any) of one variable upon another. Analysis of Variance (or ANOVA as it is often called) helps observers to avoid simplistic conclusions assuming causality between one variable and a criterion. ANOVA is commonly available on computer statistical packages.

Example: success at the end of an intermediate language course is shown to be significantly correlated with scores on an entry language test; when two other variables, age and motivation, are added to the study, it might turn out that entry scores no longer predict or do so only in relation to age and/or motivation; or that age is now so important a predictor that, when the 'variance' due to age is removed from the analysis, what remains for entry scores is trivial (see: variance, correlation, criterion, variable, predict).

Entry 3A1

Bias: 'systematic error associated with any type of group membership, sex and age group membership included'. (Jensen 1980)

Entry 3A2

Bias: 'systematic differences in test performance that are the result of differences in individual characteristics, other than the ability being tested, of test takers'. (Bachman 1990: 271)

Entry 3B

Bias: bias is defined by Jensen (1980) as 'systematic error associated with any type of group membership, sex and age group membership included'. The terms systematic error and group are important in this definition. In a trivial way all tests are biased against individuals who lack knowledge or skill. But since that is what tests are designed to do, such 'bias' or, better, discrimination is not systematic error, that is to say there will be random error as in all measurement but it is not systematic or deliberate. The group issue is more problematic in situations of norm conflict such as recent migrant communities. Should children from such communities with only a few years of schooling in the target language (eg English) take the same language tests as first language speaking children? In conflict are (1) the general educational norms and standards of the host community and (2) what it is reasonable to expect in terms of English language proficiency of the migrant children. In situations where the first consideration weighs more heavily, migrant children will take the same English test as first language children. In situations where the second consideration is more important, a more specialised test of ESL may be used.

Subject index

ability   1, 104
ability estimates   1, 55
accuracy   1
achievement   2
achievement test   2
ACTFL   2, 6
adaptive testing   3, 28
administration   4
advantage   4
affective reaction   4
agreement (in CRM)   5, 42
alpha coefficient   5, 39
ALTE   5, 12
alternate forms, alternative forms   5
American Council on the Teaching of Foreign Languages (ACTFL)   2–3, 5
analysis of covariance (ANCOVA)   6, 8
analysis of variance   6, 126
analytic scoring   7
anchoring   8
ANCOVA   6, 8
ANOVA   6, 8
answer key   8
anxiety   9, 197
a posteriori test validation   9
applied linguistics   9
appropriacy   10
appropriateness   10
a priori test validation   10
aptitude   10–11
aptitude test   10, 123
ASLPR (Australian Second Language Proficiency Ratings)   11, 87–8
assess   11, 160
assessment   11, 27, 42, 65, 68, 74, 80, 120, 147, 192

Subject index

item equating   97
item facility   95, 97
item independence   98
item ordering   98, 137
item pool   98
item response theory (IRT)   98
item writing   99

judge   100, 160, 161

Kendall's coefficient of concordance   100
Kendall's tau   100
key   8, 100
Key English Test (KET)   101
knowledge   14, 101
K-R 20/21   102
Kuder-Richardson formulae   102
kurtosis   102

language ability   1, 104
Language Aptitude Battery (LAB)   104
language(s) for specific purposes (LSP)   104
language impairment   105
language norms   105, 131
language proficiency   106, 153
language proficiency test   106, 153
language program(me) evaluation   106
language testers   106
Language Testing   106
Language Testing Update (LTU)   106
language tests   107
latent trait model(s), latent trait theory   98, 107
LD   107
leniency   107
leptokurtic distribution   102, 107
level   107
lexical density (LD)   108
Likert Scale   108
linearity   109
linear regression   109
linear structural equation modelling   109, 190
linguistic competence   109